Legalines®

Business Associations

by

GLORIA A. ALUISE
Attorney at Law

KEYED TO THE EIGHTH EDITION OF THE KLEIN CASEBOOK

GILBERT

Mat #41676477

444 Cedar Street, Suite 700
St. Paul, MN 55101
1-877-888-1330

Printed in the United States of America

ISBN: 978-1-62810-443-1

Summary of Contents

Table of Contents

Business Associations

KEYED TO THE EIGHTH EDITION OF THE KLEIN CASEBOOK

Chapter I
Agency

A. Introduction

Common throughout the field of organizations are the principles of agency. Since most businesses, at one time or another, act through third parties, it is necessary to determine when an agent can bind the principal, when the principal is liable for the wrongful acts of the agent, and what the duties and obligations of agents are to their principals and vice versa.

1. Analysis of Agency Problems

In analyzing agency problems, you can simplify the task if you first determine which of the following three types of problems is involved:

a. Is the problem between the agent and the principal?

b. Does it involve a third party trying to hold the principal to an agreement based on the agent's conduct or on an express agreement?

c. Does it involve a third party trying to hold a principal liable for the agent's torts?

2. Proving Agency

The person asserting that there is a principal-agent relationship has the burden of proving it. Note that whether an agency relationship has been created is ***not*** dependent on the intent of the parties involved. An agency relationship can arise even if the parties do not intend to be agent and principal to each other, and may not arise even if the parties so intend if certain conditions are not met. The formation of an agency relationship depends on the existence of certain factual elements. There must be an agreement between the parties that the agent will undertake some act on behalf of the principal, with the understanding that the principal is to remain in control of the undertaking.

3. Fiduciary Relationship

Every agent is a fiduciary. This means she owes a high standard of care to her principal. Fiduciaries must avoid conflicts of interest, self-dealing, disloyal acts, etc. This standard of care is similar to the duty a trustee owes his trustor and beneficiaries.

4. Gratuitous Agents

These are agents who perform their services without gain. Unlike other agents, gratuitous agents cannot be compelled to perform the duty they have undertaken. The principal may, nevertheless, be liable for the torts of gratuitous agents.

5. Principal's Duty to His Agent

The principal is under a duty to compensate his agent, including reimbursing her for out-of-pocket costs, unless the parties contract otherwise. He also has a duty to cooperate with the agent and aid her in the performance of her duties.

B. Who Is an Agent?

Agency is defined as the fiduciary relationship that results from the manifestation of consent that one person (the agent) shall act on behalf of and subject to the control of another person (the principal). The "manifestation of consent" requirement is objective—it does not matter what the principal truly intended, but rather, the agency relationship depends on what the agent believed the principal intended. Thus, an agency relationship can arise even where the principal subjectively intended no such relationship. Moreover, agency power to bind the principal can arise even absent true mutual consent.

1. Creation of the Agency Relationship

There are several ways for an actual agency relationship to be formed:

a. By Agreement

b. By Ratification

This occurs when the principal accepts the benefits or otherwise affirms the conduct of someone purporting to act for the principal, even though no actual agency agreement exists.

c. Agency by Estoppel

A principal may act in such a way that a third person reasonably believes that someone is the principal's agent; this is called agency by estoppel.

2. Agency Arising from Use of a Vehicle

Gorton v. Doty

69 P.2d 136 (Idaho 1937).

Facts. Garst was a high school football coach whose team was playing against a school in another city. Private automobiles were to be used to transport the team to and from the game. The day before the game, Doty (D) offered Garst the use of her car to help him transport some of the team members. Garst was involved in an accident while driving D's car, and one player, Gorton, was injured. Gorton's father sued D on behalf of his son to recover damages for injuries he sustained, as well as to recover the costs of his medical treatment. A jury awarded $5,000 to the son, and $870 to the father as reimbursement for medical expenses he had paid. D appeals.

Issue. Was Garst an agent of D while driving her car?

Held. Yes. Judgment affirmed.

- The evidence sufficiently supports the jury finding that the relationship of principal and agent existed between D and Garst. An agency relationship results when one person allows another to act on her behalf and subject to her control. D consented to Garst acting on her behalf in driving her car to and from the football game. She volunteered the use of her car, with the express condition that Garst drive it. She did not say anything about loaning Garst the car, and he did not say anything about borrowing it.

- Furthermore, this court has previously held that ownership of a car alone, regardless of the owner's presence in the car at the time of the accident, establishes a prima facie case against the owner because there is a presumption that the driver is the owner's agent.

Dissent. The record indicates that D simply loaned her car to Garst to enable him to transport his players to the game. The condition of Garst driving the car was a mere precaution so that the car would not be driven by any of the young players. Garst was a gratuitous bailee and not an agent of D.

---

3. Creditor Exercising Control over Debtor

A. Gay Jenson Farms Co. v. Cargill, Inc.

309 N.W.2d 285 (Minn. 1981).

Facts. In 1964, Cargill, Inc. (D), a worldwide grain dealer, entered into a contract with Warren Grain & Seed Company ("Warren"), a Minnesota firm operating a grain elevator. Under the agreement, D loaned money and working capital to Warren, and Warren appointed D its grain agent with the Commodity Credit Corporation. D had a right of first refusal to purchase grain sold by Warren. Warren purchased grain from local farmers, and shipped D 90% of the grain it purchased. Warren received funds and paid its expenses using drafts drawn on D through Minnesota banks. The drafts were imprinted with both Warren and D's names. Proceeds from Warren's sales were deposited with D. Under the contract, Warren would provide D with annual financial statements and either D would keep the books for Warren, or an independent firm would perform an audit of Warren. Warren began experiencing severe financial difficulties and in 1977, D determined that Warren's financial statements had been falsified. Following Warren's financial collapse, 86 farming concerns (Ps) sued to recover $2 million in payments for grain Ps sold to Warren. Ps also named D as a defendant, alleging that in acting as a principal, D became jointly liable for Warren's debt. A jury found that Warren was D's agent, making D liable for the debt to Ps. D appeals.

Issue. Is D liable as a principal on contracts made by Warren by virtue of its course of dealing with Warren?

Held. Yes. Judgment affirmed.

- By its control and influence over Warren, D became a principal with liability for the transactions entered into by its agent, Warren. The existence of an agency relationship, while denied by both defendants, may be proved by circumstantial evidence that shows a course of dealing between the two parties.
- D argues that it was merely a creditor of Warren, and that an agency relationship could not exist because D never consented to the agency. A creditor who assumes control of his debtor's business may become liable as principal for the acts of the debtor in connection with the business. Whatever the terms of the formal contract, when the creditor assumes de facto control over his debtor, he becomes a principal.
- In this case, the evidence shows that D continuously interfered in the internal affairs of Warren to a degree that constituted de facto control. For example, Warren was not able to make capital improvements in excess of $5,000, declare a dividend, or sell or purchase stock without D's permission. D continually reviewed Warren's operation and expenses, and recommended that certain actions be taken. D provided Warren with drafts and forms with D's name imprinted on them. D maintained a right of entry onto Warren's premises to carry out periodic checks and audits. This was clearly not an ordinary debtor-creditor relationship.
- The principal must be shown to have consented to the agency relationship. By directing Warren to implement its operational recommendations, D consented to the agency relationship. Warren fulfilled its part by acting on D's behalf in procuring grain.

- D's final argument, that its relationship with Warren was that of buyer-supplier, also fails. Under the Restatement (Second) of Agency, it must be shown that a supplier has an independent business before it can be concluded that he is not an agent. The evidence establishes that Warren's entire operation was financed by D, and that Warren sold almost all of its grain to D. Warren had no independent business.

C. Liability of Principal to Third Parties in Contract

1. Authority

After establishing that an agency relationship exists, a third party wanting to hold the principal liable must demonstrate the scope of the agent's authority to act for the principal. There are several sources of authority:

a. Actual Authority

Actual authority may be ***expressly*** conferred on the agent, or reasonably ***implied*** by custom, usage, or the conduct of the principal to the agent. Such authority may be either express or implied.

1) Express Authority

Express authority is actual authority contained within the agency agreement (*i.e.,* expressly granted by the principal).

2) Implied Authority

Implied authority comes from the words or conduct between the principal and the agent. It is often labeled to signify how it has arisen: (i) incidental to express authority; (ii) implied from conduct; (iii) implied from custom and usage; and (iv) implied because of emergency.

a) Implied from Past Conduct

Mill Street Church of Christ v. Hogan

785 S.W.2d 263 (Ky. App. 1990).

Facts. The elders of the Mill Street Church of Christ (D) hired Bill Hogan ("Hogan") to paint the church interior. Hogan had done work for the church several times in the past. For jobs with which he needed assistance, Hogan had hired his brother, Sam Hogan (P). Hogan painted most of the church himself, but when he reached a portion of the building that was very high and difficult to paint, he spoke to Dr. Waggoner, an elder of the church, about hiring a helper. Dr. Waggoner recommended Gary Petty, another church member, but stated that he might be difficult to reach. Dr. Waggoner did not tell Hogan that he had to hire Petty. Hogan instead decided to hire his brother, P. Less than one hour after Hogan and P began work, P fell from his ladder and broke his arm. Hogan reported the accident to the church elders. The church paid both Hogan and P for the hours they worked. P filed a claim against D under the Workers' Compensation Act. D contended that P was not an employee of the church, and that Hogan had no implied or actual authority to hire him. The Workers' Compensation Board found that Hogan possessed implied authority to hire P, and that P was therefore an employee entitled to benefits. D appeals.

Issue. Did Hogan have authority to hire P as an assistant?

Held. Yes. Judgment affirmed.

- ♦ The party alleging agency and resulting authority has the burden of proving the agency relationship. It must be determined whether the agent reasonably believed that the principal wished him to act in a certain way, or to have certain authority. Prior dealings between the principal and agent and the nature of the task to be carried out are factors to be considered. In this case, Hogan reasonably believed that he had authority to hire P to help him finish the painting project. In the past, the church had allowed Hogan to hire P or other persons whenever he needed assistance. Even though Hogan initially discussed a different arrangement with Dr. Waggoner, he was not told that he had to hire a specific person. In addition, it was clear from the nature of the project that Hogan would need to hire an assistant to help complete it. One person could not paint the interior of the church.
- ♦ Finally, P reasonably believed that Hogan had authority to hire him for this project, as he had done in the past. The church even paid P for the short time that he worked before the accident occurred.

---

b. Apparent Authority

Apparent authority results when a principal manifests ***to a third party*** that an agent is authorized, and the third party reasonably relies on the manifestation. There must be some holding out by the principal that causes a third party to reasonably believe that the agent has authority, and the third party must reasonably rely on the principal's manifestations.

1) Apparent Authority to Accept a Contract

Three-Seventy Leasing Corporation v. Ampex Corporation

528 F.2d 993 (5th Cir. 1976).

Facts. Three-Seventy Leasing Corporation (P) sued Ampex Corporation (D) for breach of contract in connection with the sale of computer equipment. Joyce owned P and was its only employee. Kays was a computer salesperson employed by D, and a friend of Joyce. In August of 1972, Joyce met with Kays and Mueller, Kays's supervisor, to discuss the possible sale of six computer core memory units from D to P. At the meeting, Mueller told Joyce that D could sell him the core memories if P could pass D's credit requirements. Negotiations continued until November third, when Kays submitted a written document to Joyce outlining the terms of the sale. The document provided for the sale of six memory units at $100,000 each, with a down payment of $150,000 and the remainder to be paid over the next five years. The document contained two signature lines—one for a representative of P and one for a representative of D. When the document was presented to Joyce, the signature line for D was blank. Joyce signed the contract on behalf of P. On November 17, Kays sent Joyce a letter confirming the delivery dates for the memory units. D subsequently claimed that the document was not a contract, but an offer by P to purchase, which required acceptance by D, and that D never accepted by executing the document. The district court found that there was an enforceable contract between P and D for the purchase of the core memories. D appeals.

Issue. Did D, through the conduct of its agent, demonstrate acceptance of the contract?

Held. Yes. Judgment affirmed.

- ♦ On its face, the document does not demonstrate that D had the intent necessary to form a contract in that the signature line for D was blank. In order for there to be a valid contract, we must find some act of acceptance on the part of D. We find that Kays's November 17 letter can reasonably be interpreted to be an acceptance.

- Although D's employees testified that only supervisors have the authority to enter into contracts on D's behalf, this fact was never communicated to P. There are no facts to indicate that Joyce had any reason to believe that Kays did not have authority to speak for the company. Kays was a salesperson for D. An agent has apparent authority to do those things that are usual and proper to the conduct of the business he is employed to conduct. It is reasonable for a third party to assume that a salesperson has authority to bind his employer to sell. In fact, Mueller had acknowledged in an intra-company memorandum that all communications to Joyce should be channeled through Kays, and Mueller directed Kays to submit the document in question to Joyce.
- Thus we find that Kays had apparent authority to accept the contract on behalf of D, and his letter of November 17 provided such acceptance.

---

c. Inherent Agency Power

Inherent authority is not well defined, but is thought to be analogous to the doctrine of respondeat superior in torts. That is, the doctrine of inherent authority recognizes that it is inevitable that in the course of performing her duties, either by mistake, negligence, or misinterpretation of her instructions, an agent may harm a third party or deal with one in an unauthorized manner. It is an agency power that arises even in the absence of actual or apparent authority or by estoppel. It arises from the designation by the principal of a kind of agent who ordinarily possesses certain powers. The doctrine is based on a reasonable foreseeability rationale. The test is whether the principal could reasonably foresee that an agent would take the action she did.

1) Acts of Agent in Ordinary Course of Business

Watteau v. Fenwick

1 Queen's Bench 346 (1892).

Facts. Humble owned a bar called the Victoria Hotel. He transferred ownership of the business to Fenwick (D), but continued to act as manager of the bar. The liquor license was always taken out in Humble's name, and his name was painted over the door. Under his agreement with D, Humble only had authority to buy bottled ales and mineral waters for the bar. Over several years, Watteau (P) delivered cigars and other supplies, which Humble ordered, to the bar. P sued D to recover payment for these supplies. D was found liable on the debt, and appeals.

Issue. Is an undisclosed principal liable for the acts of an agent taken in the ordinary course of business even if the principal did not authorize the agent to act, nor held the agent out as his agent?

Held. Yes. Appeal dismissed.

- Normally, when a person carries out business through a manager, he holds out his own credit and is liable for goods supplied even if the manager exceeded his authority. We have held that in such a case, proof must be given of agency in fact in order to make the principal liable. Here, however, there was no holding out by the principal. The business was carried out in the agent's (Humble's) name, and the goods were supplied on Humble's credit.
- This case is complicated due to the existence of an undisclosed principal. P indicated that he gave credit to Humble alone, and had never heard of D. The above rule, which would require P to prove actual authority, is therefore unworkable. How could P be expected to discover the existence of the secret principal, and determine the scope of the agent's authority? We hold therefore that the principal is liable for all acts of the agent that are within the authority usually confided to an agent of that character, regardless of limitations put on that authority by the principal. Very mischievous consequences could result were we to hold otherwise.

Comment. The Restatement (Second) of Agency specifically addresses the situation in *Watteau v. Fenwick.* Section 194 states that an undisclosed principal is liable for acts of an agent "done on his account if usual or necessary in such transactions, although forbidden by the principal." Section 195 makes an undisclosed principal who entrusts his agent with management of his business liable to third persons with whom the agent enters into transactions in the usual course of business even if the agent's actions are contrary to the principal's directions.

---

2. Ratification

A person may affirm or ratify a prior act supposedly done on his behalf by another that was not authorized at the time it was performed. Ratification causes the agent's act to be treated as if the principal had authorized it at the outset.

a. Ratification Requires Intent and Full Knowledge

Botticello v. Stefanovicz

411 A.2d 16 (Conn. 1979).

Facts. Mary and Walter Stefanovicz (Ds), who were husband and wife, owned a farm as tenants in common. Botticello (P) made an offer of $75,000 to purchase the farm. Mary told P that she could never sell the farm for less than $85,000. Later, P and Walter agreed on a price of $85,000 for a lease with an option to purchase. An agreement was prepared by Walter's attorney, and signed by Walter and P. P's attorney did not perform a title search, and P was unaware of Mary's legal interest in the property. At no time did Walter indicate to P, P's attorney, or his own attorney that he was acting as an agent for his wife. P took possession of the property and made substantial improvements. He then attempted to exercise his option to purchase. Ds refused to honor the option, and P sued Ds for specific performance of the contract. The court found for P and held that even though Mary was not a party to the negotiations or the contract, her husband had acted as her agent in the proceedings. The court further held that Mary had ratified the contract by her conduct. Ds appeal.

Issues.

(i) Do the facts and law support a finding that Walter acted as an agent for his wife, Mary?

(ii) Did Mary ratify the contract by her subsequent conduct?

Held. (i) No. (ii) No. Judgment reversed.

- The existence of an agency relationship is a question of fact. An agency relationship is not proven by marital status alone, nor by the fact that the parties owned the land jointly. For an agency relationship to be proven, it must be shown that the principal consented to the agent acting for her, that the agent accepted the undertaking, and that the parties understood that the principal would be in control of the undertaking.
- Although Ds admit that they discussed selling the farm, Mary's statement that she could not sell for less than $85,000 is by no means the equivalent of an agreement to sell for that amount. Although P points out that Walter customarily handled business matters for the couple, Walter had never before signed any document as agent for Mary. Mary had consistently signed any deed, mortgage, or mortgage note in connection with property the couple held jointly.
- The trial court found that even if no agency relationship existed, Mary ratified the terms of the contract by her subsequent conduct. Ratification requires acceptance of the results of a prior act with an intent to ratify, and with full knowledge of all of the material circumstances. The facts do not establish that Mary had the intent required to ratify the contract, nor do they establish that she had full knowledge of the contract's terms. While Mary observed P using the property and

making improvements, and received rental payments from P, this is not enough to indicate she had knowledge of the terms of the agreement. Walter had the power to lease his undivided one-half interest in the property, and there is nothing to indicate Mary had any reason to believe that the contract was for anything more than that. Therefore, the judgment against Mary is set aside. P may, however, proceed against Walter for specific performance or damages, and the case is remanded for a new trial on the issue of relief.

---

3. Estoppel

When a principal negligently or intentionally causes a third party to believe that his agent has authority to do an act that is actually beyond his authority, and the third party ***detrimentally relies*** on the principal's conduct, the principal is estopped from denying the agent's authority. Estoppel is different from apparent authority in that apparent authority makes the principal ***a contracting party*** with the third party with rights and liabilities on both sides. In contrast, estoppel only compensates the third party for losses arising from the third party's reliance; it creates no enforcement rights in the principal against the third party.

a. Store Owner's Negligent Surveillance May Lead to Estoppel

Hoddeson v. Koos Brothers

135 A.2d 702 (N.J. Super. Ct. App. Div. 1957).

Facts. Mrs. Hoddeson (P) was shopping at Koos Brothers (D), a large furniture store. She was approached by a man she assumed was a salesperson, and through him, placed an order for some bedroom furniture. P gave the man $168 in cash, but did not obtain a receipt. After several weeks, the furniture had not been delivered and P inquired about the delay. D told P that the store had no record of her furniture order. P went to the store, but was unable to identify the person to whom she gave the money from any of D's five salespeople. P sued D, and the lower court found for P. D appealed, arguing that the man P dealt with was not D's agent, but an imposter deceitfully impersonating a salesperson in D's store without D's knowledge.

Issue. Under these circumstances, can D be held liable for the acts of the imposter even if the imposter was not D's agent?

Held. Yes. Judgment reversed and case remanded for a new trial.

- P claims that the imposter salesperson acted as an agent for D. When a party seeks to impose liability on a principal for a contract made with an alleged agent, the burden is on P to prove the agency relationship. Clearly, the imposter salesperson did not have express or implied authority, but P claims that the evidence demonstrates that the imposter had apparent authority to bind D to the contract. However, P is unable to prove that the appearance of authority was created by the manifestations of the alleged principal. In this case, the appearance of authority was created by the manifestations of the imposter salesperson alone. Failure to prove this element of agency requires a reversal of the judgment.
- We do not find, however, that D is immune from P's complaint as a matter of law. We therefore order a new trial, which will allow P to reconstruct her complaint to state a cause of action. The proprietor of a place of business has a duty of care for the safety and security of his customers. This duty extends to reasonable care and vigilance to protect the customer from loss occasioned by the deceptions of an imposter salesperson operating on D's premises. P testified that consummation of the sale took 30–40 minutes. Through D's lack of reasonable surveillance and supervision of his store, an imposter was able to impersonate a salesperson over a lengthy period of time. We believe that the doctrine of "agency by estoppel" should apply in cases such as this, which involve a "tortious dereliction of duty to an invited customer."

4. Agent's Liability on the Contract

An agent's liability on a contract depends on the status of his principal.

a. Disclosed Principal

An agent who purports to contract for a disclosed principal is ***not personally liable*** on the contract. In such a case, the agent negotiates the contract in the name of the principal, and the agent is not a party to the contract. The parties' intent is that the principal be bound.

b. Undisclosed or Partially Disclosed Principal

In undisclosed principal cases, both the fact of agency and the principal's identity are not disclosed. In partially disclosed principal cases, the third party knows that the agent is acting as an agent, but does not know the identity of the principal. An agent acting on behalf of an undisclosed principal is ***personally liable on the contract itself.*** Courts generally apply the same rule in partially disclosed principal cases. If the agent has signed or described himself as an agent for an undisclosed person, ***he is personally liable*** on the contract unless otherwise agreed.

1) Agent Personally Liable When Principal Not Disclosed

Atlantic Salmon A/S v. Curran

591 N.E.2d 206 (Mass. App. Ct. 1992).

Facts. Atlantic Salmon and Salmonor (Ps) were Norwegian salmon exporters. Curran (D) purchased salmon from Ps and sold it to other wholesalers. In his dealings with Ps, D represented himself as a representative of Boston International Seafood Exchange, Inc. ("BISE"). D paid for the salmon with checks imprinted with the corporate name, and signed by D using the designation "Treas.," purportedly indicating that D was the treasurer of the company. D also placed advertisements for BISE in trade journals indicating that the company was established in 1982. In actuality, no corporation existed. D had formed a corporation called Marketing Designs, Inc., which was created for the purpose of selling motor vehicles. After learning that BISE corporation did not exist, Ps sued D personally to recover over $250,000 in payments for salmon they had supplied. At trial, D argued that he was acting as an agent of Marketing Designs, Inc. when he dealt with Ps, and that the corporation was responsible for the debt. D testified that he used the name BISE when doing business with salmon dealers because the name Marketing Designs would have meant nothing in the salmon industry. The lower court found for D, finding that although Ps thought they were dealing with a corporation by a different name, they were aware that they were dealing with a corporate entity, and not just an individual when they sold D their salmon. Ps appeal.

Issue. Is an agent who makes a contract on behalf of a partially disclosed principal personally liable on the contract?

Held. Yes. Judgment reversed.

- This case involves a partially disclosed principal. Ps knew that D was purportedly acting for a corporate principal, but had no notice of the principal's identity. Although D filed a certificate with the city of Boston in 1987 indicating that Marketing Designs, Inc. was doing business as BISE, D had dealt with Ps using the name BISE before then. It is not the duty of Ps to seek out the identity of the principal. It is D's duty to fully reveal it. Under the Restatement (Second) of Agency, unless otherwise agreed, a person purporting to make a contract on behalf of a partially disclosed principal is a party to the contract. To avoid personal liability, the agent must disclose that he is acting in a representative capacity and the identity of his principal. The fact that Ps could have determined the name of the principal by searching the city clerk's records is irrelevant.

D. Liability of Principal to Third Parties in Tort

1. Servant Versus Independent Contractor

a. Master-Servant

This form of agency involves a servant who, under the control of her master, renders some sort of service. A common example is the employer-employee relationship. In many cases, judges use the terms "master-servant" and "employer-employee" interchangeably. Control is the essential feature of the master-servant relationship. The employer retains control over the manner in which the employee performs services.

1) Respondeat Superior

Under the doctrine of respondeat superior, an employer is liable for all torts committed by an employee ***acting within the scope of her employment***. An injured party can proceed against both the employer and the employee—the employee being directly liable for his torts while the employer is vicariously liable. Respondeat superior imposes strict liability on the employer.

b. Independent Contractors

This situation arises when a principal retains someone to do a certain job or achieve a specific objective. The principal retains ***no right of control*** over the independent contractor as to how the work is performed. The independent contractor determines for herself how she will achieve the end goal.

1) Respondeat Superior Inapplicable

The doctrine of respondeat superior does not apply to independent contractors. In certain limited situations, an employer may be held responsible for the torts of an independent contractor, but in such cases, liability is based on the employer's own negligence or as a matter of public policy, not on respondeat superior. For example, employers may be held liable if they are negligent in selecting an independent contractor, or if the contractor is to perform highly dangerous acts (*e.g.*, blasting).

c. Issue Is a Question of Fact

Humble Oil Refining Co. v. Martin

222 S.W.2d 995 (Tex. 1949).

Facts. Mrs. Love left her car at a service station owned by Humble Oil Refining Company (D) for service. Before anyone at the station touched the car, it rolled down a hill and struck Martin and his two daughters (Ps). Ps sued Love and D for negligence and a jury awarded Ps damages. D appeals, arguing that it was not liable for Ps' injuries because the service station was operated by an independent contractor, Schneider. Ps argue that Schneider was not an independent contractor, but an employee of D.

Issue. Do the facts indicate a relationship of master and servant between Schneider and D such that D can be held liable for the negligence of Schneider and the other service station employees?

Held. Yes. Judgment affirmed.

- The question of whether a party is an independent contractor or an employee is a question of fact. In this case, the contract between D and Schneider, as well as D's exercise of control over the station's operation, demonstrate facts indicating that Schneider was an employee. The contract indicates that D owned the station, exercised financial control over the station, set the hours of operation, provided its own automotive products for sale, and set the price for those products. Under the contract, D paid 75% of the station's public utility bills, furnished the station and equipment, furnished the advertising media and the products sold, and paid a substantial part of the station's operating costs. Schneider had no business discretion except as to hiring, discharge, and payment of a handful of station employees. These facts indicate that Schneider was simply an employee and not an independent contractor. Therefore, the court properly held D liable for the negligence of its employees.

---

d. Facts Demonstrate Independent Contractor Relationship

Hoover v. Sun Oil Company

212 A.2d 214 (Del. 1965).

Facts. Hoover (P) was injured when his car caught fire while being filled with gasoline at a service station owned by Sun Oil Company (D) and operated by Barone. The accident was allegedly due to the negligence of a service station employee, Smilyk. P sued D, Barone, and Smilyk. D moved for summary judgment on the ground that Barone was an independent contractor, and therefore, D could not be held responsible for the negligence of Barone's employees.

Issue. Was Barone an agent of D such that D could be held responsible for the negligence of Barone's employees?

Held. No. Motion for summary judgment granted.

- P contends that D controlled the day-to-day operation of the station, making Barone D's agent. However, the facts indicate that Barone was an independent contractor, and D had no control over the details of the service station's operation. Barone made no written reports to D, and he alone assumed the risk of profit or loss in the operation of the business. Barone independently set the station's hours of operation, pay scale, and working conditions of his employees.
- Barone's relationship with D was typical of company-service station relationships. Barone advertised and sold gasoline and other products bearing the Sun label. D's sales representative visited the station weekly to take orders for Sun products, inspect the restrooms, and discuss any problems Barone was having. While the record indicates that D's representative made suggestions to improve sales and marketing, Barone was under no obligation to follow the advice.

---

e. Franchising Agreements and Agency

Questions of agency frequently arise in the context of franchises. Generally, in a franchising arrangement, the franchiser supplies the franchisee with a brand identification or business identity, and controls the distribution of its goods or services through a contract which regulates the activities of the franchisee in order to achieve standardization. The franchisee has the right to profit and bears the risk of loss from operation of the franchise. Most franchise agreements contain some regulatory provisions indicating how the business is to be run. This is done in the interest of providing a standard level of service upon which customers come to rely. However, if the franchise agreement gives the franchiser too much control over the day-to-day operation of the business, an agency relationship arises such that the franchiser may be held responsible for the torts of the franchisee.

1) Test Is Control

Murphy v. Holiday Inns, Inc.

219 S.E.2d 874 (Va. 1975).

Facts. Murphy (P) sued Holiday Inns Incorporated (D) for injuries she sustained in a slip and fall accident while staying at a Holiday Inn motel. D filed a motion for summary judgment on the grounds that it did not own the premises upon which the accident occurred, and that D had no relationship with the operator of the motel other than a license agreement permitting the operator/licensee, Betsy-Len Motor Hotel Corporation ("Betsy-Len"), to use the name "Holiday Inns." The trial court found for D, holding that no principal-agent or master-servant relationship existed between D and Betsy-Len. P appeals, arguing that the licensing agreement gives D authority and control over Betsy-Len sufficient to establish a master-servant relationship.

Issue. Did the licensing agreement or franchise contract create an agency relationship between D and Betsy-Len?

Held. No. Judgment affirmed.

- An agency relationship between a franchiser and franchisee arises only if the parties' agreement so regulates the activities of the franchisee as to vest the franchiser with control over the operation of the franchisee. P claims that several provisions of D's franchise agreement satisfy the control test and establish a principal-agent relationship. P points out that the agreement requires Betsy-Len (i) to construct its motel according to plans, specifications, and locations approved by D; (ii) to pay a fee for use of the trade name and for advertising of the Holiday Inns system; (iii) to conduct its business under the Holiday Inns "system"; (iv) to observe certain rules of operation; (v) to make quarterly reports to D; and (vi) to submit to periodic inspections of facilities and procedures conducted by D's representatives.
- We find that the regulatory provisions of the agreement do not constitute control within the definition of agency. The purpose of the regulatory provisions is to achieve system-wide standardization of the business identity, uniformity of service, and optimum public goodwill. The agreement does not give D control over the day-to-day operations of the business. D has no control over Betsy-Len's business expenditures or room rates, and does not demand a share of Betsy-Len's profits. While D did regulate architectural style during the construction of the motel, it has no power to control maintenance of the premises.
- The license agreement here contains the principal features of the typical franchise contract. D allowed Betsy-Len to use its trademark, and Betsy-Len agreed to pay a fee for that use. Betsy-Len retained the right to profit and bore the risk of loss. Betsy-Len agreed to certain regulatory rules of operation with respect to use of D's trademark.

---

2. Tort Liability and Apparent Agency

a. Franchisor Liability

Miller v. McDonald's Corp.

945 P.2d 1107 (Ore. App. 1997).

Facts. Miller (P) sued McDonald's Corporation (D) for injuries she received when she bit into a heart-shaped sapphire stone while eating a Big Mac. The trial court granted summary judgment for D on the grounds that D did not own or operate the restaurant; rather it was owned and operated by a franchisee, 3K Restaurants ("3K"). P appeals.

Issue. Was there an agency relationship between D and 3K that could make D liable for P's injuries?

Held. Yes. Judgment reversed.

- The franchise agreement between D and 3K laid out detailed instructions on how the restaurant was to be operated. In fact, D periodically sent inspectors to the restaurant to ensure conformity with D's standards. A jury could find that D retained sufficient control over 3K's daily operations such that an actual agency relationship existed.
- Furthermore, a jury could find that apparent agency existed. The test for apparent agency is whether the putative principal held the third party out as an agent and whether the plaintiff relied on that holding out. Everything about the appearance of the restaurant identified it with D and the common image for all of D's restaurants. D has created this image with national advertising, common signage, menus, and uniforms, etc. P has testified that she went to the restaurant under the belief that it would have the same quality of service and care as other McDonald's restaurants.

---

3. Scope of Employment

For respondeat superior to apply, the employee must have committed the tortious act within the course and scope of employment. That is, the employee must have been engaged in work for the employer of a type that he was employed to perform, during work hours. The Restatement sets forth factors to be considered in determining whether an act occurred within the scope of employment (*e.g.,* authorization of the act by the employer; the time, place, and purpose of the act; whether the act was commonly performed by employees; the extent to which the employer's interest and the employee's interest was involved; etc.). Liability extends to intentional acts if the act is related to carrying on the employer's business.

a. Acts That Are Reasonably Foreseeable

Ira S. Bushey & Sons, Inc. v. United States

398 F.2d 167 (2d Cir. 1968).

Facts. The United States (D) had a coast guard vessel, the Tamaroa, in a floating dry dock owned by Ira S. Bushey & Sons, Inc. (P). P was repairing the vessel. Late one night, one of the Tamaroa's seamen, Lane, returned to the vessel drunk. While walking to his quarters, he turned three large wheels that controlled the water intake valves on one side of the dry dock. The influx of water eventually caused the Tamaroa to fall off its blocks and against the dry dock wall. P sued D for the damage to its dock. D argued that it could not be held liable because Lane's acts were not within the scope of his employment. The district court awarded P damages, and D appeals.

Issue. Did the court err in holding D responsible for the acts of its drunken sailor?

Held. No. Judgment affirmed.

- The Restatement (Second) of Agency states that the conduct of a servant is within the scope of employment only if it is actuated, at least in part, by a purpose to serve the master. Here, Lane's turning of the wheels was in no way related to his employment. The trial court held D liable based on the doctrine of respondeat superior, contending that such a ruling would result in a more effective allocation of resources. We agree that D should be held responsible for P's damages, but we reject the allocation of resources rationale.
- Instead, we base our finding on the reasonable foreseeability test. In this case, the drunken seaman's conduct was not so unforeseeable as to make it unfair to hold D responsible. After a night out, Lane was returning to his ship as he was required to do by his employer. The proclivity for seamen to drink to excess while ashore is well known. It is immaterial that Lane's precise action could not be foreseen. The risk that seamen coming and going from the Tamaroa might cause damage to the dry dock is enough to make it fair that D bear the loss.

---

b. Battery Committed by Employee

Manning v. Grimsley

643 F.2d 20 (1st Cir. 1981).

Facts. Manning (P) was a spectator at a Baltimore Orioles baseball game. He and some other fans sitting in the right field bleachers were heckling Grimsley, an Orioles pitcher who was warming up nearby. Grimsley reportedly looked directly at the hecklers several times during the first two innings. At the end of the third inning, after the Orioles catcher had already left his position, Grimsley wound up as though about to pitch in the direction of the plate. However, when he released the ball, it traveled at more than 80 miles per hour directly toward the hecklers, who were sitting at an angle approximately 90 degrees from the plate. The ball broke through a mesh fence and struck P. P sued Grimsley and his employer, the Baltimore Baseball Club, Inc. (Ds), for battery and negligence. The district court entered a directed verdict for Ds, and P appeals.

Issue. Did the district court properly enter a directed verdict for Ds on the battery count?

Held. No. Judgment vacated and case remanded.

- In light of the fact that Grimsley was an expert pitcher who presumably could control the direction of his throw, that he looked directly at the hecklers several times, and that the ball traveled at a right angle to the direction in which he had been pitching, we find that a jury could have reasonably inferred that he intended to throw the ball in the direction of the hecklers to cause them immediate fear of being hit in retaliation for their heckling. Therefore, it was error for the court to have entered a directed verdict for Grimsley on the battery count.
- P is also entitled to vacation of the judgment in favor of the Baltimore Baseball Club. To recover damages from an employer for injuries resulting from an employee's assault, a plaintiff must show that the employee's assault was in response to the plaintiff's conduct that was interfering with the employee's ability to perform his duties. In this case P was heckling Grimsley who was warming up before entering the game. A jury could reasonably find that the purpose of P's conduct was to rattle Grimsley so that he could not pitch effectively, and that Grimsley's assault was in response to this conduct. Therefore, the lower court erred in directing a verdict for the Baltimore Baseball Club.

---

4. Statutory Claims

a. Racial Discrimination

Arguello v. Conoco, Inc.

207 F.3d 803 (5th Cir. 2000).

Facts. A group of Hispanic and African-American consumers (Ps) filed suit against Conoco, Inc. (D) alleging that D's employees discriminated against them when they attempted to purchase gasoline at D's service stations. The suit was the result of several separate incidents involving several of D's stores. In the first incident, Arguello, a Hispanic woman, and her family were pumping gas at a store D owned in Fort Worth, Texas. Arguello and her father entered the store to pay for the gas and other items. When Arguello gave the cashier, Smith, a credit card, Smith requested identification. Arguello provided her Oklahoma driver's license. Smith told her the out-of-state license was not acceptable identification. An argument ensued, and Smith began to insult Arguello and her father with racial epithets and obscene gestures. Arguello and her father left the store and called D's customer service line to complain. Smith and another employee locked the doors when the two tried to reenter the store, and continued shouting racial epithets over the store's intercom system. D's district manager investigated Arguello's complaint and found that Smith had acted inappropriately. Smith was counseled about her behavior, but she was not fired.

The second incident occurred in a Conoco-branded store in Fort Worth. Three African-American customers, Ivory, Pickett, and Ross, allege that they were followed by Conoco employees while in the store. When they complained about this, the employees told them "we don't have to serve you people" and "you people are always acting like this." The employees refused to serve them and asked them to leave. Eventually, the police were called, and they forced the employees to serve the three customers.

In the third incident, Escobedo, a Hispanic man, and his wife alleged that when they stopped at a Conoco-branded store in San Marcos, Texas an employee refused to provide toilet paper for the restroom, shouted a profanity at them, and said "you Mexicans need to go back to Mexico." Escobedo also claims that at other Conoco-branded stores he was required to prepay for gas while Caucasians were allowed to pump first and pay later. Ps filed suit against D alleging violations of 42 U.S.C. §§ 1981 and 2000a. The district court found no agency relationship between D and the Conoco-branded stores and granted summary judgment for D on all claims involving those stores. Regarding the incident at the store D owned, the court held that D's employee, Smith, acted outside the scope of her employment as a matter of law and entered summary judgment for D. Finally, the court dismissed Ps' disparate impact claims for failure to state a claim upon which relief could be granted. Ps appeal.

Issues.

(i) Did the district court err in finding that no agency relationship existed between D and the Conoco-branded stores?

(ii) Did the district court err in granting summary judgment for D on the issue of whether Smith acted within the scope of her employment?

(iii) Did the district court err in dismissing Ps' disparate impact claims?

Held. (i) No. (ii) Yes. (iii) No. Judgment affirmed in part, reversed in part, and case remanded.

- The incidents involving the Escobedos, Ivory, Pickett, and Ross occurred at Conoco-branded stores, which are independently owned. These stores have petroleum marketing agreements ("PMAs") with D which allow them to market and sell Conoco brand gasoline. The district court found that D did not control the day-to-day operations of the Conoco-branded stores, and that no agency relationship existed between D and those stores. The Supreme Court has suggested that a plaintiff must demonstrate an agency relationship between a defendant and the third party in order to impose section 1981 liability on a defendant for the racially discriminatory acts of a third party. Ps argue that the PMAs establish that D has an agency relationship with the Conoco-branded stores, and that D controls them by requiring their compliance with the PMAs. We disagree. The PMAs state that business must be conducted in a manner consistent with the standards of D, and that customers should be treated fairly and courteously. These are guidelines for the operation of Conoco-branded stores for the protection of the Conoco name. The PMAs do not establish that D has any participation in or control over the day-to-day operations of the branded stores. In the absence of an agency relationship, we find that D cannot be held liable for the unfortunate events that took place at the Conoco-branded stores.

- The events involving Arguello and her family occurred at a store owned by D. However, the district court granted summary judgment for D, finding that there was no agency relationship between D and D's employee Smith because Smith's acts of discrimination were outside the scope of her employment. We find that the court erred in granting summary judgment on this issue.
- Generally, a master is subject to liability for torts his servants commit while acting within the scope of their employment. Some factors to consider in determining whether an employee's acts are within the scope of employment include (i) the time, place, and purpose of the act; (ii) the act's similarity to acts which the employee is authorized to perform; (iii) whether the act is commonly performed by employees; (iv) the extent of the employee's departure from normal methods; and (v) whether the employer would reasonably expect such acts to be performed. Smith's discriminatory acts took place while she was on duty at the Conoco station where she was employed. The purpose of Smith's interaction with Arguello was to complete the purchase of gas and other items. The initial confrontation occurred while Smith was processing this transaction. Smith's actions, including selling gasoline and other items, completing credit card purchases, and using the store intercom, were all customary actions of gasoline station clerks. D had authorized Smith to interact with customers. Although Smith did depart from the normal methods of conducting a sale by shouting racial epithets, this does not automatically lead to the conclusion that her actions were outside the scope of her employment. There is also no evidence in the record as to whether D could have reasonably expected Smith's behavior. Even if the evidence shows D could not have anticipated Smith's conduct, a jury would be entitled to find that the other factors outweigh this consideration. For these reasons, we find that the lower court erred in granting summary judgment, and we reverse and remand the case.
- Finally, we affirm the district court's dismissal of Ps' disparate impact claims. Even if such claims are cognizable under Title II, Ps failed to allege that there was a specific Conoco policy that had a negative disparate effect on minority customers.

---

5. Liability for Torts of Independent Contractors

Employers of independent contractors cannot be held liable for their torts on a respondeat superior theory. However, in some situations, an employer may be held responsible for the torts of an independent contractor based on the employer's own negligence or as a matter of public policy. For example, an employer may be held liable if he is negligent in selecting an independent contractor, or if the contractor is performing highly dangerous acts (*e.g.,* blasting).

a. Contractor Engaged in Activity That Is a Nuisance

Majestic Realty Associates, Inc. v. Toti Contracting Co.

153 A.2d 321 (N.J. 1959).

Facts. The city of Patterson Parking Authority ("Parking Authority") hired an independent contractor, Toti Contracting Company ("Toti"), to demolish several buildings to build a parking lot. Majestic Realty Associates, Inc. (P) owned a two-story building immediately adjacent to one of the buildings to be demolished. During the course of the demolition, a large piece of debris fell onto P's building causing a huge hole in the roof. P sued Toti and the Parking Authority for damages. The trial court held that the Parking Authority could not be held liable for the negligence of its independent contractor. P appealed, arguing that an exception to the general rule applies in this case because the work done by the contractor was a nuisance per se. The appellate court agreed and reversed the decision. The Parking Authority appeals.

Issue. Can the Parking Authority be held responsible for the negligent acts of an independent contractor if the work done was a nuisance per se?

Held. Yes. Judgment affirmed.

- Generally, when a person engages an independent contractor, he is not liable for the negligent acts of the contractor in the performance of the contract. There are three exceptions to this rule. The employer will remain liable for the acts of the contractor if he: (i) retains control of the manner and means of doing the work; (ii) engages an incompetent contractor; or (iii) the work contracted for constitutes a nuisance per se.
- Courts have equated nuisance per se with activities that are "inherently dangerous." The Restatement of Torts considers an activity to be inherently dangerous if it can only be carried out safely by the exercise of special skill and care, and it involves grave risk of danger to persons or property if negligently done. Courts have reached different conclusions as to whether demolition activity necessarily involves a peculiar risk of harm to persons or property. However, we note that the current doctrine in New York is that the razing of buildings in a busy, built-up section of a city is inherently dangerous within the meaning of the Restatement. We find this doctrine to be sound and just. Thus, the judgment of the appellate court is affirmed and the matter remanded for a new trial against the parking authority.

E. Fiduciary Obligations of Agents

1. Duties During Agency

An agent is a fiduciary and, as such, he owes his principal the obligation of faithful service. This obligation requires the agent to notify the principal of all matters affecting the agency.

a. Duty of Loyalty/Conflicts of Interest

An agent is charged with the fiduciary duty of loyalty, which includes the duty not to compete with his principal. Anything that an agent obtains as a result of his employment belongs to the principal, thus effectively barring the retention of secret profits, advantages, and benefits absent the principal's consent.

b. Remedies Available to Principal

1) Damages

An agent may be liable to a principal in tort for breach of fiduciary duty.

2) Action for Secret Profits

When an agent breaches a fiduciary duty to the principal and secretly profits from it, the principal may recover the actual profits or property held by the agent.

3) Rescission

Any transaction that violates the agent's fiduciary duty is voidable by the principal.

4) Other

Other remedies available include an accounting, or imposition of a constructive trust on property the agent obtained in violation of his fiduciary duties.

c. Secret Profits

Lorry: large truck transporting goods or troops

Reading v. Regem

2 KB 268 (1948).

Facts. Reading (P) was a sergeant in the British Army stationed in Egypt in 1944. Every few weeks, P would, in full uniform, board a lorry loaded with cases, the contents of which were unknown. P would escort the lorries through Cairo. Because P wore his uniform, the lorries were able to pass the civilian police without being inspected. P was paid large sums of money for this service. When military authorities discovered P's activities, they took possession of the money for the Crown. P petitioned the court to recover the money.

Issue. Is P entitled to recover money he made outside the scope of his employment?

Held. No. Petition dismissed.

- There are many cases on the books in which a master has been held entitled to the unauthorized gains of his servant or agent. It makes no difference that in this case there was no fiduciary relationship, and P was not acting within the course of his employment. Nor does it matter that there was no loss to the Crown. If a servant unjustly enriches himself by virtue of his service without his master's sanction, the law says that he shall not be allowed to keep the money, but it shall be taken from him and given to his master. This is so because P got the money solely by reason of the position he occupied as a servant of the Crown. The uniform of the Crown and P's position as a servant of the Crown were the only reasons he was able to obtain this money, and that is sufficient to cause him to forfeit the money to the Crown.

---

d. Duty to Disclose Information

Rash v. J.V. Intermediate, Ltd.

498 F.3d 1201 (10th Cir. 2007).

Facts. J.V. Intermediate, Ltd. and J.V. Industrial Companies, Ltd. (collectively, "JVIC," Ds) manufacture, repair, expand and manage assets for industrial process plants throughout the world. Ds Rash (P) to start and manage a Tulsa, Oklahoma, division of its industrial plant maintenance business, inspecting, repairing, and maintaining oil refineries and power plants. The employment agreement provided for a salary, a bonus of 20% of the Oklahoma company's net profits, and a termination bonus of 20% of the division's equity. The contract required that P "devote [his] full work time and efforts" to Ds. Ds claim that P failed to disclose to them that he actively participated in and owned at least four other businesses, one of which was Total Industrial Plant Services, Inc. (TIPS), a scaffolding business. TIPS bid on contracts and was often chosen as a subcontractor under P's management. While P was manager, Ds started their own scaffolding business, but between 2001 and 2004, while Ds paid TIPS over $1 million, Ds' scaffolding services were never used by the Tulsa division. Claiming Tulsa purposely understated its net profits and equity, and thereby did not properly pay him his net profit and bonus, P sued Ds for breach of contract and fraud. Ds counterclaimed. At trial, the court granted P's Rule 50 motion for a judgment as a matter of law on Ds' counterclaim for breach of fiduciary duty. The jury was therefore only instructed on Ds counterclaim for breach of the duty of loyalty. P requested a damages award of $564,993 for his breach of contract claim and the jury granted him $444,933. Ds sought $143,000 in damages for its breach of the duty of loyalty claim; the jury awarded $71,500. Ds filed a motion for a new trial, a renewed motion for judgment as a matter of law on the fiduciary duty claim, a motion for the equitable relief of fee forfeiture due to P's duty of loyalty violation, a motion to alter or amend the judgment, and a motion to vacate the verdict. All of Ds' motions were denied. Ds appeal.

Issues.

(i) Is there a fiduciary relationship?

(ii) Did Rash breach his fiduciary duty?

Held. (i) Yes. (ii) Yes. Judgment reversed and case remanded.

- Under Texas law, certain relationships constitute formal fiduciary relationships, *e.g.*, trustee to beneficiary, executor to beneficiary of estates, attorney to client, and partner to partner. Under Texas common law, the agent to principal relationship also gives rise to a fiduciary duty. The Texas Supreme Court has adopted section 387 of the Restatement (Second) of Agency, which provides: "[U]nless otherwise agreed, an agent is subject to a duty to his principal to act solely for the benefit of the principal in all matters connected with his agency."
- P was employed to introduce Ds to the market, build the Tulsa division from the ground up and had sole responsibilities for Tulsa operations. P found facilities to operate the business, hired and trained employees, purchased tools and equipment and promoted the branch. P conceded that he "ran the shop;" he solicited and received bids for subcontracts and directly received the invoices for those bids; he set rates charged for work performed by the Tulsa division and kept track of all costs.
- P also contracted to perform the duties of an agent. Texas law defines an agent as "a person having a duty, created by his undertaking, to act primarily for the benefit of another in matters connected with his undertaking." P contracted to "devote [his] full work time and efforts to the business and affairs of Joint Venture Piping."
- P does not deny the agency; however, he claims that scaffolding-related ventures were outside the scope of his agency.
- P was Ds' representative in the Oklahoma region, and agreed to and was expected to act primarily for Ds' benefit P owed Ds a fiduciary duty as a matter of law.
- Rather than relying on a blanket definition of the scope of an agent's duty, Texas courts instead inquire whether a fiduciary duty exists with respect to the particular occurrence or transaction at issue.
- Among the several basic duties Texas law recognizes a fiduciary owes the principal are:

  "... the duty to account for profits arising out of the employment, the duty not to act as, or on account of, an adverse party without the principal's consent, the duty not to compete with the principal on his own account or for another in matters relating to the subject matter of the agency, and the duty to deal fairly with the principal in all transactions between them."
- For the instant appeal, the most important duty is the "duty to deal openly with the employer and to fully disclose to the employer information about matters affecting the company's business." Restatement (Second) of Agency section 13, cmt. a (1958). While there is not an absolute duty of loyalty to an employer, at a minimum, an employee's independent undertaking cannot compete or contract with the employer without the employer's full knowledge.
- P defends that he owed no duty to Ds' minor scaffolding business and that Ds' president told P he had no problem with P forming a business that might contract with Ds. These defenses fly in the face of P's obligation "to deal fairly with the principal in all transactions between them,"... "to

fully disclose to the employer information about matters affecting the company's business," and the prohibition against a fiduciary's "using the relationship to benefit his personal interest, except with the full knowledge and consent of the principal."

- If P had simply notified Ds about his association with TIPS, this case would be completely different. He did not, and Ds were entitled to judgment as a matter of law on their breach of fiduciary claim against P.

---

2. Duties During and After Termination of Agency: Herein of "Grabbing and Leaving"

Post-termination competition with a former principal is permitted, but the former agent is barred from disclosure of trade secrets or other confidential information obtained during his employment.

a. Soliciting Former Employer's Clients

Town & Country House & Home Service, Inc. v. Newbery

147 N.E.2d 724 (N.Y. 1958).

Facts. Town & Country House & Home Service, Inc. (P) was a housecleaning business. Newbery and others (Ds) worked for P for three years. After Ds left P's employment, they set up their own housekeeping business that directly competed with P, and solicited P's customers. P brought an action for an injunction and for damages. The trial court dismissed P's complaint finding that Ds were not subject to any negative covenants under any contract with P, and that Ds did not violate any duty to P by soliciting P's clients. The court of appeals reversed, finding that in their conspiring and planning of their new business, Ds breached a duty they owed to P as employees, and that P was entitled to an injunction and damages.

Issue. Can P enjoin Ds from soliciting its customers?

Held. Yes. Judgment affirmed in part.

- We agree that the trial court erred in dismissing the complaint, but would not afford as much relief as the appellate court.
- The only trade secret that could be involved in a case like this is P's list of customers. The testimony at trial established that P's customer list could not have been easily obtained. The list was painstakingly compiled by calling hundreds of homes in areas P identified as possibly being interested in P's services, which were quite uncommon at the time. P's owner's wife testified that she would make 200 or 300 phone calls, and only secure between 8 and 12 customers. At the end of the first year of business, P had only about 40 customers. P's customers were screened by P at considerable effort and expense. It would be different if Ds had gone out and solicited new customers from a pool of potential customers available to both P and Ds. The record indicates that P's current customers were the only ones Ds solicited.
- P is entitled to enjoin Ds from further solicitation of its customers.

Chapter II Partnerships

A. What Is a Partnership?

1. Introduction

a. The Basic Nature of a Partnership

A partnership is an association of two or more persons to carry on a business as co-owners for profit. [Uniform Partnership Act ("UPA") § 6] Note that a lawful partnership cannot be formed for nonprofit purposes.

b. Comparison with Other Forms of Doing Business

1) Agency

A partnership is a more complex form of organization than a sole proprietorship. It is really an extension of the sole proprietorship, which incorporates many of the principles of agency law in structuring how the partnership will function.

a) For example, A, formerly a sole proprietor, takes in B and C as partners. Now, an association has been formed, in which all (A, B, and C) will be co-owners.

b) Each partner is the agent of her co-partners, and when any partner acts within the scope of the partnership, her acts will bind the other partners.

2) Joint Venture

A joint venture is an association of two or more members, agreeing to share profits. However, a joint venture is usually more limited than a partnership; *i.e.,* it is formed for a single transaction and usually is not the complete business of the individual associated members. However, the rights and liabilities of partners and joint venturers are usually the same, and the courts usually apply the provisions of the UPA to joint ventures.

3) Other Unincorporated Associations

There are other types of unincorporated associations, such as a business trust, that are not partnerships.

c. The Uniform Partnership Act

The UPA has been adopted by most states, so that the provisions governing partnerships are usually a part of state statutory law, rather than the common law.

d. The Revised Uniform Partnership Act

The Revised Uniform Partnership Act ("RUPA") was adopted by the National Conference of Commissioners on Uniform State Laws in 1994 and applies to all partnerships formed after its adoption in any given state. The RUPA continues many of the rules of the UPA and has been adopted in most states.

e. Entity and Aggregate Characteristics of a Partnership

1) Both Characteristics

A partnership is treated both as a separate entity from its partners (for some purposes) and as though there is no separate entity but merely an aggregate of separate, individual partners.

2) Aggregate Theory

For example, the partners are jointly and severally liable for the obligations of the partnership. [*See* UPA § 15] And, for federal income tax purposes, the income and losses of the partnership are attributed to the individual partner; the partnership itself does not pay taxes (although it does file an information return).

3) Entity Characteristics

For other purposes, a partnership is treated as a separate entity apart from its individual partners.

a) Capacity to Sue or Be Sued

The jurisdictions vary as to whether a partnership can be sued and/or sue in its own name. For example, if a "federal question" is involved, then a partnership can sue or be sued in its own name in federal courts. [*See* Fed. R. Civ. P. 17(b)]

b) Ownership of Property

A partnership can own and convey title to real or personal property in its own name, without all of the partners joining in the conveyance. [UPA § 8]

4) RUPA

Unlike the UPA, the RUPA ***expressly states*** that a partnership is an entity, thus simplifying many partnership rules such as those on property ownership and litigation. [RUPA § 201]

2. Agreement to Form a Partnership

As a partnership is a voluntary association, there must be an express or implied agreement in order to form a partnership.

a. Formalities

If the partnership is to continue beyond one year, the Statute of Frauds requires that the agreement be written.

b. Duration

If no term is specified, then the partnership is terminable at the will of any partner.

c. Capacity to Become a Partner

Persons must have the capacity to contract. Some states hold that corporations cannot be partners.

d. Consent of Other Partners

A prospective partner must have the consent of all of the other prospective partners. [UPA § 18(g)]

e. Intent of the Parties

Where there is any question, the intent of the parties involved is determined from all of the circumstances, [*See* UPA § 7—the factors considered, including the sharing of profits of the business]

3. Partners Compared with Employees

Fenwick v. Unemployment Compensation Commission

44 A.2d 172 (N.J. 1945).

Facts. Fenwick (D) opened a beauty shop in New Jersey in November 1936. In 1937 or early 1938, he hired Chesire as a cashier and receptionist. In December 1938, Chesire asked for a raise, and D agreed to pay her a higher wage if warranted by the income of the shop. D and Chesire entered into a written agreement, drafted by an attorney, that provided, in relevant part: (i) "[t]hat the parties associate themselves into a partnership to commence January 1, 1939" for the operation of the beauty shop; (ii) that Chesire will not make a capital investment; (iii) "[t]hat the control and management of the business shall be vested in Fenwick"; (iv) that Chesire continue to act as cashier and receptionist at her current salary but receive a bonus of 20% of the net profits of the business if the business warrants it; (v) "[t]hat as between the partners Fenwick alone is to be liable for debts of the partnership"; (vi) "[t]hat both parties shall devote all their time to the shop"; (vii) "[t]hat the books are to be open for inspection of each party"; (viii) that, at the end of the year, D receive 80% of the profits; and (ix) "[t]hat the partnership shall continue until either party gives 10 days' notice of termination." The relationship terminated in January 1942 at Chesire's request to stop working at the shop. The Unemployment Compensation Commission considered whether Chesire was a partner or an employee of the business during the term of the agreement; if she was an employee, D was an employer under a New Jersey statute requiring employer payments into an unemployment compensation fund. The Commission determined that Chesire was an employee. The appeals court reversed, finding that a partnership existed, and the Commission appeals.

Issue. Do the agreement and the conduct of the parties evince a partnership?

Held. No. Judgment reversed.

- In determining whether a partnership exists, a court first considers the intent of the parties. Where, as here, the agreement itself is not conclusive, the court looks to other evidence. D testified that he suggested the agreement because, when Chesire requested a raise, he was unsure whether the business would make enough money to warrant it, but did not want to lose her as an employee. This suggests that the intent of the parties was to provide Chesire the possibility of an increase and retain her services while protecting D from an obligation to provide additional compensation if the business could not afford it. Additionally, after the agreement became effective, the parties continued to operate as before, with Chesire as cashier and receptionist and Fenwick in complete control of management.
- Another element to consider is the right under the agreement to share in the profits of the business, a right that existed in this case but is not conclusive on the issue of the existence of a

partnership. The court also considers the obligation to share in the losses, which did not exist in this case, the ownership and control of the property and business, which remained in D, and power of administration, which also remained in D under the terms of the agreement.

- A court also considers the language of the agreement and the conduct of the parties toward third parties. Here, while the parties call themselves partners and the business a partnership, other language clearly excludes Chesire from most of the rights ordinarily held by a partner. The parties also did not hold themselves out to be partners except on tax returns and to the Commission.
- Finally, a court considers the rights of the parties on dissolution of the relationship. In this case, the effect of the dissolution was the same as an employee quitting her employment. Chesire stopped working and no longer received compensation, and D carried on the business with a new receptionist. Thus, the evidence reveals that a partnership did not exist, and that the agreement was nothing more than a method of compensating an employee.

---

4. Partners Compared with Lenders

a. Sharing of Profits Not Conclusive Evidence of Partnership

v for D appeal affirmed

Martin v. Peyton

158 N.E. 77 (N.Y. 1927).

Facts. Knauth, Nachod & Kuhne ("KNK"), a partnership in the securities business, was in financial difficulty. Hall, a partner, arranged for a loan of some securities from Peyton and other friends (Ds), which were to be used as collateral for a bank loan to KNK. The agreement provided that (i) no partnership was intended; (ii) until the loan was repaid, Ds were to receive 40% of KNK's profits; (iii) collateral was given to Ds in the form of speculative securities owned by the firm; (iv) all dividends on the securities loaned by Ds were to be paid to Ds; (v) Ds were to be advised of and consulted on all important matters affecting the firm; (vi) Ds could inspect the books and request any information they wanted; (vii) Ds could veto any of KNK's business deemed "speculative"; (viii) all KNK partners assigned their interest in KNK to Ds as security for the loan; (ix) Ds had an option to join the firm; and (x) each KNK partner submitted his resignation, which could be accepted at any time by Ds on paying the firm member the value of his interest. But Ds could not initiate any actions for the firm or bind the firm by their actions. Creditors of KNK (Ps) claimed that the "loan" agreement was actually a partnership agreement and sought to hold Ds liable for KNK's debts. The trial court found that the transaction was a loan, and Ps appeal.

Issue. Has a partnership been formed?

Held. No. Judgment affirmed.

- A sharing of profits is considered an element of a partnership, but not all profit-sharing arrangements indicate the existence of a partner relationship. Nor is language saying that no partnership is intended conclusive. The entire agreement will be looked at in making this determination.
- All of the features of the agreement are consistent with a loan agreement, so no partnership has been formed.

Comment. Had KNK been organized as a corporation, limited liability company, or limited liability partnership, Ds would have avoided any risk of liability. Under those forms of business organization, as equity investors, Ds could not have been held personally liable for the firm's debts.

---

b. Lack of Intent to Form a Partnership

Southex Exhibitions, Inc. v. Rhode Island Builders Association, Inc.

279 F.3d 94 (1st Cir. 2002).

Facts. In 1974, Rhode Island Builders Association, Inc. (D) entered into an agreement with Sherman Exposition Management, Inc. ("SEM"), predecessor-in-interest to Southex Exhibitions, Inc. (P), regarding future productions of D's home shows at the Providence, Rhode Island civic center. The agreement stated that D "wishes to participate in such [s]hows as sponsors and partners," and had a fixed term of five years, renewable by mutual agreement. In the agreement, (i) D agreed to sponsor and endorse only SEM shows, (ii) to persuade its members to have exhibits at SEM shows, and (iii) to allow SEM to use its name for promotions. SEM, in turn, agreed (i) to obtain licenses, leases, permits, and insurance; (ii) to indemnify D for show-related losses; (iii) that D could accept or reject any potential exhibits; (iv) to audit the income of the shows; and (v) to advance all necessary capital to finance the shows. The agreement provided that the parties would mutually determine show dates, admission prices, and the bank at which to transact show-related business. If the civic center were to become unavailable for reasons beyond SEM's control, SEM would be excused from its duties but could not promote another home show in Rhode Island, while D could conduct a home show at another venue after notifying SEM. During conversations contemporaneous to the making of the agreement, SEM's president informed D's executive director that he "wanted no ownership of the show" and added that "after the first year, if I'm not happy, we can't produce the show properly or make any money, we'll give you back the show."

In 1994, P acquired SEM's interest under the 1974 agreement. In 1998, P determined that the agreement had to be renegotiated or allowed to expire in 1999 according to its terms. Instead, D expressed its dissatisfaction with P's performance and entered into a management contract with another producer. P sued to enjoin D from holding its 2000 home show on the grounds that the 1974 agreement established a partnership between D and P's predecessor-in-interest and/or that, by D's silence, a partnership-by-estoppel had been formed, and that D had breached its fiduciary duty to P through wrongful dissolution of their partnership and appointment of another producer. The district court found that a partnership did not exist under Rhode Island law, and P appeals.

Issue. Does a partnership exist between the parties?

Held. No. Judgment affirmed.

- Whether a partnership exists is normally assessed under a "totality-of-the-circumstances" test. Here, while the agreement contained some terms common to partnerships, there was ample evidence that a partnership did not exist. First, the 1974 agreement was entitled "Agreement," not "Partnership Agreement." Second, the agreement was for a fixed term as opposed to an indefinite duration. Third, under the agreement, SEM was responsible not only for advancing all money required to produce the shows but also for indemnifying D for all show-related losses. Generally, a presumption exists that partners share equally or proportionately in partnership losses. Fourth, SEM was responsible for the majority of management decisions in the relationship. The evidence revealed that, since succeeding SEM, P entered into contracts and conducted business with third parties in its own name, not that of the alleged partnership, that the alleged partnership was actually never given a name, and that P had never filed a federal or a state partnership tax return. Fifth, aside from cash receipts, the relationship never generated any tangible property, and determining the existence of an intention to share intangible properties, such as client lists, goodwill, and business expertise, would involve significant speculation. Finally, SEM's president testified that he regarded SEM merely to be the producer of D's shows, and D's executive director testified that SEM specifically disclaimed any ownership interest in the home shows in 1974.

- While evidence of profit sharing is prima facie evidence of the existence of a partnership, and D failed to show that any of the enumerated exceptions applied, a finding of partnership formation is not compelled in light of other factors indicating the absence of an intent to form a partnership.
- The labels parties assign to their intended relationship may be probative of intent to form a partnership, but are not necessarily dispositive. The agreement describes the parties as "partners," but the court could consider extrinsic evidence to determine whether the parties, in fact, intended to be partners.

---

5. Partnership by Estoppel

a. Liability of Alleged Partner

One who holds herself out to be a partner, or who expressly or impliedly consents to representations that she is such a partner, is liable to any third person who extends credit in good-faith reliance on such representations. [UPA § 16]

1) For example, A represents to C that she has a wealthy partner, B, in order to obtain credit. B knows of the representation and does nothing to inform C that he is not a partner. C makes the loan.
2) For the purposes of the loan, B will be held to be a partner with A, but he has no other rights to participation in A's business.

b. Liability of Partners Who Represent Others to Be Partners

In the above example, if A were part of an actual partnership, then she would make B an agent of the partnership by her representation that B was also a partner. As such, B could bind A as though they were in fact partners (but only those other partners of A who made or consented to A's representations would be bound).

c. Liability of an Affiliated Company

Young v. Jones

816 F. Supp. 1070 (D.S.C. 1992).

Facts. Price Waterhouse Bahamas ("PW-Bahamas") is a Bahamian general partnership, and Price Waterhouse United States ("PW-US") is a New York general partnership. Investors (Ps) invested $550,000 in Swiss American Fidelity and Insurance Guaranty ("SAFIG") based on an unqualified audit letter on SAFIG by PW-Bahamas. After the funds disappeared and Ps learned that SAFIG had falsified its financial statement, Ps sued both PW-Bahamas and PW-US, as well as certain partners of PW-US, in a federal district court for damages, claiming that PW-Bahamas was negligent in issuing the letter on which Ps relied in investing in SAFIG. Ps further allege that although the two firms are separately organized, the firms are partners by estoppel and that, therefore, PW-US and its individual partners are liable for the negligent acts of PW-Bahamas. In support of its partnership by estoppel argument, Ps refer to the letter-head on which the audit letter was written, which identified PW-Bahamas only as "Price Waterhouse," bore a "Price Waterhouse" trademark, and was signed "Price Waterhouse." Furthermore, Price Waterhouse advertised in a brochure that it is a worldwide organization with 400 offices throughout the world. PW-Bahamas and PW-US move to dismiss the lawsuit.

Issue. Do a United States firm and its foreign affiliate operate as partners by estoppel when the foreign affiliate uses the firm name and trademark, and the United States firm makes no distinction in its advertising between itself and its foreign affiliates?

Held. No. Case dismissed.

- As the two firms are organized separately, there is no partnership in fact.
- According to UPA section 16, a person who represents himself, or permits another to represent him, to anyone as a partner in an existing partnership or with others who are not actual partners is liable to any such person to whom a representation is made who has, on faith in the representation, given credit to the actual or apparent partnership. This is an exception to the rule that persons who are not actual partners as to each other are not partners as to third persons.
- Here, Ps do not contend that they saw the PW-US brochure or that they relied on it in investing, nor does the brochure say that affiliated entities are liable for each other's actions. Furthermore, UPA section 16 creates liability to third persons who, in reliance on representations as to a partnership, "give credit" to the partnership. In this case, no credit was extended to the alleged partnership. Moreover, Ps have not shown that they relied on any act of PW-US that there was a partnership with PW-Bahamas.

B. The Fiduciary Obligations of Partners

1. Duties of Partners to Each Other

The duties of one partner to all others are based on a fiduciary relationship. Specifically, a partner owes certain duties of care and of loyalty.

2. Duties with Regard to Outside Opportunities

Meinhard v. Salmon

164 N.E. 545 (N.Y. 1928).

Facts. Gerry leased a hotel to Salmon (D) for 20 years. Under the agreement, D was obligated to spend $2 million in improvements. Shortly thereafter, D entered a joint venture with Meinhard (P) for P to pay one-half of the money needed to alter and manage the property, receiving 40% of the net profits for five years and 50% thereafter. D had the sole power to manage the property. D's interest in the lease was never assigned to P. Gerry owned a substantial amount of adjoining property and, near the end of the lease term, tried to put together a deal to level all of the property and put up one large building. Failing that, Gerry approached D, and they entered a lease on all of the ground (renewable for a period up to 80 years), eventually calling for the destruction of the hotel and the building of a new, larger building. P found out about the new lease and demanded that it be held in trust as an asset of their joint venture. The lower court held that P was entitled to a half interest in the new lease and must assume responsibility for half of the obligations. D appeals.

Issue. Does the new lease come within D's fiduciary obligation to his joint venture partner as a joint venture "opportunity"?

Held. Yes. Judgment for P affirmed.

- Joint venture partners owe the highest obligation of loyalty to their partners. This includes an obligation not to usurp opportunities that are incidents of the joint venture. The duty is even higher of a managing co-adventurer.
- There was a close nexus between the joint venture and the opportunity that was brought to the manager of the joint venture, as the opportunity was essentially an extension and enlargement of the subject matter of the old one.

- Because D was to control the project, he should receive 51 shares of the corporation that holds the lease on the new project, and P should have 49 shares.

Dissent. This is not a general partnership; it is a joint venture, entered into by D to get financing for his project. There was no expectancy of a renewal of the lease, and no intention that P be part of D's business forever. P, for example, never received an assigned interest in D's lease with Gerry, and P could not have renewed the lease had there been a renewal provision. P and D's relationship was that of a limited venture for a limited term. Thus, the new opportunity was not an extension of the old one.

---

3. Definition of Joint Venture Expanded

Sandvick v. LaCrosse

747 N.W.2d 519 (N.D. 2008).

Facts. Sandvick, Bragg, LaCrosse, and Haughton purchased three oil and gas leases (the Horn Leases) in Golden Valley County, North Dakota in May, 1996. These standard, paid-up, five-year term leases did not contain any provision for extension or renewal. Record title for the leases was held by Empire Oil Company, owned by LaCrosse. The leases were purchased from the parties' credits in the Empire Oil Company JV checking account. Testimony revealed the parties' initial intent was to try to sell the leases during the five-year term. The parties owned other oil and gas leases together; one party owned with one or others or all. Haughton and LaCrosse purchased three oil and gas leases on the Horn property in November 2000. Referred to as the "Horn Top Leases," these leases had a five-year term, covered the same acreage as the Horn Leases, and were set to start when the Horn Leases expired. Title was held in the name of Empire Oil Company. The *Manual of Oil and Gas Terms* 1285 (8th ed. 1991), defines a "top lease" as a "lease granted by a landowner during the existence of a recorded mineral lease which is to become effective if and when the existing lease expires or is terminated." The top leases were not recorded until December 2001. Before buying the top leases, LaCrosse and Haughton offered on two occasions to purchase Sandvick's and Bragg's interests in the Horn leases, but Sandvick and Bragg refused. Neither Sandvick nor Bragg (Ps) was told about the purchase of the top leases; they sued LaCrosse and Haughton (Ds), claiming they breached their fiduciary duties by not offering Ps a chance to join them in the purchase the top leases. After the bench trial, the district court concluded no partnership or joint venture existed. Ps appeal.

Issues.

(i) Did the district court err in concluding a partnership did not exist?

(ii) Did the district court err in concluding a joint venture did not exist?

(iii) Were any fiduciary duties breached by Ds?

Held. (i) No. (ii) Yes. (iii) Yes. Judgment reversed.

- Under state law, a partnership is "an association of two or more persons to carry on as co-owners a business for profit." The necessary elements of a partnership are (i) the parties' intention to be partners, (ii) co-ownership of the business, and (iii) a profit motive.
- Here, the district court found the parties' venture was too limited to be characterized as a business; the court said the parties' activity was limited to one occurrence rather than a series of acts as required by Comment 1 to section 202 of the Revised Uniform Partnership Act and state law. In fact, the parties were parties to other leases with other people as well as the parties involved here. There was testimony that Haughton had jointly owned other leases with LaCrosse and Sandvick. The court found that the Horn leases were a separate investment and we agree.
- Ps argue that the district court erred in concluding a joint venture did not exist. Common law holds that: "For a business enterprise to constitute a joint venture, the following four elements

must be present: (1) contribution by the parties of money, property, time, or skill in some common undertaking, but the contributions need not be equal or of the same nature; (2) a proprietary interest and right of mutual control over the engaged property; (3) an express or implied agreement for the sharing of profits, and usually, but not necessarily, of losses; and (4) an express or implied contract showing a joint venture was formed." . . . To determine whether a joint venture relationship exists, each case will depend upon its own unique facts.

♦ The district court supported its conclusion that a joint venture did not exist based on the following findings of fact: (i) Bragg never spoke to Haughton about the purchase of the Horn leases and there was no agreement about the purchase of additional leases or leases on minerals near the Horn property; (ii) Sandvick had no written agreement with Ds regarding purchasing a new lease after the Horn leases expired; (iii) when the Horn leases were acquired, Bragg did not have an agreement with LaCrosse regarding the development of those leases; (iv) LaCrosse never agreed to make Ps a part of any subsequent lease of the Horn minerals; (v) there was no agreement of any kind limiting the parties abilities to engage in future undertakings not involving each other, and (vi) the parties knew the others would continue to do business that did not include them. These circumstances indicate the parties had no expectations that the other parties would not invest in the area without offering the other parties the opportunity to join the investment.

♦ However, the court also made findings that support a joint venture. The court found: (i) a checking account was opened under the name Empire Oil JV Account; (ii) the leases were purchased from the parties' credits in the Empire Oil Company JV account in equal shares; (iii) title to the leases was held in Empire Oil Company's name; and (iv) the parties' intent in acquiring the leases was to sell them. At trial, three of the parties testified that any profits resulting from a sale of the leases would have been shared. This testimony, combined with the court's findings above, demonstrates the existence of a joint venture.

♦ Under UPA (1997) section 404(a) and N.D.C.C. section 45–16–04(1), a partner owes duties of loyalty and care to the other partners. The duty of loyalty is set forth in UPA (1997) section 404(b) N.D.C.C. section 45–16–04(2):

> "a. To account to the partnership and hold as trustee for it any property, profit, or benefit derived by the partner in the conduct and winding up of the partnership business or derived from a use by the partner of partnership property, including the appropriation of a partnership opportunity;
>
> b. To refrain from dealing with the partnership in the conduct or winding up of the partnership business as or on behalf of a party having an interest adverse to the partnership; and
>
> c. To refrain from competing with the partnership in the conduct of the partnership business before the dissolution of the partnership."

♦ Like co-partners, while the venture exists, joint venturers owe to one another the duty of the finest loyalty.

♦ Here, six months before the Horn leases expired, Ds purchased the top leases, essentially an extension of the Horn leases. The top leases were identical to the Horn leases except for the fact that Ps were not told of their purchase.

♦ Once Ds purchased the top leases, they created a conflict of interest. It became Ds' best interest not to sell the Horn leases before they expired. By excluding Ps, Ds potentially stood to benefit more by waiting until the end of the Horn leases term to sell. Ds breached their fiduciary duties of loyalty by taking advantage of a joint venture opportunity when they purchased the top leases without informing Ps. Ps should have been afforded the opportunity to purchase the top leases with Ds.

Concurrence and Dissent. While I concur that the parties were not partners, I dissent regarding the finding of a joint venture. Under state law, the parties to a partnership and a joint venture can limit their duties of loyalty. The majority assumes there was a duty of full loyalty, ignoring the district court's findings that with the absence of a written contract, the parameters of the activity were not clear; there was no conversation regarding the purchase of additional leases; no expectations were communicated to Haughton regarding the development of the Horn leases; the parties had other and separate lease undertakings; and Haughton had had an interest in the area of the Horn leases and had had leases there dating from 1991, about which the parties were aware. Our standard of review requires that we respect the trier of fact's assessment of the testimony and its determination of the scope of the obligations at issue in this case. We have not done that.

---

4. Withdrawing Partners Removing Clients from Firm

Meehan v. Shaughnessy

535 N.E.2d 1255 (Mass. 1989).

Facts. Parker, Coulter (P) was a large law firm and a partnership. In June 1984, two key partners, Meehan and Boyle (Ds), litigators, began discussing forming their own firm. Together their profit interest in the firm was 10.8%. On July 5, Ds met with Cohen, a junior partner in charge of P's appellate division, and asked her to join the new firm. Boyle gave Cohen a list of all of his cases that he intended to take with him. Cohen was asked to keep the meeting confidential. Several other associate lawyers were targeted by Ds to go to the new firm. All were asked to make lists of cases they would take to the new firm. Boyle met with one associate and his source of clients to gain assurances that they would continue to send work to the new firm. By late in the summer, the group had turned from recruiting people to making arrangements for the firm (office space, etc.). Near the end of November, the group had prepared letters to present clients and referring attorneys asking for their authorization to remove their cases from P. The trial court found that during all of this time, Ds continued to work for P and to handle their cases appropriately and fairly. Three times during this period, firm partners, having heard rumors, approached Ds and asked if they intended to leave the firm. The rumors were denied. Finally, Meehan was asked the same question on November 30; Ds then decided to give notice that afternoon that they were leaving December 31. On December 3, the firm formed a separation committee and indicated that it intended to communicate with clients in an effort to keep them with the firm. They asked Ds for a list of clients they intended to take; the firm did not get such a list until December 17. In the meantime, Ds immediately sent out their notice of leaving to clients and asked for permission to remove their work from the firm.

The partnership agreement allowed a retiring partner to remove any case that had come to the firm as a result of his efforts on paying a "fair charge" to the firm, subject to the right of the client to stay with the firm if he wished. On December 31, Ds left P, taking many of P's clients with them. P sued, charging Ds with a breach of the fiduciary duty they owed to P and with a violation of the partnership agreement. The trial court found that Ds had handled all of their cases appropriately while at the firm and that the firm had failed to prove that the clients who left did not freely choose to leave (so there was no breach of fiduciary duty). P appeals.

Issue. Did the partners who left the firm breach their fiduciary duty to the partnership in taking clients from the firm?

Held. Yes. Judgment reversed and case remanded.

- We affirm that Ds did not handle cases while with the firm in an improper manner for their own benefit.

- The fiduciary duty of a partner to his firm does not prevent that partner from secretly preparing to start his own law firm.
- But there has been a breach of duty by Ds in the manner in which they acted to take clients from the firm. To gain the consent of firm clients to remove them from the firm, they acted in secret and they obtained an unfair advantage over the firm in communicating with these clients by denying that they were leaving the firm, by preparing notices to go out immediately to the clients, by delaying giving information to the partners' separation committee, etc. Also, the letter to the clients did not indicate to these clients that they had a choice to remain; it simply indicated that they were leaving and wanted permission to remove the clients' files from the firm.

---

5. Expulsion of a Partner

Lawlis v. Kightlinger & Gray

562 N.E.2d 435 (Ind. Ct. App. 1990).

Facts. Lawlis (P) became a senior partner at the law partnership Kightlinger & Gray (D) in 1975. Under the partnership agreement, partners were compensated by participating in partnership profits according to the number of units assigned to them each year by the partnership. In 1982, P began abusing alcohol and, as a result, did not practice law for several months in early 1983 and again in mid-1984 while seeking alcoholism treatment. When P revealed his problem to the partnership in July 1983, the partnership "promptly contacted and met as a group with a physician who had expertise in the area of alcoholism" and drafted a document, which P signed in August 1983, setting forth conditions for P's continuation in the partnership and providing, "It must be clearly understood that there is no second chance." When P began abusing alcohol again in 1984, however, the firm gave him a second chance, requiring him to meet certain conditions specified by the firm's Finance Committee, including meetings with selected specialists and favorable reports regarding the likelihood of a favorable treatment outcome. P was informed that, if he complied with the conditions, he would return to full partnership status. P did not consume alcoholic beverages after March 1984.

Under the 1984 partnership agreement, executed by P and the other partners, the number of units assigned to each partner, the involuntary expulsion of partners, and the involuntary retirement of partners was to be decided by a majority vote of the senior partners. During P's struggle with alcohol, his units of participation were reduced by annual addendums to the partnership agreement, all signed by P. On October 1, 1986, having ceased his consumption of alcohol and after being congratulated by Wampler, a senior partner and member of the Finance Committee, and others as to his "100% turnaround," P met with the Finance Committee and proposed that his units of participation be increased from 60 to 90 units in 1987. On October 23, however, Wampler informed P that the Finance Committee would recommend severance of P's relationship as senior partner no later than June 30, 1987, and, two days later, all of the firm's files were removed from P's office. At the year-end 1986 senior partners' meeting, all except P voted to accept the recommendation. A compensation arrangement permitting P to remain a senior partner and continue insurance coverage while he sought other employment became part of a 1987 addendum to the partnership agreement, but P refused to sign it, instead retaining counsel to represent his interests. On February 23, 1987, by a seven-to-one vote, P was expelled from the partnership. P sued for damages for breach of contract, the lower court entered summary judgment against him, and P appeals.

Issues.

(i) Did the notification that the Finance Committee intended to recommend his severance in the future and the removal of files from his office two days later constitute an expulsion in contravention of the terms of the partnership agreement?

(ii) Was P expelled in bad faith?

Held. (i) No. (ii) No. Judgment affirmed.

- On October 23, 1986, Wampler merely informed P about what might happen in the future, and the removal of the files from P's office was immaterial. These facts do not constitute a dissolution of the partnership. To the contrary, following these incidents, P continued to participate in the firm's profits, the partnership otherwise continued to treat P as a senior partner, and the firm decided to move P's name to the bottom of the list of partners on the firm's letterhead rather than to remove it. The evidence also reveals that P continued to consider himself to be a senior partner after those incidents, refusing to sign the 1987 addendum and casting a dissenting vote on his expulsion, actions that could be taken only by a senior partner under the partnership agreement. Finally, under Indiana law and the UPA as well as the partnership agreement at issue, P's expulsion occurred when the partners voted for it on February 23, 1987, in the manner prescribed by the partnership agreement.
- When a partner is involuntarily expelled from a business, his expulsion must be bona fide or in good faith. P asserts that a five-year plan, proposed by the finance committee in a November 25, 1986, memorandum, to "improve our lawyer to partner ratio" and increase partners' shares revealed a "predatory purpose" to take advantage of P's weakened position in the partnership caused by his alcoholism. The same memorandum, however, recommended that P not be expelled immediately, as permitted under the partnership agreement, but allowed to remain a partner for a maximum of eight months while sharing in partnership profits and retaining insurance coverage. Additionally, the facts reflect that, despite the fact that P was significantly less productive while struggling with his alcoholism and had initially concealed his alcoholism from his partners for months, the firm worked with him and allowed him to remain a partner, even after he violated a "no second chance" clause. Thus, there is no genuine issue that the firm acted in good faith in expelling P.

C. Partnership Property

1. What Constitutes Partnership Property

A frequent issue involves whether property is partnership property or the individual property of a partner. All property originally brought into the partnership or subsequently acquired, by purchase or otherwise, for the partnership, is partnership property. [UPA § 8(1)]

a. Proof of Intent

Where there is no clear intention expressed as to whether property is partnership property, then courts consider all of the facts related to the acquisition and ownership of the asset in question. Some of the factors considered are: (i) how title to the property is held; (ii) whether partnership funds were used in the purchase of the property; (iii) whether partnership funds have been used to improve the property; (iv) how central the property is to the partnership's purposes; (v) how frequent and extensive the partnership's use is of the property; and (vi) whether the property is accounted for on the financial records of the partnership.

2. Rights and Interests

a. Individual Partner's Interest in the Partnership

The property rights of an individual partner in the partnership property are (i) her rights in specific partnership property, (ii) her interest in the partnership, and (iii) her right to participate in the management of the partnership. [UPA § 24]

1) Rights in Specific Partnership Property

Each partner is a tenant-in-partnership with her co-partners as to each asset of the partnership. [UPA § 25(1)] The incidents of this tenancy are as follows: (i) each partner has an equal right to possession for partnership purposes; (ii) the right to possession is not assignable, except when done by all of the partners individually or by the partnership as an entity; (iii) the right is not subject to attachment or execution except on a claim against the partnership (the entity theory); (iv) the right is not community property, hence it is not subject to family allowances, dower, etc.; and (v) on the death of a partner, the right vests in the surviving partners (or in the executor or administrator of the last surviving partner). Hence, partnership property is not part of the estate of a deceased partner but vests in the surviving partner, who is under a duty to account to the deceased partner's estate for the value of the decedent's interest in the partnership (*see* below).

2) Partner's Interest in the Partnership

A partner's interest in the partnership is her share of the profits and surplus, which is ***personal property*** [UPA § 26]

a) Consequences of Classification as Personal Property

A partner's interest is personal property, even if the firm owns real property. Thus, the partner's rights to any individual property held by the partnership are equitable (the partnership holds title), and this equitable interest is "converted" into a personal property interest. This can be important in inheritance situations where real property may be given to one heir and personal property to another.

b) Assignments

A partner may assign her interest in the partnership (unless there is a provision in the partnership agreement to the contrary), and unless the agreement provides otherwise, such an assignment will not dissolve the partnership. [UPA § 27(1)]

(1) The assignee has no right to participate in the management of the partnership (*i.e.,* he is not a partner; he only has rights to the assigning partner's share of the profits and capital).

(2) But the assignee is liable for all partnership obligations.

b. Creditor's Rights

A creditor of an individual partner may not attach partnership assets. He must get a judgment against the partner and then proceed against the individual partner's interest (by an assignment of future distributions, a sale of the interest for proceeds, etc.).

3. Effect of Conveying a Partnership Interest

Putnam v. Shoaf

620 S.W.2d 510 (Tenn. Ct. App. 1981).

Facts. The Frog Jump Gin Company ("the gin") was originally operated as an equal partnership between E. C. Charlton, Louise Charlton, Lyle Putnam, and Carolyn Putnam. By agreement, Carolyn Putnam succeeded her husband Lyle's interest after his death. On February 19, 1976, Carolyn Putnam decided to sever her relationship with the other partners to relieve herself of liability for a debt owed by the gin to the Bank of Trenton and Trust Company. The Shoafs agreed to take over her position and one-half interest in the partnership as well as to assume personal liability for all of the partnership's debts if Carolyn Putnam and the Charltons each paid $21,000 into the partnership account. At the time, the gin had a negative financial position of approximately $90,000. The parties agreed, the money was paid into the account, and the Shoafs assumed the agreed-to obligations. All of the gin's assets, including the land upon which it was located, were held in the partnership's name, and Carolyn Putnam conveyed her interest in the partnership to the Shoafs by a quitclaim deed.

When the Shoafs became partners, the old bookkeeper was terminated and a new one hired. In April 1977, the partnership learned that the former bookkeeper had systematically embezzled from the gin from the time of Lyle Putnam's death until the bookkeeper's termination. Lawsuits were filed by the gin against the former bookkeeper and banks that had honored his forged checks. Carolyn Putnam was allowed to intervene to claim an interest in any fund paid by the defendant banks. Ultimately, the banks paid into the court a sum in excess of $68,000. One-half of that sum was paid to the Charltons by agreement, and the present lawsuit involves a dispute between the Shoafs and Carolyn Putnam's estate over the remaining half of the sum.

Issue. When a partner conveys her partnership interest to another, can she later claim an interest in a recovery resulting from a chose in action unknown to the parties at the time she conveyed her interest?

Held. No.

- Under the UPA, a partner's property rights in a partnership consist of rights in specific partnership property, an interest in the partnership, and a right to participate in the management of the partnership. The right in "specific partnership property" is a partnership tenancy possessory right of equal use or possession and is not an "interest" in the partnership's assets. Instead, the "real interest of a partner" is in her share of the profits and surplus as well as the partnership's losses. Accordingly, the partnership, not the partner, actually owns the property and assets. When a partner conveys her interest in a partnership, she does not convey property held by the partnership but only her interest in the partnership. She does not have a specific interest in unknown choses in action relating to partnership property.
- It is evident that Carolyn Putnam intended to convey her entire interest in the partnership to the Shoafs. Had she intended to convey less, she would have remained a partner unknown to the other parties as well as to herself. Obviously, had the partnership failed and left a sizeable deficit, Carolyn Putnam would not want to accept a partner's share of the liabilities for a share of the banks' refunds.

D. Raising Additional Capital

Often, partnerships are faced with the need to raise additional capital to finance their activities and attempt to find the lowest-cost method to raise such funds. Sometimes, the issue is addressed within the partnership agreement itself. One type of provision, allowing for what is often called "pro rata dilution," permits a call to each partner for a certain sum and provides for the reduction in partnership shares of any partner who does not contribute the requested sum. Other provisions might allow partners to invest in the firm at a reduced price or require partners to make loans that will bear interest at a higher rate. Some partnership agreements provide for the sale of new partnership assets to people outside of the partnership, similar to a corporation's placing new shares on the stock market.

E. The Rights of Partners in Management

1. Equal Rights

All partners have equal rights in management (even if sharing of profits is unequal). [UPA § 18(e)]

a. One Partner Cannot Escape Responsibility by Notifying Creditor

National Biscuit Company v. Stroud

106 S.E.2d 692 (N.C. 1959).

Facts. Stroud (D) and Freeman entered a partnership to sell groceries under the name Stroud's Food Center. There were no restrictions in the partnership agreement on the management functions or authority of either partner. Several months prior to February 1956, D notified National Biscuit Company (P) that he would not be responsible for any additional bread delivered to the Food Center. Nevertheless, on Freeman's order, P delivered $171 worth of bread over a two-week period in February. At the end of this time, D and Freeman dissolved the partnership, and D was responsible for winding up its affairs. D refused to pay P's bill. The trial court found for P, and D appeals.

Issue. If there are no restrictions in the partnership agreement as to the partners' authority, can an equal partner escape responsibility for partnership obligations by notifying a creditor that he will not be responsible for partnership debts incurred with that creditor?

Held. No. Judgment affirmed.

- The acts of a partner within the scope of the partnership business bind all partners.
- A majority of partners can make a decision and inform creditors and will thereafter not be bound by acts of minority partners in contravention of the majority decision. But here there could be no majority decision, as they are equal co-partners.
- Hence, the partnership is liable for the debt to P.

Comment. Had D dissolved the partnership and given P notice prior to the order by Freeman, D would not have been personally liable for the partnership debt to P.

---

b. Differences Must Be Resolved by the Majority

Summers v. Dooley

481 P.2d 318 (Idaho 1971).

Facts. Summers (P) and Dooley (D) entered into a partnership, operating a trash collection business. Both worked in the business, each providing and paying for a substitute when he could not work. P asked D to hire a third person and D refused; P hired one anyway, paying him with his own funds. When D discovered this, he objected. P sued for reimbursement from partnership funds for monies he paid the third person. The trial court found for D, and P appeals.

Issue. In a two-person partnership, can one partner, over the objection of the other partner, take action that will bind the partnership?

Held. No. Judgment affirmed.

- Where equal partners exist (*i.e.,* partners have equal rights in conduct of the affairs of the partnership), differences on business matters must be decided by a majority of the partners.
- Here, one of two partners refused to consent to the hiring of a third person and objected immediately upon discovering that a third person had been hired. D did not sit idly by and acquiesce in his partner's actions. Thus, it would be unjust to grant P recovery.

---

2. Partners May Fashion an Agreement as to Who Makes Decisions

Day v. Sidley & Austin

394 F. Supp. 986 (D.D.C. 1975), *aff'd,* 548 F.2d 1018 (D.C. Cir. 1976).

Facts. Day (P) was a senior underwriting partner for the law firm of Sidley & Austin ("S&A"). He had a long history with the firm and was instrumental in establishing the firm's Washington office. The position of senior underwriting partner entitled P to a certain percentage of the firm's profits as well as the privilege to vote on certain, specified matters. In early to mid-1972, the firm's executive committee, of which P was not a member and which managed the day-to-day affairs of the firm in accordance with the partnership agreement, considered a merger with the Liebman law firm. On July 17, 1972, the committee revealed its merger proposal at a meeting of the underwriting partners, all of whom, including P, voiced approval of the merger idea and favored pursuit of the possibility. The merger was discussed at four subsequent meetings of which P had notice but did not attend. The final partnership agreement, dated October 16, 1972, was executed by all of the firm's partners, including P.

On October 16, 1972, the executive committee of the firm created by the merger met and decided to combine the Washington offices of the two predecessor firms. The committee created a Washington Office Committee, chaired by the former chairmen of the Washington office committees of the two firms. Later that month, upon the new Washington Office Committee's recommendation and despite P's objections, a decision was made to set up the combined Washington office at a new location. Effective December 31, 1972, P resigned from the firm, contending that the appointment of the co-chairmen to the new Washington Office Committee and the relocation of the Washington office made his continued service with the firm intolerable. P then filed a lawsuit against S&A and some of his fellow partners (Ds), seeking damages resulting from loss of income, damage to his professional reputation, and personal embarrassment resulting from his allegedly forced resignation. Day asserted that he had a contractual right to be the sole chairman of the Washington office. He also maintained that the decision to appoint the co-chairmen was made prior to the merger but was concealed, and that he would not have voted to approve the merger had he been aware of the plan. Furthermore, he alleged that the executive committee made several active misrepresentations that had the effect of voiding the approval of the merger. Ds moved for summary judgment.

Issue. Was P's resignation precipitated by any illegality?

Held. No. Judgment for Ds.

- The primary misrepresentation alleged by P is that no S&A partner would be worse off because of the merger. P believes this statement meant that he would continue to be the sole chairman of the Washington office and have commanding authority over matters such as office space. The partnership agreement to which P was a party, however, does not mention the Washington office or P's status with regard to the office, although special arrangements are specified for other partners. Also, the partnership agreement gave the executive committee complete authority to decide firm policy and to create, control, or eliminate firm committees. P has not shown that he had any legal right to remain chairman of the Washington office.

- ♦ Under the partnership agreement, majority approval of the merger was all that was required. P cites no law to support his contention that a unanimous vote was required to approve the merger, particularly where the partners have agreed otherwise. Thus, a change in P's vote would have no effect.
- ♦ P also contends that Ds breached their fiduciary duty because they began merger negotiations without informing those partners outside the executive committee and did not reveal changes that might occur subsequent to the merger, such as the co-chairmen arrangement for the Washington office. No court, however, has recognized a fiduciary duty to disclose information regarding changes in the internal structure of a partnership when, as here, its concealment does not result in a profit for the alleged wrongdoers or financial loss to the partnership. The alleged wrongdoers also did not gain any more power within the firm as a result of their actions. Thus, there was no breach of fiduciary duty.

F. Partnership Dissolution

1. Introduction

Dissolution of a partnership does not immediately terminate the partnership. The partnership continues until all of its affairs are wound up. [UPA § 30]

2. Causes of Dissolution

Unless otherwise provided for in the partnership agreement, the following may result in a dissolution:

a. Expiration of the Partnership Term

1) Fixed Term

Even where the partnership is to last for a fixed term, partners can still terminate at will (but it will be a breach of the agreement by the terminating partner, which may result in damages charged to the terminating partner).

2) Extension of Term

The partners can extend the partnership by creating a partnership at will on the same terms.

b. Choice of a Partner

Any partner can terminate the partnership at will (because a partnership is a personal relationship which no one can be forced to maintain). Where the partnership is for a term or even where it is a partnership at will, however, if dissolution is motivated by bad faith, it may be a breach of the agreement.

c. Assignment

Note that an assignment of a partner's interest is not an automatic dissolution, nor is the levy of a creditor's charging order against a partner's interest. But an assignee or the creditor can get a dissolution decree on expiration of the partnership term or at any time in a partnership at will. [UPA §§ 30–32]

d. Death of a Partner

On the death of a partner, the surviving partners are entitled to possession of the partnership assets and are charged with winding up the partnership affairs without delay. [UPA § 37] The surviving partners are also charged with a fiduciary duty in liquidating the partnership and must account to the estate of the deceased partner for the value of the decedent's interest.

e. Withdrawal or Admission of a Partner

Most partnership agreements provide that losing or admitting a partner will not result in dissolution. New partners may become parties to the preexisting agreement by signing it at the time of admission to the partnership. [UPA § 13(7)] When an old partner leaves, there are usually provisions for continuing the partnership and buying out the partner who is leaving.

f. Illegality

Dissolution results from any event making it unlawful for the partnership to continue in business.

g. Death or Bankruptcy

Without a provision in the partnership agreement to the contrary, the partnership is dissolved on the death or bankruptcy of any partner. [UPA § 31(4), (5)]

h. Dissolution by Court Decree

A court, in its discretion, may in certain circumstances dissolve a partnership. These circumstances include insanity of a partner, incapacity, improper conduct, inevitable loss, and/or wherever it is equitable. [UPA § 32]

3. The Right to Dissolve

a. Significant Disagreements Between Partners

Owen v. Cohen

119 P.2d 713 (Cal. 1941).

Facts. On January 2, 1940, Plaintiff (P) and Defendant (D) made an oral agreement to become partners in the operation of a bowling alley business. The agreement did not contain a statement of duration. P advanced $6,986 to the partnership for the purpose of securing necessary equipment with the understanding that he was making a loan that would be repaid out of the prospective profits of the partnership. P and D opened a bowling alley on March 15, 1940, and it operated at a profit during the three-and-one-half months between its opening and the commencement of the case at bar. During this period, the partners paid off part of the debt and each took a salary of $50 per week. The partners also, however, began to have disputes regarding management and their respective rights and duties under the agreement, which had a negative effect on the profits of the business. On June 28, 1940, with much of the partnership's indebtedness unpaid, P sued for the dissolution of the partnership and the sale of its assets in connection with the settlement of its affairs. The trial court found that the partners disagreed about most matters essential to the operation of the partnership, that D had breached the partnership agreement, and that D had conducted himself in such a way that it was "not reasonably practicable to carry on the partnership business with him." In view of these circumstances, the court concluded that the partnership was dissoluble under the California Civil Code. The court adjudged the partnership dissolved, ordered the assets to be sold by the receiver it had previously appointed to manage the business, and decreed that the proceeds of the sale be applied, after allowance for the receiver's fees and expenses, to pay off the partnership debts, including P's loan, that half of any remaining sum be paid to P along with $100 in costs, and that the remainder be paid to D. D appeals.

Issues.

(i) Under these circumstances, was a decree of dissolution warranted?

(ii) Was it proper for the court to decree that P's loan be paid from the proceeds of the sale of the partnership's assets when the partnership agreement provided that the loan would be repaid through the profits of the business, a profitable enterprise?

Held. (i) Yes. (ii) Yes. Judgment affirmed.

- Under California law, a court may order the dissolution of a partnership if the partners are having such quarrels and disagreements that they can no longer act in confidence and harmony, or if one partner, by his misdeeds, materially hinders the carrying on of the business. Here, while viewed separately D's actions might appear petty, together they severely undermined the success of the partnership. Ample evidence revealed the existence of bitter, antagonistic feelings between the parties while the arrangement made by the parties requires cooperation, coordination, and harmony. Clearly, the partners were no longer able to carry on the business to their mutual advantage. Thus, California law and the UPA support dissolution of the partnership.
- D is correct that a party to a contract may limit his right to receive payments to a specified source. Where, as here, however, the other party's conduct rendered it impossible for the partners to carry on the business from which the payments would be made, it would be inequitable to enforce that part of the agreement.

---

b. Breach of Agreement

Collins v. Lewis

283 S.W.2d 258 (Tex. Civ. App. 1955).

Facts. Collins (P) and Lewis (D) entered into a partnership agreement wherein P would put up the money to build and equip a large cafeteria, and D would supervise its development and manage it. P and D entered into a lease for space in a building being built. The partnership agreement provided that P was to be paid back from net income, then P and D would share profits equally. The estimated cost to develop was $300,000. The construction of the building was delayed and so was the development of the cafeteria; costs at opening two years later were in excess of $600,000. On opening, the cafeteria operated at a loss, and P demanded that it show a profit. D indicated that there were costs of development that were being paid out of operating revenue, rather than by P as promised. Accusations went back and forth. P sued for a receiver, for dissolution, and for foreclosure of a mortgage he held on D's partnership interest. The agreement provided that D was to repay $30,000 of P's investment the first year and $60,000 each year thereafter. D filed a cross-action alleging that P had breached the partnership agreement, and asked for damages if dissolution were granted. The trial court found: (i) that D was competent to manage the cafeteria; (ii) that without P's conduct there was an expectation of profit; (iii) that P had breached his agreement to put up the funds; and (iv) that D had earned more than $30,000 in the first year, but that, due to P's refusal to pay costs of development, profits had gone to make these payments. The trial court denied the petition for a receiver and all of the other remedies sought by P. P appeals.

Issue. Under these circumstances does P have the right to dissolve the partnership?

Held. No. Judgment affirmed.

- P has the power to dissolve the partnership, but not the right to do so without damages because his conduct is the source of the partnership problems and amounts to a breach of the partnership agreement.
- P can either continue the partnership and perform on the agreement or dissolve the partnership and subject himself to possible damages for breach of the agreement.

---

c. Partnership at Will

Page v. Page

359 P.2d 41 (Cal. 1961).

Facts. P and D were partners in a linen supply business. P supplied essentials to the business, and as a result the partnership owed him $47,000. P also was the managing partner. Each partner contributed $43,000 in capital. There was no written agreement. For eight years, the business lost money. Then, when Vandenberg Air Force base opened near the town, it started making a profit. P sued to dissolve the business. D claimed (i) that there was an agreement to continue the business until all debt was paid back, and (ii) that P is terminating the business to take advantage of the opportunity himself. The trial court found that the partnership existed for a "reasonable term necessary to repay the partners' contributions of capital," and P appeals.

Issue. Was the partnership for a term rather than at will?

Held. No. Judgment reversed.

- D testified that there were no understandings about continuation for a term or until money was paid back, and conceded that another partnership that P and D were in expressly provided for a term. Some cases do hold that the partnership shall continue for a term necessary to repay debt, but only if there is evidence showing this intention. There is no such evidence here.
- Instead, the evidence reveals the existence of an at-will partnership. Thus, P has the power to dissolve the partnership upon express notice to D.
- If P is acting in bad faith in seeking dissolution, then he may be violating his fiduciary duty as a partner. Dissolution must be in good faith. State law provides for damages in that case. A separate action could determine this issue. But a partner at will is not bound to remain in a partnership just because it is profitable.

---

4. The Consequences of Dissolution

a. Distribution of Assets

1) Partnership Debts

The debts of the partnership must first be paid.

2) Capital Accounts

Then amounts are applied to pay the partners their capital accounts (capital contributions plus accumulated earnings and less accumulated losses).

3) Current Earnings

Finally, if there is anything left over, the partners receive their agreed share of current partnership earnings. [UPA § 40]

4) Distributions in Kind

Where there are no partnership debts, or where the debts can be handled from the cash account, partnership assets may not be sold, but they may be distributed in kind to the partners.

5) Partnership Losses

Where liabilities exceed assets, the partners must contribute their agreed shares to make up the difference. [UPA § 18(a)]

b. Rights of the Partners

1) No Violation of Agreement

If the dissolution does not violate the partnership agreement, then the partnership assets are distributed as set forth above, and no partner has any cause of action against any other partner.

2) Dissolution Violates Agreement

If the dissolution does violate the partnership agreement (*e.g.,* the fixed term of the agreement), then the innocent partners have rights in addition to those listed above.

a) Right to Damages

Innocent partners have a right to damages (*e.g.,* lost profits due to dissolution, etc.) against the offending partner. [UPA § 38(2)]

b) Right to Continue the Business

The innocent partners also have the right to continue the partnership business (*i.e.,* not sell off and distribute the assets) by purchasing the offending partner's interest in the partnership. [UPA § 38(2)(b)—provision for posting bond and beginning court proceedings] Alternatively, of course, the innocent partners may simply dissolve and wind up the business, paying the offending partner her share, less damages.

c. Effects of Dissolution

1) Partners Are Liable Until Debts Discharged

The liability of partners for existing partnership debts remains until they are discharged.

2) New Partnership Remains Liable for Old Debts

When there has been a dissolution due to death, withdrawal, or admission of a new partner and the partnership business is continued, the new partnership remains liable for all the debts of the previous partnership. [UPA § 41]

3) Retiring Partner's Liability for Debts Incurred by Partners Continuing the Business

Dissolution ends the power of a partner to bind the partnership except to the extent necessary to wind up its affairs. [UPA § 33] If, however, third parties do not know of the dissolution, contracts entered into with a partner bind the partnership. Hence, a retiring partner must make sure that prescribed procedures are followed to terminate any possible liability for partnership obligations. The UPA provides that notice of withdrawal or dissolution may be published in a newspaper of general circulation. [UPA § 35(1)]

d. A Partner May Bid for the Partnership's Assets at Dissolution

Prentiss v. Sheffel

513 P.2d 949 (Ariz. App. 1973).

Facts. Plaintiffs (Ps) and Defendant (D) were the three partners of a partnership created to acquire and operate the West Plaza Shopping Center ("Center") in Phoenix, Arizona. Ps filed suit seeking the dissolution of the partnership, contending that D had been derelict in his duties and specifically had failed to contribute the balance of his share of the Center's operating losses. Ps also sought permission to continue the partnership business and requested that a value be placed on D's partnership interest. D counterclaimed, seeking a winding up of the partnership as well as the appointment of a receiver, and contended that he had been wrongfully excluded from the partnership in violation of his rights as a partner. The trial court found that, while no detailed partnership agreement had ever been reached, a partnership at will existed, which was dissolved as a result of Ps' freezing out or excluding D from the management and affairs of the partnership. The court appointed a receiver to protect the partnership property until it could be sold, a partition made, and its assets distributed. At the sale of the Center, Ps were the high bidders. The court entered an order confirming the sale of the Center to Ps, and D appeals that order.

Issue. Under the facts of the case, should two majority partners in a three-person partnership, who have excluded the third partner from management and affairs, be allowed to purchase the partnership assets at a judicially supervised dissolution sale?

Held. Yes. Judgment affirmed.

- ♦ While D was excluded from the management of the partnership, his exclusion was not done for the wrongful purpose of obtaining the partnership's assets in bad faith but was rather the result of the partners' failure to relate harmoniously for the benefit of the partnership. Additionally, D actually benefitted by Ps' purchase of the property, as the evidence reflected that Ps' bid was much higher than any of the other bids, thus increasing the value of D's interest.

---

e. The Partnership Agreement and the UPA at Dissolution

Pav-Saver Corporation v. Vasso Corporation

493 N.E.2d 423 (Ill. App. 1986).

Facts. Pav-Saver Corporation (P) owned the Pav-Saver trademark as well as patents for the design and marketing of concrete paving machines. Dale, P's majority shareholder, invented P's " 'slip-form" paver. Meersman, an attorney, is the owner and sole shareholder of Vasso Corporation (D). In 1974, Dale individually, Dale and P, and Meersman formed Pav-Saver Manufacturing Company for the manufacture and sale of Pav-Saver machines. Dale agreed to contribute his services to the venture, P contributed the necessary patents and trademarks, and Meersman agreed to obtain financing. Meersman drafted a partnership agreement, which was approved by Peart, P's president. In 1976, this partnership was dissolved and replaced with an identical one between P and D, eliminating the individual partners.

In 1981, the business ceased to thrive according to the expectations of the partners, and the principals disagreed as to how to help the business. On March 17, 1983, Peart, acting on P's behalf, wrote to Meersman, terminating the partnership and invoking paragraph 11 of the partnership agreement, which provided that if one party terminated the relationship, the terminating party would pay to the other party a royalty equal to four times the gross royalties received by P in the fiscal year ending July

31, 1973, to be paid over 10 years. In response, Meersman moved into an office on the premises of Pav-Saver Manufacturing Company, physically ousted Dale, and began day-to-day management of the business. P then sued for a court-ordered dissolution of the partnership, the return of its patents and trademark, and an accounting. D counterclaimed for a declaratory judgment that P had wrongfully terminated the relationship and that, among other things, D could continue the business. The trial court, after considering the partnership agreement and the controlling UPA provisions, found that P had wrongfully terminated the partnership, and that D could continue the business and possess the partnership's assets, including P's trademark and patents. The court then valued P's interest in the partnership and concluded that D was entitled to $384,612 in liquidated damages under paragraph 11 of the partnership agreement. Both parties appeal. P appeals the court's failure to return its patents and trademarks or, in the alternative, to assign a value to them when it determined the value of the partnership's assets. P and D both disagree with the trial court's enforcement of their liquidated damages agreement; P asserts that the amount determined under paragraph 11 is a penalty, while D, agreeing with the sum at which the court arrived, contends that the installment payout method should not be enforced.

Issue. Do the terms of the partnership agreement control at dissolution if the result of following them would likely run afoul of the purpose of a UPA provision?

Held. No. Judgment affirmed.

- Under the partnership agreement, this was a "permanent partnership," terminable only on mutual approval of both parties. It is undisputed that P's unilateral termination contravened the agreement. While the partnership agreement provided that P's patents would be returned to it upon dissolution, the UPA governs the right to possess partnership property and to continue a business upon a wrongful termination. Section 38 of the UPA grants the partner who has not wrongfully terminated the partnership the right to continue the business in the same name for the agreed term of the partnership and to possess the partnership property for that purpose. Here, the evidence reflects that the business could not be continued without P's patents and trademark. The purpose of section 38 was "to cover comprehensively the problem of dissolution [and] to stabilize business." Thus, section 38 controls over the contract and the court was correct in allowing D to use P's patents and trademark to continue the business.
- The trial court was also correct in refusing to assign a value to P's patents and trademark when determining the value of the partnership assets. The only evidence adduced at trial to show the value of the patents and trademark was testimony relating to goodwill, and section 38 of the UPA explicitly states that "the value of the goodwill of the business shall not be considered."
- The liquidated damages awarded do not constitute an unenforceable penalty.

Concurrence and dissent. D should not be permitted to retain P's patents. The partnership agreement made provisions for wrongful termination, including the return of the patents and trademark. There is no conflict between the terms of the contract and the statutory option to continue the business upon wrongful termination; the option to continue the business does not carry with it a guarantee that the business will be successful. In any event, even if there was a conflict, the contract, not the statute, should prevail.

---

5. The Sharing of Losses

Kovacik v. Reed

315 P.2d 314 (Cal. 1957).

Facts. In late 1952, Kovacik (P) asked Reed (D) to be his job superintendent and estimator for P's opportunity to remodel kitchens in San Francisco. P stated that he would invest approximately

$10,000 in this venture and that he would share the profits on a 50–50 basis if D would perform these services. D accepted the proposal. At no time did the parties discuss what they would do in the event of loss. The parties subsequently obtained several jobs, for which D acted as superintendent, and P provided all financing and kept the financial records. In August 1953, P informed D that their venture had lost money and demanded that D pay a portion of the losses. D refused, arguing that he had never agreed to share the responsibility for any losses. P then sued D, seeking an accounting as well as the recovery from D of one-half of the venture's losses. The trial court concluded as a matter of law that P and D were to share all profits and losses equally. After an accounting, judgment was rendered awarding P the sum of $4,340, one-half of the monetary loss found to have been sustained by the joint venture. D appeals.

Issue. Is a party who has contributed only his services and not capital to a joint venture liable for a portion of the venture's losses?

Held. No. Judgment reversed.

- As a general rule, in the absence of an agreement to the contrary, it is presumed that partners and joint venturers intended to share equally in profits and losses.
- Where, however, as here, one partner or joint venturer contributes the capital while the other contributes skill and labor, neither party is liable to the other for losses. The rationale behind this rule is that, where one party contributes money and the other contributes services, in the event of a loss, each party loses the value of his own capital or contribution.

Comment. Section 401(b) of the RUPA provides, "Each partner is entitled to an equal share of the partnership profits and is chargeable with a share of partnership losses in proportion to the partner's share of the profits," following the general language of section 18(a) of the UPA. The comment to section 401(b) expressly cites and rejects *Kovacik,* stating that losses are shared even when one or more partners do not contribute any capital.

---

6. Buyout Agreements

G & S Investments v. Belman

700 P.2d 1358 (Ariz. Ct. App. 1984).

Facts. Century Park, Ltd. is a limited partnership formed to receive ownership of an apartment complex. In 1982, its general partners were G & S Investments (51%) and Nordale (25½%), and the remaining partnership interest was owned by limited partners Jones and Chaplin. In 1979, Nordale began using cocaine and underwent a personality change, becoming suspicious of the other partners, ceasing to keep regular business hours, making threats to "get" and "fix" some of the other partners, and having irrational ideas for the direction of the business, among other things. He also lived in the apartment complex, refusing to give up possession or pay rent on an apartment the partnership had allowed him to use temporarily during his divorce, sexually soliciting an underage female tenant, and causing such a disturbance in the complex that tenants were frightened and at least one moved out. In 1981, Gibson and Smith (Ps) of G & S Investments decided to seek a dissolution of the partnership that would allow them to carry on the business and buy out Nordale's interest. After they filed the complaint, Nordale died, and Ps filed a supplemental complaint invoking their right under the partnership's articles to continue the partnership and acquire Nordale's interest. Nordale's estate (D) took the position that the filing of the complaint operated as a dissolution of the partnership, requiring a liquidation of the partnership's assets and a distribution of the net proceeds to the partners. Ps asserted that the filing of the complaint did not cause a dissolution but that Nordale's wrongful conduct, which made it impracticable to continue in partnership with him, gave the court the power to dissolve the partnership and to allow Ps to carry on the business.

Issues.

(i) Can Ps continue the partnership after the death of a partner?

(ii) Is a partnership buyout agreement valid even if the agreed-upon purchase price is less or more than the actual value of the interest at the time of the buyout?

Held. (i) Yes. (ii) Yes.

- Nordale's conduct was in contravention of the partnership agreement. Under section 32 of the UPA, the court has the power to dissolve the partnership and to permit the remaining partners to carry on the business. The mere filing of a complaint does not operate as a dissolution; dissolution occurs when decreed by the court or brought about by other acts. When Nordale died before the court entered a decree, Ps could take advantage of article 19 of the Articles of Partnership, providing, in part, that upon the death of a general partner, the remaining general partners may continue the partnership business.
- Because partnerships result from contract, the partners' rights and liabilities are subject to the agreements made among them. Here, article 19 contained a buyout provision, requiring the remaining partners who desire to continue the business to purchase the interest of the departed partner. Here, the buyout formula takes the capital account of the deceased partner and adds to that amount the average of the prior three years' earnings. "Capital account" means the partner's capital contribution to the partnership plus profits minus losses and reduced by the amount of any distributions already made. While the fair market value of Nordale's interest would have been higher than the formula provided by article 19, modern business practice mandates that parties be bound by the contracts into which they enter, absent a showing of fraud or duress in the inducement.

G. Limited Partnerships

1. The Modern Limited Partnership

Limited partnerships are entities created by modern statutes. They were developed to facilitate commercial investments by those who want a financial interest in a business but do not want all the responsibilities and liabilities of partners. Prior to 1976, most states had adopted the Uniform Limited Partnership Act ("ULPA"). In 1976, the ULPA was revised to make it applicable to large partnerships and to reflect new business practices. Most states have now adopted the Revised Uniform Limited Partnership Act ("RULPA"). Another revision in 1985 was only slightly different from the 1976 Act. A new revision of the ULPA was drafted in 2001 and has been adopted by several states.

a. In General

1) Definition

A limited partnership is a partnership formed by two or more persons and having as its members one or more general partners and one or more limited partners.

a) General Partner

The "general partner" assumes management responsibilities and full personal liability for the debts of the partnership.

b) Limited Partner

The "limited partner" makes a contribution of cash, other property, or services rendered to the partnership and obtains an interest in the partnership in return, but is not active in management and has limited liability for partnership debts. [RULPA § 303(b)]

c) A Person Can Be Both at the Same Time

A person may be both a general and a limited partner in the same partnership at the same time. In such a case, the partner has, with respect to her contribution as a limited partner, all the rights that she would have if she were not also a general partner. [ULPA § 12]

2) Purposes

A limited partnership may carry on any business that a partnership could carry on. [ULPA § 3]

3) Liability

As noted above, the general partner is personally liable for all obligations of the partnership. A limited partner, however, has no personal liability for partnership debts, and her maximum loss is the amount of her investment in the limited partnership. [ULPA § 1] *Exception:* When a limited partner takes part in the management and control of the business, she becomes liable as a general partner. [RULPA § 303(b)]

4) Rights of Limited Partners

The rights of a limited partner are substantially the same as those of a partner in an ordinary partnership, except that she has no rights with regard to management. Hence, she has rights of access to the partnership books, to an accounting as to the partnership business, and to a dissolution and winding up by decree of court. [ULPA § 10]

a) A limited partner may lend money to, or transact business with, the partnership. [ULPA § 13]

b) A limited partner's interest is assignable, unless the agreement provides otherwise. The assignment vests in the assignee all rights to income or distribution of assets of the partnership, but unless and until the certificate of limited partnership is amended with the consent of all other partners, the assignee is ***not*** entitled to inspect partnership books, obtain an accounting, etc. [RULPA § 702]

b. Formation of Limited Partnership

While formalities are usually not required to create a partnership, there are certain requirements for the formation of a limited partnership: (i) the partners must execute a certificate setting forth the name of the partnership, the character of the business, the location of the principal office, the name and address of each of the partners and their capital contributions, a designation of which partners are "general" and which are "limited," and the respective rights and priorities (if any) of the partners; and (ii) a copy of the certificate must be recorded in the county of the principal place of business. [ULPA § 2] The certificate may be amended or canceled by following similar formalities. [ULPA § 25]

1) If the certificate contains false statements, anyone who suffers a loss by reliance thereon can hold all of the partners (general and limited) liable. [ULPA § 6]

2) The purpose of the certificate is to give all potential creditors notice of the limited liability of the limited partners.

3) The ULPA requires at least "substantial compliance in good faith" with these requirements. If there has been no substantial compliance, the purported limited partner may be held liable as a general partner. A purported limited partner, however, can escape liability as a general partner if, upon ascertaining the mistake, she "promptly renounces her interest in the profits of the business or other compensation by way of income." [ULPA § 11]

2. Limited or General Partner?

Holzman v. de Escamilla

195 P.2d 833 (Cal. App. 1948).

Facts. In early 1943, Hacienda Farms, Limited, a business raising vegetable and truck crops, was created as a limited partnership with de Escamilla as the general partner and Russell and Andrews as limited partners. In late 1943, the partnership went into bankruptcy, and Holzman (P) was appointed as trustee. P later filed suit, contending that Russell and Andrews were liable as general partners to the partnership's creditors because they had taken part in the control of the business. The court decreed that all three partners were liable as general partners, and Russell and Andrews appeal.

Issue. Are purported limited partners who controlled the finances of the partnership business and controlled the actions of the general partner liable as general partners?

Held. Yes. Judgment affirmed.

- Under the California Civil Code, "A limited partner shall not become liable as a general partner, unless, in addition to the exercise of his rights and powers as a limited partner, he takes part in the control of the business."
- In this case, the evidence revealed that Russell and Andrews always conferred with de Escamilla regarding the planting of crops, that they overruled de Escamilla's opinion as to what should be planted on more than one occasion, that they eventually asked de Escamilla to step down as manager and appointed another, and that they had the power to withdraw all funds without the knowledge or consent of de Escamilla, but de Escamilla could not withdraw money without one of their signatures. Under these circumstances, it is clear that Russell and Andrews took part in the control of the business of the partnership. Thus, they are liable as general partners.

Chapter III

The Nature of the Corporation

A. Promoters and the Corporate Entity

In the course of forming the corporation, promoters often contract for products or services on behalf of the corporation (not yet formed).

1. Promoter Liability

a. The General Rule

If the promoter contracts in the name of, and solely on behalf of, the corporation to be, the promoter cannot be held liable if the corporation is never formed. Of course, if the promoter contracts in his own name, then the promoter may be held liable. A court will attempt to determine the "intent" of the parties, and various factors enter into the determination of this intent.

b. Corporate Liability

If the corporation ratifies or accepts the contract after incorporation, the corporation may be held liable on the pre-incorporation promoter contract (and may enforce the contract). Ratification may be express or implied from adoptive conduct of the corporation.

1) Quasi-Contractual Recovery

If the corporation repudiates the contract, it is still liable for the value of anything that it makes use of (in quasi-contract).

2) Adoption by Implication

The general rule is that ratification is retroactive and adoption is not. For a corporation to adopt a contract, it must have knowledge of the terms of the contract. (But who must know of the contract to impute this knowledge to the corporation?) Most jurisdictions recognize that adoption may be by implication. Also, adoption is not generally held to be a novation (although some argue it should be), and thus the promoter is not relieved of personal liability by the adoption.

2. Consequences of Defective Incorporation

a. Introduction

Once there has been an attempt to incorporate, the first issue is whether or not a corporation has actually been formed, and if not, what the consequences are. For example, any one of a number of the formal requirements for incorporation may have been omitted or improperly performed. Or, even though the articles have been properly filed, the steps necessary to complete the company's internal organization (adoption of bylaws, etc.) may not have been completed. What is the effect? The question normally arises where an outside party (such as a creditor) wants to disregard the corporate shield against liability and hold one or more of the shareholders personally liable for "corporate" debts. Note also the relationship of this topic to that of "piercing the corporate veil," discussed *infra.*

b. "De Jure" Corporation

A corporation that has complied strictly with all of the mandatory provisions for incorporation cannot be attacked by any party (even the state). What is mandatory and what is "directory" is a matter of judicial construction of the state's incorporating laws.

c. "De Facto" Corporation

There is a body of common law indicating that, even if a corporation has not complied with all of the mandatory requirements to obtain de jure status, it may have complied sufficiently to be given corporate status vis-à-vis third parties (although not against the state).

d. Corporation by Estoppel

When a corporation is not given de jure or even de facto status, its existence as a corporation may be attacked by any third party. However, there are situations where courts will hold that the attacking party is "estopped" to treat the entity as other than a corporation.

e. Conduct of the Parties

Southern-Gulf Marine Co. No. 9, Inc. v. Camcraft, Inc.

410 So. 2d 1181 (La. Ct. App. 1982).

Facts. On December 6, 1978, pursuant to a Letter of Agreement, Southern-Gulf Marine Co. No. 9, Inc. (P), a company that had not yet been formed, became obligated to purchase a supply vessel from Camcraft, Inc. (D) for $1,350,000. Among other details, D was given authority to begin purchasing components to build the boat. On May 30, 1979, the parties executed the vessel construction contract. P was listed in the preamble as a corporation organized under Texas law, appearing through Barrett, its president. One condition of the contract provided that P was a citizen of the United States within the meaning of the Shipping Act of 1916. Subsequently, Barrett informed Bowman, D's president, that P had finally become incorporated on February 15, 1980, but in the Cayman Islands rather than the United States for economic reasons. By his signature, Bowman accepted and agreed to the letter.

D subsequently defaulted on its obligation. P sued D for breach of contract. D defended that no cause of action existed because P lacked any corporate existence at the time of the contract, and P later incorporated under the laws of a sovereign other than that represented in the contract. The motion was sustained, and P appeals.

Issue. Should a party to a contract be permitted to escape performance by raising an issue as to the character of the organization to which it is obligated if its substantial rights are not affected?

Held. No. Judgment reversed.

- If a party contracts with an entity it acknowledges to be and treats as a corporation, and incurs obligations in its favor, and is later sued for performance, it is generally estopped from arguing lack of corporate existence as a defense. This principle comports with the rules of construing contracts so as to give them effect and of interpreting contracts in accordance with justice and fair dealing, with any doubts resolved against the seller.
- Here, both parties relied on the contract, P securing financing and D beginning construction of the vessel. There is no evidence that D's substantial rights were affected by P's de facto status.

B. The Corporate Entity and Limited Liability

1. The Corporate Form

a. Characteristics of the Corporation

1) Separate Legal Entity

A corporation is a separate legal entity (created by the law of a specific state), apart from the individuals that may own it (shareholders) or manage it (directors, officers, etc.). Thus, the corporation has legal "rights" and "duties" as a separate legal entity.

2) Limited Liability

The owners (shareholders) have limited liability; debts and liabilities incurred by the corporation belong to the corporation and not to the shareholders.

3) Continuity of Existence

The death of the owners (shareholders) does not terminate the entity, because shares can be transferred.

4) Management and Control

Management is centralized with the officers and directors. Each is charged by law with specific duties to the corporation and its shareholders. The rights of the corporate owners (shareholders) are spelled out by corporate law.

5) Corporate Powers

As a legal entity, a corporation can sue or be sued, contract, own property, etc.

b. Limited Liability

1) Liabilities Belong to Corporation Itself

Because a corporation is held to be a separate legal entity, the corporation normally incurs debts and obligations in its own name that are not the responsibility of its owners (shareholders). At the same time, the corporation is not responsible for the debts and obligations of its owners (shareholders).

2) Exceptions to the Limited Liability Rule

There are exceptions to the rule of limited liability. In those exceptional situations, a court is said to "pierce the corporate veil" and to dissolve the distinction between the corporate entity and its shareholders so that the shareholders may be held liable as individuals despite the existence of the corporation.

a) Situations Where the Corporate Veil May Be Pierced

(1) Fraud or Injustice

Where the maintenance of the corporation as a separate entity results in fraud or injustice to outside parties (such as creditors).

(2) Disregard of Corporate Requirements

Where the shareholders do not maintain the corporation as a separate entity but use it for personal purposes (for example, corporate records are not maintained, required meetings are not held, money is transferred back and forth and commingled between individuals and the corporation, etc.). The rationale here is that if the shareholders have disregarded the corporate form, then the entity is really the alter ego of the individuals and decisions are being made for their benefit and not the entity's—the individuals should not complain if the courts likewise disregard the entity. This is most likely to occur with close corporations.

b) Undercapitalization

A prime condition for piercing exists where the corporation is undercapitalized given the liabilities, debts, and risk it reasonably could be expected to incur.

(1) Liability Insurance as Evidence of Undercapitalization

Walkovszky v. Carlton

223 N.E.2d 6 (N.Y. 1966).

Facts. Walkovszky (P) was severely injured in a taxicab accident. P sued the cab driver, the corporation owning the cab, and Carlton (D), who owned that corporation and nine others, each corporation having two cabs with the minimum $10,000 liability insurance coverage required by state law. The complaint alleged that the corporations operated as a single entity and constituted a fraud on the public. D moves for dismissal, asserting that P had not alleged a cause of action.

Issue. Does P's complaint state a cause of action?

Held. No. Dismissed as a faulty complaint, with leave for P to amend.

- Courts will pierce the corporate veil when necessary to prevent fraud or to achieve equity.
- There is nothing wrong with one corporation being part of a larger corporate enterprise (*i.e.,* a subsidiary corporation, or one corporate member of a group owned by common shareholders). The issue is whether the business is really carried on in a corporate form but by and for another entity or person with a disregard of the corporate formalities. It was not alleged by P that the business was really being carried on for "personal" rather than corporate purposes.
- On the undercapitalization issue, the state has set the minimum insurance requirements and thousands of individuals driving cabs have incorporated and taken out the minimum insurance. If the insurance protection provided is inadequate, the remedy is the state legislature. This being the case, the corporate veil cannot be pierced due to fraud in undercapitalization.

Dissent.

- An action lies against the shareholders if they incorporate a business without sufficient assets to meet prospective liabilities and possible business risks. Legislative setting of minimum insurance does not prevent the court from requiring that incorporating shareholders provide adequate capital for the intended business. This capital can be provided by insurance and/or other assets.
- Here, the corporation was undercapitalized. I would hold that a participating shareholder of a corporation vested with a public interest that is organized with insufficient capital to meet liabilities which will certainly arise due to the nature of the business may be held personally liable.

c) Requirements of Fairness

The veil may also be pierced in any other situation where it is only "fair" that the corporate form be disregarded.

(1) Cannot Differentiate Between Corporation and Individual

Sea-Land Services, Inc. v. Pepper Source

941 F.2d 519 (7th Cir. 1991).

Facts. Sea-Land Services, Inc. (P) was an ocean carrier who shipped peppers on The Pepper Source's ("PS") behalf. After PS refused to pay its substantial freight bill, P sued. The district court entered judgment in default for P, but P could not obtain any recovery because PS had been dissolved. P then brought this action against PS's sole shareholder, Marchese (D), individually, and against the other business entities D owns. P's plan was to pierce PS's corporate veil so that D could be held personally liable, and then "reverse pierce" D's other corporations. The court granted P's summary judgment motion, holding all Ds jointly liable. Ds appeal.

Issue. May the corporate veil be pierced when the court can no longer differentiate between the corporation and the individual and it would be unjust to protect the individual?

Held. Yes. Judgment reversed and case remanded.

- A corporate veil may be pierced if two requirements are met: (i) there must be such unity of interest and ownership that the separate personalities of the corporation and the individual no longer exist; and (ii) circumstances must be such that adherence to the fiction of separate corporate existence would sanction a fraud or promote injustice.
- In determining whether a corporation is so controlled by an individual or another corporation that the court would be justified in disregarding their separate identities, Illinois courts look to the following four factors: (i) a failure to comply with corporate formalities or to keep sufficient business records, (ii) a commingling of corporate assets, (iii) undercapitalization, and (iv) one corporation's treatment of another corporation's assets as its own.
- In this case, D used the same office, phone line, and expense account to run the majority of his corporations. Furthermore, none of D's corporations ever held a meeting. D would borrow funds from his corporations for personal expenses, and his corporations would borrow money from each other. D did not even have a personal bank account. Clearly, the first part of the test for piercing the corporate veil has been met.
- The second part of the test requires a finding that failing to allow the veil to be pierced would sanction a fraud or promote an injustice. Illinois courts that have properly pierced a corporate veil to avoid "promoting injustice" have concluded that a failure to pierce would result in some wrong that lies beyond the fact that a creditor may not be able to recover, *e.g.*, that a party would be unjustly enriched. Here, P must present evidence of such a wrong.

Comment. On remand, the court found in P's favor, entering a judgment against D for $86,768 plus costs and concluding that protecting D would "sanction a fraud or promote injustice." On appeal, the judgment was affirmed with the observation that by receiving countless benefits at the expense of P and other creditors, D "insur[ed] that his corporations had insufficient funds with which to pay their debts."

---

(2) Liability Between Subsidiaries

Roman Catholic Archbishop of San Francisco v. Sheffield

93 Cal. Rptr. 338 (Cal. Ct. App. 1971).

Facts. While traveling through Switzerland, Sheffield (P) visited a monastery of the Roman Catholic order operated by the Canons Regular of St. Augustine. There, P contracted with Father Cretton to purchase a St Bernard dog for $175, payable in $20 installments. The dog was to be shipped to P's home in Los Angeles. P made two additional installments, but did not receive the dog. P was told that the dog would not be shipped until the entire purchase price was paid, along with additional "fees" to cover Father Cretton's trip to Geneva to deliver the dog to the airline. P was also told that he could not receive a refund of the money he had already paid. P filed suit in a California state court against the Roman Catholic Church, The Roman Catholic Archbishop of San Francisco (D), the Bishop of Rome (*i.e.,* the Pope), the Holy See (*i.e.,* the Vatican), the Canons Regular of St. Augustine, and Father Cretton. P alleged that the Roman Catholic Church, the Pope, and the Vatican controlled D and the Canons Regular of St. Augustine, and thus all were liable. D filed a motion for summary judgment, but was denied. D appeals.

Issue. When a parent corporation controls several subsidiaries, is each subsidiary liable for the actions of all other subsidiaries?

Held. No. Judgment reversed.

- D submitted an affidavit that D had no knowledge of the contract and had no business or dealings with P or the Canons Regular of St. Augustine. D also claimed that it is a distinct legal entity. P argued that the Roman Catholic Church and its congregations are one worldwide entity. P did not contend that D was directly involved in the transaction at issue, but sought to reach D through the alter ego theory. To prove this theory, P must show that not only is D influenced and governed by the other entity, but also that there is such a unity of interest and ownership that the individuality or separateness of each has ceased, and the facts are such that an adherence to the fiction of a separate existence would sanction a fraud or promote injustice.
- The affidavits may have raised a triable issue of fact as to whether the Canons Regular of St. Augustine is an "alter ego" of the Church, but it does not show that the Canons Regular of St. Augustine is an "alter ego" of D. D had no dealings with the organization. There is no respondeat superior between subagents.
- It is not enough that P would not be able to collect if not permitted to sue D. The purpose of the doctrine is not to protect every unsatisfied creditor, but to afford him protection when some conduct, amounting to bad faith, makes it inequitable for the owner of a corporation to hide behind its corporate veil.

(3) Liability of Parent to Subsidiary

In re Silicone Gel Breast Implants Products Liability Litigation

887 F. Supp. 1447 (N.D. Ala. 1995).

Facts. Bristol-Myers Squibb Company (D) is the sole shareholder of a major breast implant supplier, Medical Engineering Corporation ("MEC"). MEC purportedly had a three-member board of directors consisting of two of D's executives and MEC's president, although many of MEC's past presidents did not recall that MEC had a board or that they were members. Evidence revealed that MEC prepared regular reports for D, that D required MEC to submit a five-year plan for its review, that MEC submitted budgets to D for approval, that D controlled MEC's money and kept any interest earned, that D required MEC to obtain its approval for capital appropriations, that D was highly involved in MEC's personnel issues, that D performed auditing and review functions for MEC, and that D otherwise played a regular part in MEC's business. Additionally, D's public relations department issued statements regarding the safety of breast implants, D's name and logo were in package inserts and promotions regarding breast implants, and D's name was used in sales and communications to physicians regarding breast implants. In 1991, D's executive vice president suspended MEC's sales of the product, and MEC ceased all operations later that year, selling its urology division with D's approval and turning the proceeds from the sale over to D. Plaintiffs (Ps) brought a products liability suit, seeking to hold D responsible for MEC's actions and pleading strict liability, negligence and negligence per se, fraud, misrepresentation, and participation. D moves for summary judgment.

Issue. May an entity, which is the sole shareholder of a corporation that makes a product subject to a products liability action, but which does not itself manufacture or market that product, be found liable through piercing the corporate veil or under a theory of direct liability?

Held. Yes. Summary judgment denied.

- Because this is a federal multi-district proceeding, the court looks to the laws of several states to determine the issues at hand.
- A parent corporation is expected to exert some control over its subsidiary. When, however, a corporation is controlled to such an extent that it is merely the alter ego or instrumentality of its shareholder, the corporate veil should be pierced in the interest of justice. Here, the evidence would provide significant support for a finding at trial that MEG is D's alter ego.
- In Delaware, courts can pierce the corporate veil absent a finding of fraud or like misconduct if a subsidiary is found to be an alter ego or mere instrumentality of its sole shareholder. Many states that do require a fraud finding do so only in contract cases, not tort cases. Moreover, the fact that MEC's funds may be insufficient to handle Ps' claims and that D may have induced people to believe D was vouching for MEC's product through its actions support a finding that allowing D to escape liability would be unjust.
- D may also be liable under at least one direct theory of liability, that of negligent undertaking under section 324A of Restatement (Second) of Torts, which provides, "One who undertakes, gratuitously or for consideration, to render services to another which he should recognize as necessary for the protection of a third person or his things, is subject to liability to the third person for physical harm resulting from his failure to exercise reasonable care to [perform] his undertakings" under certain circumstances. Thus, D is not entitled to summary judgment.

---

(4) No Improper Actions

Frigidaire Sales Corp. v. Union Properties, Inc.

562 P.2d 244 (Wash. 1977).

Facts. Frigidaire Sales Corporation (P) contracted with Commercial Investors ("Commercial"), a limited partnership. Mannon and Baxter (Ds) were limited partners of Commercial as well as officers, directors, and shareholders of Commercial's only general partner, Union Properties, Inc. ("Union"). Ds controlled Union and, through that control, exercised the day-to-day management and control of Commercial. Commercial breached the contract, and P filed suit. The trial court found that Ds did not incur general liability for Commercial's obligations. The appeals court affirmed, and P appeals.

Issue. Do limited partners incur general liability for the limited partnership's obligations merely because they are directors, officers, or shareholders of the corporation's general partner?

Held. No. Judgment affirmed.

- Under Washington law, parties may form a limited partnership with one corporation as its only general partner. If that general partner is inadequately capitalized, a creditor is protected under the corporation law doctrine of piercing the corporate veil. Mere undercapitalization is no reason to open liability to limited partners who control the general partner.
- Additionally, P was never misled into believing that Ds were acting outside their corporate capacities. Where, as here, persons who are directors, officers, and shareholders of a corporation keep the corporation's affairs separate from their personal affairs, and do not perpetrate fraud or manifest injustice upon parties dealing with the corporation, the corporation's separate entity should be respected.
- P entered into the contract with Commercial, and Ds signed the contract only through their capacities as officers of Union, Commercial's general partner. In the eyes of the law, it was Union that entered into the contract with P and controlled Commercial.
- Finally, there is no evidence that P mistakenly assumed that Ds were general partners. P entered into the contract knowing that Union was the only party with general liability. P could have, but did not, insist that Ds personally guarantee contractual performance. Thus, there is no justification for holding that Ds incurred general liability.

Comment. The major difference between tort and contract cases is that in contract cases, the plaintiff had an opportunity in advance to investigate the financial resources of the corporation and had then chosen to do business with it. Thus, in contract cases, the intention of the parties and knowledge of the risks assumed in entering into a contract are factors to be assessed in making a determination as to whether the corporate veil should be pierced.

C. Shareholder Derivative Actions

1. Direct and Derivative Suits

A shareholder may sue to enforce management's duties. The suit may be direct or derivative depending on the nature of the claim. If the claim is that management's breach reduced the residual value of the business (*e.g.,* shirking or self-dealing), the shareholder must sue derivatively in the name of the corporation. If the claim is that management's breach deprived the shareholder of some other right (other than her contingent right to that residual value, *e.g.,* right to inspect shareholder list), the shareholder must sue directly in her own name. It is sometimes difficult to distinguish the two types of claims, especially because direct suits may be brought as class actions.

2. The Threat of Derivative "Strike" Suits

A person with a relatively small stake in the residual value of a business might be tempted to bring a derivative suit for the primary purpose of being bought off. Requiring the defendants to make payment to the corporation reduces this temptation for the complaining shareholder. It makes little difference to the complaining shareholder's attorney, however, who is usually the real party in interest. The attorney for a prevailing shareholder suing derivatively may obtain his fee from the corporation. He may therefore legitimately demand some payment in connection with a settlement.

3. Limits on the Derivative Action

In an effort to limit "strike" suits and otherwise protect against over-deterrence, virtually all corporation statutes limit the shareholders who may bring derivative suits, and many states have enacted statutes requiring the plaintiff-shareholder in a derivative suit, under certain circumstances, to post a bond or other security to indemnify the corporation against certain of its litigation expenses in the event that the plaintiff loses the suit.

a. When Security Must Be Posted

There is great variety in the requirements of state statutes. Some provide that the plaintiff must post security if she owns less than a specified percentage of stock. Others state that security is discretionary with the court (and it is demanded only when there is no reasonable possibility that the action could benefit the corporation).

b. Who Is Entitled to Security

In most states, only the corporation may demand security and only its expenses may be paid. Some states allow officers and directors to demand security and to receive reimbursement.

c. Covered Expenses

Normally, all expenses, including attorneys' fees, are covered. Also covered may be expenses of officers and directors that the corporation is obligated to pay because it has indemnified them (it may indemnify officers and directors for actions taken in good faith and pursuant to their business judgment, but normally not for fraudulent actions).

d. Application in Federal Diversity Cases

Cohen v. Beneficial Industrial Loan Corp.

337 U.S. 541 (1949).

Facts. Cohen's decedent (P) brought a shareholders' derivative action in federal court in New Jersey against Beneficial Industrial Loan Corporation and certain of its managers and directors (Ds). The complaint alleged that since 1929, the individual defendants had engaged in a continuing conspiracy to enrich themselves at the corporation's expense. P owned only approximately .0125% of the outstanding stock of the corporation. After the lawsuit commenced, New Jersey enacted a statute that requires plaintiffs owning less than 5% of a corporation's outstanding shares of stock (unless those shares have a market value over $50,000) to be liable for reasonable expenses and attorney's fees of the defense if his derivative suit fails. The corporate defendant moved to require P to post a security bond of $125,000. P appeals a court of appeals judgment requiring P to post bond as a condition to further prosecution of the lawsuit.

Issue. Must a federal court sitting in diversity apply a statute of the forum state providing for the posting of security for the corporation?

Held. Yes. Judgment affirmed.

- ♦ A stockholder who brings a derivative action assumes a position of a fiduciary nature. He sues as a representative of a class that did not elect him as a representative as they elected the corporate director or manager. The state has plenary power to impose standards promoting accountability, responsibility, and liability upon such a representative without offending the Constitution. The statute at issue does not offend the Due Process Clause, as it imposes liability and requires security for only ***reasonable*** expenses. It also does not offend the Equal Protection Clause by making a classification based on the financial interest the representative has in a corporation; the classification serves only to insure some measure of good faith and responsibility.

- Under the doctrine resulting from *Erie R.R. Co. v. Tompkins,* 304 U.S. 64 (1938), federal courts sitting in diversity apply the substantive law of the forum state while following the federal rules of procedure. The New Jersey statute imposes a new liability, which is substantive, along with the procedure of entitling the corporate defendant to a bond of indemnity in order to effectuate the law. Thus, federal courts must apply the New Jersey statute in diversity cases.

---

e. Determining Whether Statute Is Applicable on Its Terms

Eisenberg v. Flying Tiger Line, Inc.

451 F.2d 267 (2d Cir. 1971).

Facts. In mid-1969, The Flying Tiger Line, Inc. (D), a Delaware corporation, organized a wholly owned subsidiary in Delaware called the Flying Tiger Corporation ("FTC"). The following month, FTC organized a Delaware wholly owned subsidiary, FTL Air Freight Corporation ("FTL"). These three Delaware corporations then created a plan of reorganization, subject to shareholder approval, under which D would merge into FTL. The stockholders approved the plan by a two-thirds vote. When the merger took effect, D ceased to operate, FTL took over all operations, and D's shares were converted into equal FTC shares. FTL then changed its name to Flying Tiger Line, Inc. Essentially, the merger resulted in all business operations being confined to a wholly owned subsidiary of a holding company whose stockholders are the former stockholders of D.

Eisenberg (P), purportedly on his own behalf and on behalf of all other stockholders of D, filed suit in a New York state court to enjoin the reorganization and merger. P asserted that the purpose of the plan was to dilute his voting rights. D, who removed the action to a New York federal court, moved for an order that P comply with section 627 of the New York Business Corporation Law, which provides that a plaintiff filing a derivative suit against a corporation must post security for the corporation's costs. The trial judge granted D's motion, giving P 30 days to post security. P failed to comply, the court dismissed his action, and P appeals.

Issue. Is an action asserting that stockholders have been deprived of any voice in the affairs of the company derivative for purposes of the statute?

Held. No. Judgment reversed.

- Under *Cohen, supra,* a federal court in a diversity action must apply a state statute requiring the posting of security for costs if the state court would require the security under similar facts. New York courts have indicated that section 627 applies in its courts even when another state's substantive law controls the merits of the case. Thus, even if, as P contends, Delaware law, which has no security requirement, controls the merits of this case, this court must look to the New York statute regarding the issue of security.
- Section 627 applies exclusively to derivative actions. Here, P contends that the reorganization deprived him and the other stockholders of their right to vote on the operating company's affairs. In essence, he claims that he and his fellow stockholders have been deprived of any voice in the operation of their company. He is not challenging the management of the company on behalf of the corporation. Thus, P's cause of action is personal and not derivative within the meaning of section 627. Therefore, P is not required to post security.

---

4. Settlements and Attorneys' Fees

When derivative suits reach settlement rather than proceeding to judgment, the company can pay the parties' attorneys' fees. When a judgment is rendered against the defendants, however, except as covered by insurance, the defendants generally will be responsible for attorneys' fees and possibly costs. Often, the real beneficiary on the plaintiff's side is his attorney, who may accept a generous fee from the corporation to settle the lawsuit while the corporate managers who brought harm to the corporation are relieved of the risk of any personal loss.

5. Individual Recovery

In *Lynch v. Patterson,* 701 P.2d 1126 (Wyo. 1985), the plaintiff, one of three shareholders, brought a derivative suit against the other shareholders who, in managing the corporation, had increased their own salaries, ultimately paying themselves an extra $266,000. The court awarded the plaintiff damages in his individual capacity, reasoning that allowing a corporate recovery would merely put the funds back in the hands of the wrongdoers.

6. The Demand Requirement

All corporation statutes regulate settlement of derivative claims as well as requiring the complaining shareholder to exhaust internal remedies before bringing suit. Typical of these statutes is Rule 23.1 of the Federal Rules of Civil Procedure.

a. Federal Rule of Civil Procedure 23.1

"In a derivative action . . . , the complaint shall be verified and shall allege . . . that the plaintiff was a shareholder or member at the time of the transaction of which [he] complains or that [his] share or membership thereafter devolved on [him] by operation of law. . . . The complaint shall also allege with particularity the efforts, if any, made by the plaintiff to obtain the action [he] desires from the directors . . . [or] the reasons for [his] failure to obtain the action or for not making the effort. The derivative action may not be maintained if it appears that the plaintiff does not fairly and adequately represent the interests of the shareholders or members similarly situated in enforcing the right of the corporation. . . . The action shall not be dismissed or compromised without the approval of the court, and notice of the proposed dismissal or compromise shall be given to shareholders or members in such manner as the court directs."

b. The Delaware Approach

Delaware's demand requirement parallels Federal Rule of Civil Procedure 23.1. Interpreting the "futility" exception to this requirement in *Aronson v. Lewis,* 473 A.2d 805 (Del. 1984), the Delaware Supreme Court held that a plaintiff would have to allege particularized facts that would create a reasonable doubt about the independence or disinterestedness of the directors or whether the challenged transaction is "otherwise the product of a valid exercise of business judgment."

c. "Universal Demand"

Some critics of the Delaware approach have advocated "universal demand." The American Law Institute ("ALI"), for example, would require a written demand unless "the plaintiff makes a specific showing that irreparable injury to the corporation would otherwise result." [2 ALI, Principles of Corporate Governance: Analysis and Recommendations § 7.03(b) (1992)] If a board rejects a demand, however, the ALI would subject the board's decision to "an elaborate set of standards that calibrates the deference afforded the decision of the directors to the character of the claim being asserted." The Model Business Corporation Act section 7.42 (1995 Supp.) requires demand, but permits the derivative plaintiff to file suit within 90 days of the demand unless the demand is rejected earlier and to file even earlier if the corporation would otherwise suffer irreparable injury. The legislatures of at least 12 states—

Arizona, Connecticut, Florida, Georgia, Michigan, Mississippi, Montana, Nebraska, New Hampshire, North Carolina, Virginia, and Wisconsin—have adopted a universal demand requirement.

d. The New York Approach

The New York Court of Appeals interpreted demand futility in *Barr v. Wackman,* 329 N.E.2d 180 (N.Y. 1975), which arose in connection with the decision by the board of Talcott National Corporation ("Talcott") to reject a merger proposal from Gulf & Western Industries ("Gulf & Western") in favor of a cash tender offer from Associates First Capital Corporation, a Gulf & Western subsidiary. Under the merger proposal, Talcott holders would have received for each share $17 in cash and .6 of a warrant to purchase Gulf & Western stock, worth approximately $7; pursuant to the cash tender offer, Talcott holders received $20 per share. Talcott's board consisted of 13 outside directors, a director affiliated with a related company, and four interested inside directors. The derivative plaintiff claimed that the board abandoned the merger proposal after the four "controlling" inside directors received pecuniary and personal benefits from Gulf & Western in exchange for ceding control of Talcott on terms less favorable to Talcott's shareholders. The plaintiff also claimed that the outside directors failed "to do more than passively rubber-stamp the decisions of the active managers," whereas, had they discharged their duty of care, they would have been "put on notice of the claimed self-dealing of the affiliated directors." The court held that futility excused demand. The court noted, however, that "[i]t is not sufficient merely to name a majority of the directors as parties defendant with conclusory allegations of wrongdoing or control by wrongdoers" to justify failure to make demand.

e. Abdication Claims

Grimes v. Donald

673 A.2d 1207 (Del. 1996).

Facts. Grimes (P), a shareholder in DSC Communications Corporation, claimed that the board of directors had failed to use due care, committed waste, approved excessive compensation, and unlawfully delegated its duties and responsibilities by entering into an agreement with the CEO, Donald (D), which provided that D was entitled to damages if the board of directors "unreasonably interfered" with D's management of the company. P sought a declaration that the delegation provision was invalid. The court of chancery analyzed the claim as a direct claim, and D appeals.

Issue. May a shareholder proceed directly on an "abdication" claim when he seeks only a declaration that an agreement between the board and its CEO is invalid?

Held. Yes. Judgment affirmed.

- Whether a claim may proceed as a direct or a derivative action depends on the nature of the wrong alleged and the relief sought. Claims seeking injunctive or prospective relief, such as P's abdication claim, are more likely to qualify as direct.

Comment. The court's focus on the nature of the relief sought is consistent with the idea that the function of the shareholder derivative claim mechanism is to avoid the problems of fashioning compensatory relief that would plague a class action claim.

---

f. Futility Exception

Marx v. Akers

666 N.E.2d 1034 (N.Y. 1996).

Facts. Without making a demand on IBM's board of directors (Ds), Marx (P) filed a shareholder derivative suit alleging that the board had wasted corporate assets by awarding excessive compensation to IBM's executive officers and to its outside directors. The complaint alleged that during a five-year period, Ds increased their compensation rates from a base of $20,000 plus $500 for each meeting attended to a retainer of $55,000 plus 100 shares of IBM stock. The appellate division dismissed P's complaint for failure to make a demand, and P appeals.

Issues.

(i) When a majority of a board consists of outside directors, does futility excuse a derivative plaintiff shareholder from making a demand in connection with claims of excessive compensation paid to executive officers?

(ii) When a majority of a board consists of outside directors, does futility excuse a derivative plaintiff shareholder from making a demand in connection with claims of excessive compensation paid to outside directors?

(iii) Does a claim that the compensation paid to outside directors "bears little relation to the part-time services rendered by [them] . . . or to the profitability of [the company]" and that the compensation increased in excess of the cost of living during a period when the "board's responsibilities [had] not increased [and] its performance, measured by the company's earnings and stock price, ha[d] been poor" state a cause of action?

Held. (i) No. (ii) Yes. (iii) No. Judgment affirmed.

- ♦ The demand requirement (i) creates a form of alternative dispute resolution by providing corporation directors with opportunities to correct alleged abuses, (ii) helps insulate directors from harassment by litigations on matters clearly within the discretion of directors, and (iii) discourages "strike suits" commenced by shareholders for personal gain rather than for the benefit of the corporation. The "futility" exception to the demand requirement permits shareholders to bring claims on behalf of the corporation when it is evident that directors will wrongfully refuse to bring such claims.
- ♦ The futility exception would swallow the rule if conclusory allegations of wrongdoing against each member of the board excused demand. To qualify for the futility exception, a shareholder must allege with particularity that (i) a majority of the board of directors is interested in the challenged transaction, by virtue of self-interest in the transaction or "control" by a self-interested director, (ii) that the board of directors did not fully inform themselves about the challenged transaction to the extent reasonably appropriate under the circumstances, or (iii) that the challenged transaction was so egregious on its face that it could not have been the product of sound business judgment of the directors.
- ♦ P's claim of excessive executive compensation did not show futility as P's allegations that less than a majority of the directors received such compensation indicate that the board was not interested, and P's conclusory allegations of faulty accounting procedures used to calculate executive compensation levels do not qualify as allegations of particular facts that the board failed to deliberate or exercise its business judgment in setting those levels.
- ♦ P's claim of excessive outside director compensation did show futility because P's allegation that outside directors comprised a majority of the board indicates that a majority of the board was self-interested.

- P's claim of excessive compensation of outside directors did not state a cause of action because P did not allege compensation rates excessive on their face or other facts that would have called into question whether the compensation was fair to the corporation when approved, the good faith of the directors setting those rates, or that the decision to set the compensation could not have been a product of valid business judgment. P's conclusory allegations are not factually based allegations of wrongdoing or waste that would, if true, sustain a verdict in P's favor.

---

7. Special Committees

a. Committee Recommendation Valid

Auerbach v. Bennett

393 N.E.2d 994 (N.Y. 1979).

Facts. The management of General Telephone & Electronics Corporation investigated the possibility that the company or its subsidiaries had made improper payments to public officials or political parties in foreign countries. The board of directors furthered the investigation. It was determined that approximately $11 million had been paid in bribes and kickbacks and that four of the 15 directors (Ds) had been personally involved in certain of the transactions.

Auerbach (P), a shareholder, brought this derivative suit on behalf of the corporation against the corporation's directors, its independent auditors, and the corporation, seeking to compel these defendants to account for the money paid in bribes and kickbacks.

The board of directors then created a special litigation committee composed of three disinterested directors who had joined the board after the challenged transactions occurred. This committee concluded, among other things, that it was not in the best interests of the corporation for the derivative action to proceed. Ds moved for dismissal, which the trial court granted. P appealed. The appellate court found for P, and Ds appeal.

Issues.

(i) Is the decision by the special committee that a continuation of the derivative suit would not be in the best interests of the corporation protected from judicial inquiry by the business judgment doctrine?

(ii) Does the business judgment doctrine preclude inquiry into the disinterested independence of the members of the special committee or the appropriateness and sufficiency of the investigative procedures pursued by that committee?

(iii) Is an investigative committee authorized by the board of which the defendant directors were members incapable of determining whether to continue suit against those directors?

(iv) Should summary judgment be withheld upon a motion for disclosure made by an intervenor before an appellate court?

Held. (i) Yes. (ii) No. (iii) No. (iv) No. Judgment reversed. Summary judgment for Ds granted.

- Shareholder derivative suits present a special situation for application of the business judgment rule. Normally, before a shareholder may bring such a suit, he must request that the directors bring the suit, and they must refuse. If the directors refuse on the basis of a good faith business judgment, the court will dismiss the derivative suit. However, the directors may sometimes refuse, in bad faith, when the suit is brought against the directors themselves, as it was here.
- Thus, courts may inquire into the disinterested independence of the members of the board who are chosen to pass on whether the derivative suit should be dismissed. Here, the special committee was composed of disinterested directors. The risk that such board members will be hesitant to

investigate fellow board members is inescapable, but to require that persons outside the board do the investigation would require that the board abdicate its fiduciary duty to the corporation to manage its affairs.

- The substantive decision of the special committee to dismiss the suit may not be inquired into by the court. This is within the province of the business judgment rule. (In other words, the court will not inquire into the merits of the various considerations taken into account by the committee.)
- The court may, however, inquire into the investigative methods selected and the prosecution of those methods, which go to whether the committee acted in good faith. Here, it appears that the committee adopted appropriate procedures—it hired outside counsel, reviewed prior work of the audit committee, held interviews with the defendant directors, questioned the other directors and the accounting firm, etc.
- Taking the record below as it stands, there is nothing to indicate, and P has shown nothing further, that allowing further discovery would raise issues concerning the independence of members of the committee, the procedures they used, or whether they acted in good faith. Thus, there are no issues of fact to be considered, and summary judgment is appropriate.

Dissent. The continuation of this lawsuit requires knowledge of Ds' and the committee's motives and actions, knowledge that "is peculiarly in the possession of the defendants themselves." Summary judgment is inappropriate at this juncture, prior to disclosure proceedings.

---

b. Termination by a Special Litigation Committee

Zapata Corp. v. Maldonado

430 A.2d 779 (Del. 1981).

Facts. Maldonado (P), a stockholder in Zapata Corporation (D), instituted a derivative action on D's behalf. The suit alleged breaches of fiduciary duty by 10 of D's officers and directors. P brought this suit without first demanding that the board bring it, on the grounds that the demand would be futile because all directors were named as defendants. Several years later, the board appointed an independent investigating committee. By this time, four of the defendants were off the board, and the remaining directors appointed two new outside directors. These new directors comprised the investigating committee. After its investigation, the committee recommended that the action be dismissed. Its determination was binding on D, which moved for dismissal or summary judgment. The trial court denied the motions, holding that the business judgment rule is not a grant of authority to dismiss derivative suits, and that a stockholder sometimes has an individual right to maintain such actions. D has filed an interlocutory appeal.

Issue. Did the committee have the power to cause this action to be dismissed?

Held. Yes. Trial court interlocutory order reversed and case remanded for proceedings consistent with this opinion.

- A stockholder does not have an individual right, once demand is made and refused, to continue a derivative suit. Unless it was wrongful, a board's decision that the suit would harm the company will be respected as a matter of business judgment. A stockholder has the right to initiate the action himself when demand may be properly excused as futile. However, excusing demand does not strip the board of its corporate power. There may be circumstances where the suit, although properly initiated, would not be in the corporation's best interests. This is the context here.
- The court must find a balancing point where bona fide stockholder power to bring corporation causes of action cannot be unfairly trampled on by the board, but where the corporation can rid itself of detrimental litigation. A two-step process is involved. First, the court must recognize that the board, even if tainted by self-interest, can legally delegate its authority to a committee of

disinterested directors. However, the court may inquire on its own into the independence and good faith of the committee and the bases supporting its conclusions. If the court is satisfied on both counts, the second step is to apply its own business judgment as to whether the motion to dismiss should be granted. Thus, suits will be heard when corporate actions meet the criteria of the first step, but where the result would terminate a grievance worthy of consideration.

---

c. Burden of Persuasion on Committee

In re Oracle Corp. Derivative Litigation

824 A.2d 917 (Del. Ch. 2003).

Facts. Certain stockholders of Oracle Corp. brought a derivative complaint based on alleged insider trading by four members of Oracle's board of directors: Ellison, Henley, Lucas, and Boskin. Oracle formed a special litigation committee ("SLC") to investigate the claims and determine the best course of action for the company. Two Oracle board members, Garcia-Molina and Grundfest, were named to the SLC. Both joined the board after the events in question took place and both were tenured professors at Stanford University. Both were paid an hourly wage to serve on the SLC, but agreed to waive their compensation if a court deemed it necessary to maintain the SLC's impartiality. The SLC also retained some expert advisors to assist in the investigation, and their independence is not at issue. The SLC conducted an extensive and thorough investigation. The SLC concluded that Oracle should not pursue the plaintiffs' claims and have made a motion to terminate the action.

Issue. Has the SLC met its burden of persuasion and shown that there is no material issue of fact calling into doubt its independence?

Held. No. Motion to terminate denied.

- The SLC takes the position that its members are independent. In support of this position, they note that neither Grundfest nor Garcia-Molina were on the board at the time of the alleged wrongdoing; that neither has received compensation from Oracle other than as directors; and that there is a lack of any material ties between Grundfest and Garcia-Molina and the accused directors. The SLC did disclose in its report that defendant director Boskin was also a Stanford professor; that the SLC was aware that defendant director Lucas had made donations to Stanford; and that one of these donations was allocated for use by Grundfest in his personal research.
- The report failed to disclose, however, several shocking key facts that were only revealed during discovery. First, defendant director Boskin taught Grundfest when Grundfest was a Ph.D. candidate, and the two have remained in contact over the years, with both serving together on a Stanford steering committee. Next, defendant director Lucas is a very well-known alumnus of Stanford and a very generous contributor to the school. Finally, defendant director Ellison, who was one of the wealthiest men in America, had made major charitable contributions to Stanford and had talked publicly about endowing a graduate interdisciplinary studies program at Stanford in the future, although it should be noted that Stanford recently denied Ellison's child admission to the school.
- The SLC contends that despite this information, none of the defendants had the practical ability to deprive either Grundfest or Garcia-Molina of their positions at Stanford, as both have tenure. However, this is not the only motivating factor in human behavior. Social influences may also direct behavior. The SLC has not met its burden to show the absence of material factual question about its independence. The ties among the SLC, the defendants, and Stanford are so substantial that they raise reasonable doubt about the SLC's ability to impartially decide whether the defendants should face suit. This inference is based on common human nature.

D. The Role and Purpose of Corporations

1. Theories

Both business and legal theory agree that a corporation must have a purpose or goal. They tend to disagree about what this purpose should be.

a. Business Theory

When business theory addresses "corporate purposes," it tends to deal in terms of "strategy." "Strategy" is the determination of the basic long-term goals and objectives of the company and the adoption of courses of action and the allocation of resources necessary to carry out the basic goals. Strategy includes:

1) Selection of target markets, definition of basic products to address markets, and determination of the distribution systems (all from among many alternatives).
2) Matching corporate resources and capabilities with necessary resources and capabilities for possible market alternatives, and, once alternatives have been selected, planning the necessary resources and their allocation.
3) Selection of alternatives in terms of management's personal preferences and values.
4) Selection of alternatives according to perceived obligations by management to segments of society other than the stockholders.

b. Legal Theory

Legal theory asks what purposes are within those bounds set by the articles and the statutory law under which the corporation was formed. In effect, the articles are a contract between the state and the incorporators.

1) Originally, the issue was whether a corporation had exceeded the powers granted under a state-given charter.
2) More recently, with general incorporation laws, the issue is whether the corporation has remained within the purposes set by the incorporators and the state law.
3) Closely related to the issue of proper purposes is the issue of proper "powers." State law often sets forth the acts that a corporation may legally perform. These acts should be in aid of a proper corporate purpose.
4) If the corporation engages in an improper purpose or uses an improper power, that purpose or act is said to be "ultra vires" (beyond the corporation's powers).

c. Distinction Between Purposes and Powers

There is a distinction in meaning between purposes and powers. A "purpose" means the end or objective and usually is a statement of the type of business that the corporation will engage in. A "power" means the kind of acts (such as mortgaging property) that a corporation may engage in to pursue its corporate purpose. Discussions involving purposes or powers often confuse these terms.

2. Powers of a Corporation

a. Express Powers

A corporation has express power to perform any act authorized by the general corporation laws of the state and those acts authorized by the articles of incorporation.

1) General Powers

Most states have express statutory provisions allowing corporations to sue and be sued, own property, make gifts to charity, borrow money, acquire stock in other companies, redeem or purchase corporate stock, etc.

2) Limitations

Most states also have some express limitations on corporate powers. For example, a transfer of substantially all of a corporation's assets normally requires the approval of a majority of the voting power of the shareholders.

b. Implied Powers

In most states, corporations also have implied power to do whatever is "reasonably necessary" for the purpose of promoting their express purposes and in aid of their express powers, unless such acts are expressly prohibited by common or statutory law. The trend is to construe broadly what is reasonably necessary.

1) There may still be some limits on what the corporation may do. For example, some states limit the right of a corporation to enter into partnerships, because a partner may bind the corporate partner (removing management responsibility from the corporation's board). Shareholders may give this power in the articles, however.

2) Some states have continued the common law prohibition on corporations practicing a profession (law, etc.).

c. Constructive Notice

All parties dealing with a corporation are held to have constructive notice of the corporation's articles and of state corporation law.

3. The Objective of the Corporation

The issue here is the extent to which a corporation may act in a manner not intended to maximize profits.

a. Social Responsibility of Corporations

In early days, corporate charters were granted by the government on the theory that the corporation would contribute to the public interest as well as make money for shareholders only. In the 1930s, a debate began about the responsibility of corporations; this debate is still going on (with inconclusive results). Some argue that a corporation's objective should be to produce the best possible goods and services, that no other legal standard is enforceable, and that any other standard allows an unhealthy divorce between management (making such decisions) and ownership. Others argue that corporations have a "social responsibility" and that they must balance the interests of stockholders, employees, customers, and the public at large.

b. Charitable Contributions

A.P. Smith Manufacturing Company v. Barlow

98 A.2d 581 (N.J. 1953), *appeal dism'd,* 346 U.S. 861 (1953).

Facts. The corporation, formed in 1896, gave a $1,500 gift to Princeton University. It was challenged by a shareholder. The president and other executives testified that the gift was a sound investment, that it created a favorable environment for the company, and that the public had a reasonable expectation of such "socially" oriented contributions by corporations.

Issue. Is such a gift to a university by a corporation an ultra vires act?

Held. No. The gift was within the implied powers of the corporation.

- Control of economic wealth has passed to corporations. The common law has, therefore, begun to recognize the doctrine that such donations tend reasonably to promote corporate objectives. This is, therefore, an implied corporate power.
- A 1930 statute had been passed in the state allowing such donations (in limited amounts); it applied (although it was passed after the corporation was formed), as the legislature has power to amend corporate charters.
- There is no wrongdoing by the corporate officers (concerning contributions to their personal benefit).

---

c. Accumulation of Surplus

Dodge v. Ford Motor Co.

170 N.W. 668 (Mich. 1919).

Facts. Shareholders of Ford Motor Company (Ps) brought an action to prevent the expansion of a new plant and to compel the directors to pay additional special dividends. The company had capital stock of $2 million and $12 million in surplus. Profits for the year were expected to be $60 million. Testimony of the majority shareholder (D) and his counsel revealed that D wanted to build a new plant, increase production and employment, and cut the price of cars to the public in order to pass on part of the benefit of the company's earning power to the public. The company had paid large dividends in the years prior to this change in policy by D. D's policy is now to pay only a regular dividend (60% on stated capital) and reserve the remainder of the earnings for expansion and price reductions. Ps charge that D's new purposes are charitable in nature and unlawful. The lower court enjoined the building of the new plant and ordered the payment of a $19.3 million dividend.

Issue. When the directors' purpose in not paying a dividend (when there is adequate surplus to do so) is to benefit the interests of persons other than the shareholders, will the court intervene to force payment?

Held. Yes. Judgment affirmed as to the order to pay the dividend and reversed as to the order enjoining the building of the new plant.

- Corporations are organized primarily for the profit of the shareholders. The directors are to use their powers primarily for that end. They have reasonable discretion, to be exercised in good faith, to act for this end. Here, their discretion to expand the business and cut car prices will be upheld—it is part of a long-range business plan; past experience shows Ford management has been capable and acted for the benefit of the shareholders, and it does not appear that the interests of the shareholders are menaced.

- Directors also have the responsibility to declare dividends and their amounts. Their discretion will not be interfered with unless they are guilty of fraud, misappropriation, or (when there are sufficient funds to do so without detriment to the business) bad faith.
- Here, D's expansion plans may be carried out and there will still be a large amount of surplus available for dividends. Thus, the trial court's order that $19 million be paid in additional dividends is upheld.

---

d. Absence of Misconduct

Shlensky v. Wrigley

237 N.E.2d 776 (Ill. App. Ct. 1968).

Facts. Shlensky (P), a minority shareholder in the corporation (D) that owns Wrigley Field and the Chicago Cubs, brought a shareholder's derivative suit against the directors of the corporation for their refusal to install lights at Wrigley Field and to schedule night games for the Cubs as other teams in the league had done to increase revenues. The directors' motivation was allegedly the result of the views of Mr. Wrigley (also a defendant), the majority shareholder, president, and director of the corporation, who wanted to preserve the neighborhood surrounding Wrigley Field and who believed that baseball was a daytime sport. The lower court dismissed P's action.

Issue. May a shareholder bring a derivative action where there are no allegations of fraud, illegality, or conflict of interest?

Held. No. Judgment affirmed.

- The court will not disturb the "business judgment" of a majority of the directors, absent fraud, illegality, or a conflict of interest. There is no conclusive evidence that the installation of lights and the scheduling of night games will accrue a net benefit in revenues to D, and there appear to be other valid reasons for refusing to install lights, *e.g.,* the detrimental effect on the surrounding neighborhood.
- Corporations are not obliged to follow the direction taken by other, similar corporations. Directors are elected for their own business capabilities and not for their ability to follow others.

Chapter IV
The Limited Liability Company

A. Introduction

Every state has adopted a limited liability company ("LLC") statute. Each one of them cloaks "members"—as the principals of an LLC are usually known—with limited liability. No LLC statute contains a "control rule." In fact, all but a handful of these statutes vest partnership-like decisionmaking authority in the members—absent a provision to the contrary in the articles of organization or the operating agreement. Indeed, the LLC was designed for key actors seeking (i) the opportunity to participate in day-to-day management, (ii) limited liability, and (iii) partnership "flow-thru" tax treatment. Until the late 1980s, efforts to combine these features in a noncorporate organizational form failed because the IRS took the position that limited liability precluded classification of an enterprise as a partnership for tax purposes. The legislative rush began when the IRS reversed this long-held position. *Note*: It is possible to combine these features in a corporate organizational form by electing Subchapter S status if the principals, their business activities, and the organization of their enterprise qualify for this status. A corporation does not qualify if it has: (i) more than 35 shareholders, (ii) a corporate shareholder, (iii) a nonresident alien shareholder, or (iv) more than one class of stock.

Many of the statutes (most patterned after RULPA) reflect a determined effort by their drafters to insure "flow-thru" tax treatment under the IRS "Kitner" rules for classifying business organizations for tax purposes as "partnerships," which received such treatment, and "corporations," which did not. To insure this classification, an LLC statute had to resolve the control and duration issues so that a limited liability company would possess no more than two of the following three "corporate characteristics:" (i) centralized management; (ii) free transferability of interests; and (iii) continuity of [the enterprise's] life. The IRS has rescinded these rules and now simply permits members to choose "flow-thru" treatment.

B. Formation

An LLC is formed by filing articles of organization with the secretary of state. Most states require the articles of organization to include the names of the LLC, the address of its registered office and registered agent, whether the LLC is a term company and, if so, the length of the term, and if management of the company is vested in managers, whether any member or members are to be liable for all or certain debts of the LLC.

1. No Limited Liability for LLC Members Who Fail to Disclose Existence of Their Business Organization to Third Parties

Water, Waste & Land, Inc. d/b/a Westec v. Lanham

955 P.2d 997 (Colo. 1998).

Facts. Larry Clark (D), a manager and member of Preferred Income Investors, LLC ("P.I.I.") (D), a limited liability company organized under the Colorado Limited Liability Company Act ("LLC Act"), contacted Water, Waste & Land, Inc. d/b/a Westec (P) about doing some engineering work for a development project. During preliminary discussions, Clark gave P's representatives his business card, which contained an address and, above the address, the letters "P.I.I." The address was that of Donald Lanham (D), another member of P.I.I., LLC and its primary manager; the same address was listed as the principal office and place of business of P.I.I., LLC in its articles of organization filed with the secretary of state. After further negotiations, Clark entered into an oral agreement with P's representatives and instructed them to send a written work proposal to Lanham. They did so in April 1995. In August, they sent Lanham a proposed contract along with a request that Lanham sign it and return it to P. P never received it, but in mid-August, Clark orally authorized them to begin work. When the work was done, P sent a bill for $9,183.40 to Lanham, but P received no payment. P sued Clark and Lanham individually as well as P.I.I. P.I.I. admitted liability. The county court found that P's representatives understood Clark to be Lanham's agent and so dismissed Clark from the suit. The county court also found that P's representatives "did not have knowledge of any business entity" and dealt with Clark and Lanham "on a personal basis," so the court entered judgment against Lanham as well as P.I.I. Lanham appealed. The district court reversed principally on the grounds that, since Clark's business card contained the letters "P.I.I.," P had constructive notice that it was dealing with a limited liability company under the notice section of the LLC Act (section 7–80–208), which provides: "The fact that the articles of organization are on file in the office of the secretary of state is notice that the limited liability company is a limited liability company and is notice of all other facts set forth therein which are required to be set forth in the articles of organization." The district court also cited P's failure to investigate or request a personal guarantee. P appeals.

Issue. Is a member-manager of an LLC personally liable on a contract entered into by another member-manager and a third party if the third party lacks knowledge of the business entity and believes that the member-manager with whom he dealt was acting as an agent for the other member-manager?

Held. Yes. Judgment reversed and case remanded.

- While Lanham was an agent of P.I.I., LLC, the trier of fact found that he failed to fully disclose his principal to a third party with whom his agent dealt, and, under agency law, this failure rendered him liable on the contract with the third party.
- The notice section of the LLC Act does not address the issue presented.

  To interpret the notice section as providing that the filing of an article of organization puts third parties who deal with a member of an LLC on constructive notice of the LLC's limited liability status even if they lack knowledge of the LLC's existence would invite sharp practices and outright fraud. Such an interpretation would permit an agent of an LLC to mislead a third party into believing that the agent would make good on a contract, conduct that the legislature did not mean to protect.

  A more plausible interpretation is that notice of an LLC's name puts a third party who deals with someone that he knows is a member of an LLC on constructive notice of the LLC's limited liability status and that managers and members bear no liability simply because of their status. This interpretation is consistent with the sections of the LLC Act that (i) require the name of an LLC to include the words "Limited Liability Company" or the initials "LLC" and (ii) expose members to individual liability when they engage in "improper actions" or fail "to observe the formalities or requirements relating to the management of its business and affairs when coupled with some other wrongful conduct."

Courts should interpret statutes in derogation of the common law narrowly, particularly when a broad interpretation would depart radically from the settled rules of agency and create uncertainty about accepted rules that govern business relationships.

When Lanham received the proposed contract from P that demonstrated that P believed that Lanham was the principal, he could have easily corrected P's mistake.

---

2. Limited Liability Partnerships

Registering a partnership as an LLP—by filing a "registration statement" with the secretary of state—typically gives the partners limited liability in connection with "debts and obligations of the [LLP] arising from negligence, wrongful acts, or misconduct . . . by another partner or an employee, agent, or representative of the partnership" unless that "person [is] under his direct supervision and control." [Del. Code Ann., tit. b, ch. 15, 1515 (1992)]

C. The Operating Agreement

Although LLCs are governed by statute, LLC statutes generally provide that the members can adopt an operating agreement with provisions different from the LLC statute. Generally, the operating agreement will control.

1. Operating Agreement Controls If No Conflict with Statute

Elf Atochem North America, Inc. v. Jaffari and Malek LLC

727 A.2d 286 (Del. 1999).

Facts. Elf Atochem North America, Inc. (P) manufactured a solvent-based product that was used in the aviation and aerospace industries. Jaffari was the president of Malek, Inc., and had developed a water-based, more environmentally friendly product. When the Environmental Protection Agency ("EPA") began to regulate solvent-based products as hazardous chemicals, P and Jaffari agreed to undertake a joint venture to market Jaffari's product. The parties formed Malek LLC, a Delaware limited liability company. P contributed capital to the project in exchange for a 30% interest in Malek LLC, and Malek, Inc. contributed its rights to the new product in exchange for a 70% interest in Malek LLC. P, Jaffari, and Malek, Inc. entered into an agreement ("the Agreement") providing for the governance and operation of the LLC. The Agreement contained an arbitration clause covering all disputes arising out of the Agreement, and a forum selection clause providing for exclusive jurisdiction of the state and federal courts sitting in California. Two years later, P filed suit in Delaware against Jaffari and Malek LLC (Ds), individually and derivatively on behalf of Malek LLC. P claimed that Jaffari breached his fiduciary duty to the LLC, used LLC funds for personal use, interfered with prospective business opportunities, failed to make disclosures to P, and breached their contract. Ds filed a motion to dismiss due to lack of subject matter jurisdiction. The court of chancery held that P's claims arose under the Agreement, and that, therefore, the Agreement controlled the question of jurisdiction. Because the Agreement states that only a court of law or arbitrator in California may decide claims arising under it, the court granted Ds' motion and dismissed P's complaint. P appeals.

Issue. May the members of a limited liability company, through the use of a forum selection clause in their membership agreement, vest jurisdiction in a particular forum?

Held. Yes. Judgment affirmed.

- The Delaware Limited Liability Company Act provides broad discretion in drafting the LLC agreement and furnishes default provisions only when the members' agreement is silent. It is designed to give maximum effect to the freedom to contract and to the enforceability of limited liability company agreements. Only when the agreement is inconsistent with mandatory statutory provisions will the members' agreement be invalidated.
- P argues that the dispute resolution provision in the Agreement is invalid under the Delaware Limited Liability Company Act because the Act prohibits the parties from vesting exclusive jurisdiction in a forum outside of Delaware. We find nothing in the Act or elsewhere to indicate that members cannot alter the default jurisdiction provisions of the statute and contract away their right to file suit in Delaware. The policy of the Act is to give maximum effect to the members' freedom of contract to govern their relationship provided that they do not violate any mandatory provisions of the Act. Thus, we find that members may contract to vest jurisdiction where they please. In this case, the Agreement clearly states that no action based on any claim arising out of this Agreement may be brought except in California, and then only to enforce arbitration in California.
- Finally, P argues that Malek LLC, although in existence when the Agreement was executed, did not sign the Agreement and, thus, never assented to the arbitration and forum selection clauses within it. Therefore, P argues, it is suing derivatively on behalf of Malek LLC. We disagree. Malek, Inc. and P, the members of the limited liability company, executed the agreement. P's claims are subject to the arbitration and forum selection provisions notwithstanding Malek LLC's failure to sign the Agreement.

---

2. Failure to Allege Breaches of Duties Found in the LLC Agreement

Fisk Ventures LLC v. Segal

C.A. No. 3017–CC (Del.Ch. January 13, 2009),
aff'd sub nom., Segal v. Fisk Ventures, LLC, 984 A.2d 124 (Del.2009).

Facts. Segal (D) worked on projects relating to how the human immune system could be manipulated effectively to attack cancer and infectious diseases for the Whitehead Institute from 1994 to early 1996. When he left, D obtained a license to certain patent rights related to his research and formed Genitrix, LLC in 1996 in Maryland to market biomedical technology. Originally, the terms of D's employment were governed by a contract ("Segal Employment Agreement") that provided that any intellectual property rights developed by D during his tenure with Genitrix would be assigned to the company. Dr. H. Fisk Johnson invested heavily in Genitrix, and at his urging, the company moved to Delaware. The company's equity shares are divided into three classes of membership. Segal retained 55% of the Class A membership; his capital account was credited with $500,000 in exchange for the patent rights. Others not involved in this suit held the remainder of the Class A interest. Johnson holds a Class B interest with Rose and Fisk Ventures (P). Other contributors hold membership in Class C. The power in Genitrix is divided by the LLC Agreement (the "Agreement") between Class A and Class B members. The Agreement provides that the business affairs of the company are managed by the Board of Member Representatives (the "Board"). Originally, there were four Board members, two appointed by Johnson and two by Segal. Later, when the company failed to meet certain benchmarks, the Board was expanded and the Class B members were able to appoint a representative. As a Class B member, Fisk is entitled to appoint one person to the Board. H. Fisk Johnson owns 99% of Fisk Ventures LLC. However, because the Agreement requires 75% approval by the Board for most actions, Johnson's and Fisk Venture's combined 60% stake is not sufficient to control the company.

Johnson appointed Rose and Freund as Class B Representatives on the Board. Both men are employed by Johnson outside of Genitrix. D alleges both men are dependent on Johnson for their livelihood.

Genitrix has had money problems from the beginning; D worked for little or no pay at the start and the company moved forward with grants and limited financing. Johnson and other investors contributed more cash to no avail. In 2003, D told the Board $2.6 million would be needed to allow for human trials of the technology. Johnson had already contributed about $1.4 million to the company and he and Fisk contributed another $2 million only after Genitrix agreed to try to raise an additional $5 million from other investors over the following two years.

During the parties' negotiations concerning the Fisk Venture Note, D proposed a suspension of the "Put Right" of the Class B investors to allow him to more easily encourage other investors. Under the Agreement, the Class B Members may, at any time, force the company to purchase any or all of their Class B membership interests at a price determined by an independent appraisal. If the purchase price exceeds 50% of the company's tangible assets, the Members who exercised the Put Right receive notes secured by all of the assets of the company. Thus, if the Put were exercised, it would subrogate what would otherwise be senior claims of new investors. The Class B members refused to give up their right, but said they had no intention in the immediate future of exercising the right.

Almost two years after the Fisk Ventures Note, Genitrix had failed to raise the $5 million. D said he could not attract high-net-worth investors because their initial interest was quelled by the Class B Put Right. Nevertheless, the Class B members again refused to relinquish or suspend the right. D alleges that he was forced to draft a proposed private placement memorandum ("PPM") for use in connection with any investment by the high-net-worth individuals because the company's legal counsel "was busy." The Class B representatives refused to consent and again refused to suspend or relinquish their Put Right. The Class B members instead offered a counterproposal of $500,000 in convertible debt from Fisk Ventures. The terms of that note would have required Genitrix to meet certain benchmarks. If it failed to do so, the Class B members would obtain control of the Board. Tilson, a Class C investor, agreed to provide the necessary funds if Class B members suspended their Put Right for 3 years, which they refused to do.

Class B representatives then replaced D with another Genitrix employee, Pugh, as "interim" CEO. When Genitrix ran out of cash in 2006, Fisk provided capital to pay the employees. D and the Class B Board members could not agree on an action. In August 2006, Pugh left the company; the only other employee except for D left in May 2007. The company has no office, no capital funds, no grant funds, and generates no revenue. The Board has not met since the fall of 2006 because the Class A representatives have refused to participate in any meetings. D proposed terms under which Class B members might buy his interest in the company in May 2007 at the suggestion of the Class B members. D's terms were rejected and P filed suit, seeking to dissolve Genitrix.

D counterclaimed against P and filed third-party claims against Johnson, Rose and Freund, contending that they breach the LLC Agreement, the implied covenant of good faith and fair dealing implicit in the LLC Agreement, breached their fiduciary duties to the Company, and tortiously interfered with the Segal Employment Agreement. D argues that the Class B defendants failed to comply with their duties by standing in the way of proposed financing.

Issue. Has D stated claims for which relief can be granted?

Held. No. Case dismissed.

- An actionable breach cannot be determined without a duty. With a limited liability company, a creature of contract, duties and obligations must be found in the LLC Agreement. D's claims fail to allege breaches of duties found in the Genitrix Agreement.

- D may be correct in claiming Genitrix suffered because Class B members failed to agree to his proposals regarding research, financing, and other matters, but the opposite is true as well. If D had agreed with the Class B members, the company might be thriving today. The Agreement does not obligate one class to comply with the proposals of the other because the other believes its ideas are better. For the court to decide whose business judgment was more in keeping with the LLC's best interests would undercut the policy underlying the LLC Act promoting freedom of contract.
- There is an implied covenant of good faith and fair dealing in every contract that "requires a 'party in a contractual relationship to refrain from arbitrary or unreasonable conduct which has the effect of preventing the other party to the contract from receiving the fruits' of the bargain." This implied covenant is not a cure-all and may be used to fill a gap in a contract only if it is clear from the language of the contract that the parties would have agreed to that term if they had thought to negotiate the matter. The implied covenant of good faith and fair dealing protects the spirit of the agreement rather than the form. Where the contract specifically covers an issue, the implied covenant cannot be invoked.
- Here, the LLC Agreement did not give D the right to unilaterally decide what financial opportunities Genitrix should pursue. The LLC Agreement specifically requires the approval of 75% of the Board in financial matters. Implicit in such a requirement is the right of the Class B Board representatives to disapprove of and therefore block D's proposals. The Class B Board members were merely exercising their rights and negotiating forcefully and within the bounds of the LLC Agreement.

Comment. In a later stage of the litigation, Fisk Venture's motion for a judicial order of dissolution was granted.

D. Piercing the "LLC" Veil

While state statutes generally set forth the requirements for formation and operation of an LLC, some issues have not been settled by statute and continue to be the subject of debate. For example, the scope of fiduciary duties of members of an LLC have not been clearly defined. It also remains unclear whether corporate principles of law, such as piercing the corporate veil, will be applied to LLCs. At least one court has held that the LLC veil may be pierced in a manner similar to piercing the corporate veil. (*See Kaycee Land and Livestock v. Flahive, infra.*) The Uniform Limited Liability Company Act ("ULLCA") was promulgated in 1996. The ULLCA attempts to provide uniformity and consistency to disparate state legislation. It has had limited acceptance, however, in part because it contains more partnership concepts than most existing state LLC statutes.

1. LLC Veil May Be Pierced

Kaycee Land and Livestock v. Flahive

46 P.3d 323 (Wyo. 2002).

Facts. Kaycee Land and Livestock (P) entered into a contract with Flahive Oil & Gas LLC ("FOG"), which enabled FOG to use P's real property. Roger Flahive (D) is the managing member of FOG. P alleges that during its use of the property in question, FOG caused environmental contamination of the property. FOG currently has no assets, and P sought to pierce the LLC veil and hold D individually liable for the contamination. The district court requested that the Wyoming Supreme Court decide a certified question.

Issue. In the absence of fraud, may a court pierce the limited liability entity veil in the same manner as a court would pierce a corporate veil?

Held. Yes.

- Every state that has enacted LLC piercing legislation has not developed a separate LLC standard, but has chosen to follow corporate law standards. We can find no reason to treat LLCs differently than we treat corporations. While some of the factors that justify piercing in the corporate situation, such as failure to follow corporate formalities, will be inapplicable to LLCs, a multitude of cases have developed sufficient other factors to consider.

E. Fiduciary Obligation

1. Limiting Fiduciary Duties by Agreement

McConnell v. Hunt Sports Enterprises

725 N.E.2d 1193 (Ohio Ct. App. 1999).

Facts. In October of 1996, Columbus Hockey Limited ("CHL"), a limited liability company, was formed. Its members included McConnell, Hunt, and several other wealthy individuals and their controlled entities. CHL's operating agreement indicated that the business of CHL was to invest in and operate a National Hockey League ("NHL") franchise for the city of Columbus. CHL applied to the NHL for a franchise. After city funding for a hockey arena fell through, Hunt began negotiating with Nationwide Insurance Company ("Nationwide") to privately finance an arena. In May of 1997, Nationwide representatives met with Hunt and members of his company, the Hunt Sports Group, to discuss a lease proposal. Hunt indicated that Nationwide's lease proposal was unacceptable. The parties met again in June with the same result. In the meantime, McConnell told both the NHL and Nationwide that if CHL would not lease the arena from Nationwide, McConnell would personally do so. The investors thereafter fell into two camps, McConnell and his allies, and Hunt and his allies. At a final meeting on June 9, 1997, the NHL representative required that an owner of the franchise be identified, and sign a lease term agreement. Hunt stated that he still found the lease terms unacceptable. McConnell then signed the agreement as owner of the franchise. McConnell and two other investors then formed Columbus Hockey, Limited, which became the owner of the franchise. Hunt and his allies have no interest in the franchise. McConnell and his allies (Ps) filed this action requesting a declaration that section 3.3 of CHL's operating agreement allowed members of CHL to compete with CHL for an NHL franchise. McConnell's complaint also charged Hunt with breach of contract in unilaterally rejecting Nationwide's lease proposal and wrongfully usurping control of CHL. Hunt and Hunt Sports Group filed a counterclaim, on its own behalf and on behalf of CHL (Ds), against McConnell for breach of contract, breach of fiduciary duty, and interference with prospective business relationships. Ps allege that Hunt breached the operating agreement by failing to obtain the approval of the other members prior to filing, in CHL's name, the answer and counterclaim in this suit. The trial court granted summary judgment in favor of Ps, stating that the operating agreement allowed them to compete, and that McConnell did not breach the operating agreement by competing. A jury rendered a decision in favor of McConnell on the counterclaim. The court then entered a directed verdict for Ps, finding that Hunt violated the CHL operating agreement in failing to obtain authorization of CHL members before filing the answer and counterclaim. Ds appeal.

Issue. Can an operating agreement of a limited liability company limit or define the scope of fiduciary duties imposed upon its members?

Held. Yes. Judgment affirmed.

- Section 3.3 of the operating agreement states: "Members May Compete. Members shall not in any way be prohibited from or restricted in engaging or owning an interest in any other business venture of any nature, including any venture which might be competitive with the business of the Company." The language here is clear and unambiguous. By its very terms, the agreement clearly allowed the members to compete. Accordingly, Ps were entitled to a declaration that section 3.3 permitted them to request and obtain an NHL franchise to the exclusion of CHL.

- The participants in CHL agreed to abide by the terms of the operating agreement. Because that agreement specifically allowed competition, the duties the members assumed upon formation of the company did not include the duty not to compete. Thus, it cannot be said that McConnell himself breached any fiduciary duty.
- The evidence also fails to show that Ps tortiously interfered with Ds' prospective business relationships with Nationwide or the NHL. McConnell stated that he would lease the arena and obtain the franchise only if Hunt did not. It was only after Hunt, on behalf of CHL, rejected the lease proposal on several occasions that McConnell stepped in. It was Hunt's own actions that caused the termination of any potential relationship with Nationwide and the NHL.
- Finally, we affirm the lower court's directed verdict for Ps holding that Ds violated the CHL operating agreement by failing to obtain approval from CHL members prior to filing an answer and counterclaim. Section 4.1 of the operating agreement states that no member may take any action on behalf of the company unless such action was approved by a majority of the members. Ds failed to obtain this permission from a majority of CHL's members. Hunt claims that section 4.4 of the agreement makes members liable to other members only for their own willful misconduct in the performance of their duties under the agreement. However, section 4.4's provisions are in the context of members carrying out their duties under the operating agreement. There was no duty on Ds' part to unilaterally file the actions at issue. Even if this provision were applicable, the evidence shows Ds engaged in willful misconduct in filing these actions, because the operating agreement clearly states that majority approval is required for such action.

F. Additional Capital

1. No Capital Call to Satisfy a Judgment

Racing Investment Fund 2000, LLC v. Clay Ward Agency, Inc.

320 S.W.3d 654 (Ky. 2010).

Facts. Racing Investment Fund 2000, LLC, (D) was created to purchase, train and race thoroughbred horses. During the course of litigation, D entered into an agreed judgment with Clay Ward (P), its former insurance firm, for past-due insurance premiums in the amount of $57,139.68. D was then defunct and tendered all of its remaining assets in partial payment of the debt. After D failed to pay the remaining debt, P succeeded in having the company held in contempt of court for failing to pay the judgment. The trial court, invoking a provision in D's Operating Agreement which allowed the limited liability company's Manager to call for additional capital contributions, as needed, from all members on a pro rata basis for "operating, administrative or other business expenses" ruled that this provision provided a means of satisfying the judgment. The trial court ordered Racing to satisfy the Judgment within a reasonable period of time. The court of appeals affirmed and we granted discretionary review.

Issue. Can the LLC Operating Agreement provision allowing for periodic capital calls from the Manager be invoked by a court to obtain funds from the limited liability company's members in order to satisfy a debt judgment against the limited liability company in the absence of members' written agreement to subject themselves to personal liability?

Held. No. Judgment reversed.

- In 1994, when Kentucky recognized limited liability companies (LLCs) through the adoption of the Kentucky Limited Liability Company Act, commentators noted that the " 'centerpiece' of a limited liability company is its 'provision for limited liability of its members and managers in regard to the debts and obligations of the LLC. . . .' " One example of the strength of that protection is recognition by the IRS that federal employment tax liabilities incurred by an LLC cannot be collected from the LLC's members.

- The Kentucky statute provides that "no member, manager, employee, or agent of a limited liability company, including a professional limited liability company, shall be personally liable by reason of being a member, manager, employee, or agent of the limited liability company, under a judgment, decree, or order of a court, agency, or tribunal of any type, or in any other manner, in this or any other state, or on any other basis, for a debt, obligation, or liability of the limited liability company, whether arising in contract, tort, or otherwise."
- A member or manager of an LLC may agree to be obligated personally for the debts of the company under a written agreement, but because most LLCs are created for the purpose of obtaining limited liability, few allow their members to waive limited liability.
- D's Operating Agreement, in the section entitled "Additional Capital Contributions" provides:

  > "The Investor Members *(including, but not limited to,* any Investor Assignees) shall be obligated to contribute to the capital of the Company, on a prorata basis in accordance with their respective Percentage Interests, such amounts as may be reasonably deemed advisable by the Manager from time to time in order to pay operating, administrative, or other business expenses of the Company which have been incurred, or which the Manager reasonably anticipates will be incurred, by the Company. *Except* under unusual circumstances, such additional capital contributions ("Additional Capital Contributions") shall not be required more often than quarterly and shall be due and payable by each Investor Member *(including, but not limited to,* each Investor Assignee) within fifteen (15) days after such Investor Member receives written notice from the Company of the amount due (a "Quarterly Bill"). The Manager shall not be required to make any additional capital contributions." (emphasis in original).

- P argues that D incurred a legitimate business expense for its insurance, and that the LLC members by agreeing to the periodic capital contribution provision, are subject to a "last call" to satisfy the outstanding balance on the judgment.
- By agreeing with P's interpretation, the trial court and court of appeals basically concluded that D's individual members are legally responsible for their pro rata share of the entity's business debt. Thus, any of D's unpaid debt can be satisfied through application for a court-ordered capital call. This construction of D's Operating Agreement is contrary to the plain terms of the Operating Agreement and the letter and spirit of the Kentucky law.
- D's "Additional Capital Contributions" provision is designed to assure additional capital to advance D's thoroughbred racing venture. The insurance premiums are a legitimate business expense for which the Manager could have made a capital call, but that alone does not lead to the relief ordered by the trial court. The provision is capital infusion mechanism, not a debt-collection provision that can be used by a court to impose personal liability on the LLC's members for the LLC's outstanding debt.
- Under Kentucky law, members may not be held responsible for an LLC's debt unless they have agreed through the operating agreement or another written agreement to assume personal liability. Because such assumption of liability is so contrary to the advantage of an LLC, it must be clearly stated in "unequivocal" language, leaving no room for doubt. D's Operating Agreement does not come close to this standard.

G. Dissolution

An LLC will dissolve upon (i) the expiration of any period of duration stated in the articles; (ii) the consent of all members; (iii) the death, retirement, resignation, bankruptcy, incompetency, etc., of a member unless the remaining members vote to continue the business; or (iv) a judicial decree or administrative order dissolving the LLC for violation of law. The filing of articles of dissolution and notification of creditors is normally required.

1. Personal Liability Following Dissolution

New Horizons Supply Cooperative v. Haack

590 N.W.2d 282 (Wis. Ct. App. 1999) (unpublished disposition).

Facts. New Horizon Supply Cooperative (P) issued a gas card to Kickapoo Valley Freight, LLC ("Kickapoo"). The gas card agreement was signed by Haack (D). D gave no indication whether her signature was given individually or in a representative capacity on behalf of Kickapoo. When the account was in arrears, P contacted D, who indicated that she would begin paying $100 per month on the account. After no payments were received, P again contacted D. D stated that Kickapoo had dissolved, but that she had the assets of the business, which included a truck and some accounts receivable, from which D would begin to make payments. P never received any payments and sued D for the amount of the debt. At trial, D testified that she could not be held personally liable on the debt because she and her brother had organized Kickapoo as an LLC. However, she could not produce articles of organization or an operating agreement. D did produce documents that indicated the company was taxed as a partnership. D testified that she had not filed articles of dissolution or notified creditors of the company's termination of business. The lower court held that the company in actuality operated as a partnership and that D, as the only remaining partner, was liable for the debt. D appeals.

Issue. Can D be held personally responsible for the debt?

Held. Yes. Judgment affirmed.

- We find that the lower court's decision was right, but its reasoning was incorrect. The lower court held D personally liable under the rationale of piercing the LLC veil because the company actually operated as a partnership. However, in arriving at this finding, the trial court erroneously deemed Kickapoo's treatment as a partnership for tax purposes to be conclusive. There is little evidence in the record that would show that D organized, controlled, and conducted the company's affairs to the extent that it had no separate existence of its own but was D's mere instrumentality. This is the test for piercing, and it is not satisfied on these facts.
- However, we find that the entry of judgment against D was proper because D failed to establish that she took appropriate steps to shield herself from liability for the company's debts following the LLC's dissolution and distribution of assets.

Chapter V

The Duties of Officers, Directors, and Other Insiders

A. THE OBLIGATIONS OF CONTROL

1. Duty of Care

a. Introduction

Directors are normally, by law, held to have the duty of management of the corporation. These duties are normally delegated to the officers; thus, the directors must supervise the officers. The legal duties of the directors and officers are owed to the corporation; thus, performance of these duties is usually enforced by an action on behalf of the corporation brought by an individual shareholder (called a "derivative suit").

b. The Fiduciary Relationship of Directors to the Corporation

Directors are said to occupy a "fiduciary" position in relationship to the corporation and the management of its affairs (since they manage on behalf of the shareholders). This relationship has resulted in several legal standards that are applied to directors.

1) Duties of Loyalty and Good Faith

Directors are bound by rules of fairness, loyalty, honesty, and good faith in their relationship, dealings, and management of the corporation (as are officers).

2) Duty of Reasonable Care

In addition, directors must exercise reasonable care, prudence, and diligence in the management of the corporation.

3) Business Judgment

Finally, in relationship to the duty of care, there has been another standard imposed on directors—that of the "business judgment" rule.

a) There is some confusion in the courts over the negligence standard to be applied to directors. Are directors really responsible for management? Or is there a more limited role for directors? If so, then negligence is the failure to perform with the care expected of directors (but not necessarily failure to perform with the prudence that a director would give to her own personal business dealings; thus, a different standard of care would apply to directors than to officers).

b) Because of the reluctance of the courts to hold directors truly responsible for the management of the corporation, courts have also adopted the "business judgment rule," which states that, when a matter of business "judgment" is involved, the directors meet their responsibility of reasonable care and diligence if they exercise an honest, good-faith, unbiased judgment. When this standard is applied, a director acting in good faith would only be liable for gross negligence or worse.

c. Damages

1) Cause of Action

To form a cause of action, it must be shown that the director failed to exercise reasonable care and that, as a direct and proximate result, the corporation has suffered damages.

2) Joint and Several Liability

Either one director may be held liable for her own acts, or all directors may be held liable (all those participating in the negligent act). If more than one director is held responsible, liability is joint and several.

d. The Duty of Reasonable Care

1) Introduction

The ambivalence and change in the trend of authority in this area is represented by *Hun v. Cary*, 82 N.Y. 65 (1880) (directors bought property and erected a new bank building on borrowed money even though the company was insolvent; the building was foreclosed). In that case the court held that the standard of care was the prudence that directors would exercise "in their own business dealings." The current New York statute indicates that the duty is that care that persons "in similar positions" would exercise.

2) Specific Traits, Backgrounds, and Abilities of Directors

There is language in the court opinions that indicates that the specific circumstances of each director must be considered in determining whether that director violated her duty of due care.

a) For example, if the director is not a resident of the state where the corporation is located, perhaps the director's duty of care would be less than that for resident directors.

b) For example, if a director is a lawyer with experience in corporate matters, perhaps her standard of care would be higher than that for a schoolteacher without corporate experience.

3) The Standard Really Used

What the courts really appear to do, no matter what standard of negligence they purport to use, is to look at all of the facts and determine whether the total situation is one in which the directors or officers should be held liable. Thus, they determine whether the director knew or reasonably should have known of the situation, and whether the director could reasonably have done anything about it. This standard is applied to each director individually.

4) Reliance on Advice of Counsel

Normally, if there is no conflict of interest involved, the directors may rely on the advice of counsel in making business decisions and not violate the duty of due care (although there are exceptions to this rule).

e. Informed Business Judgment

1) In Declaring a Dividend

Kamin v. American Express Co.

383 N.Y.S.2d 807 (N.Y. Sup. 1976), *aff'd on opinion below*, 387 N.Y.S.2d 993 (N.Y. App. Div. 1976).

Facts. Two minority stockholders (Ps) sued American Express Company (D) derivatively. Ps are requesting a declaration that a certain dividend in kind that is to be paid by D is a waste of corporate assets. Ps allege that in 1972 D acquired for investment nearly two million shares of publicly traded common stock of Donaldson, Lufken and Jenrette, Inc. ("DLJ") at a cost of $29.9 million, and that the current market value of those shares is about $4 million. In July 1975, the board of directors of D declared a special dividend, pursuant to which the shares of DLJ would be distributed in kind to the shareholders. Ps believed that if D were to sell the DLJ shares on the market, it would sustain a capital loss of $25 million, which could be offset against taxable capital gains on other investments in order to generate a tax savings of about $8 million to D. Such a savings would not be available with a distribution of the DLJ shares. Ps demanded that D rescind the distribution of the shares. The board of directors rejected the demand. Ps then brought this suit seeking to stop the distribution or, in the alternative, for money damages. D moves for an order dismissing the complaint for failure to state a cause of action and, alternatively, for summary judgment.

Issue. Minus a showing of bad faith, fraud, oppression, arbitrary action, or breach of trust, are the business judgment decisions of corporate directors judicially rescindable for alleged imprudence or mistaken judgment?

Held. No. D's motion for summary judgment and dismissal of the complaint is granted.

- All of the allegations of the complaint go to the question of the exercise by the board of directors of business judgment in deciding how to deal with the DLJ shares. There is no claim of fraud or self-dealing, and no contention that there was any bad faith or oppressive conduct.
- The question of whether a dividend should be declared or a distribution of some kind should be made is exclusively a matter of business judgment for the board of directors. Mere errors of judgment are not sufficient as grounds for equity interference, for the powers of those entrusted with corporate management are largely discretionary. It is, therefore, not enough to allege that the directors made an imprudent decision. More than imprudence or mistaken judgment must be shown. To allege that some course of action other than that pursued by the board of directors would have been more advantageous gives rise to no cognizable cause of action.
- The objections raised by Ps were carefully considered and unanimously rejected by the board of directors. This is not a situation in which the defendant directors totally overlooked facts called to their attention. They gave them consideration and attempted to view the total picture in arriving at their decision.
- There is no basis for superimposing judicial judgment as long as it appears that the directors have been acting in good faith.

---

2) Informed Judgment in Merger Proposals

Smith v. Van Gorkom

488 A.2d 858 (Del. 1985).

Facts. Shareholders (Ps) of Trans Union sued Trans Union seeking rescission of a merger into New T Company (a wholly owned subsidiary of defendant Marmon Group, controlled by Pritzker), or alternatively, damages against members of Trans Union's board (Ds).

Trans Union was a profitable, multi-million dollar leasing corporation that was not able to use all of the tax credits it was generating. Several solutions were explored. Van Gorkom (chairman) asked for a study by Romans (financial officer) regarding a leveraged buy-out by management. Romans reported that the company would generate enough cash to pay $50 per share for the company's stock, but not $60 per share. Van Gorkom rejected the idea of this type of buy-out (conflict of interest) but indicated he would take $55 per share for his own stock (he was 65 and about to retire). On his own, Van Gorkom approached Pritzker, a takeover specialist, and began negotiating a sale of Trans Union. He suggested $55 per share and a five-year payout method without consulting the board or management. The price was above the $39 per share market value, but no study was done by anyone to determine the intrinsic value of Trans Union's shares. In the final deal, Trans Union got three days to consider the offer, which included selling a million shares to Pritzker at market, so that even if Trans Union found someone else who would pay a better price, Pritzker would profit: For 90 days Trans Union could receive—but not solicit—competing offers.

Van Gorkom hired outside legal counsel to review the deal, ignoring his company lawyer and a lawyer on the board. He called a board meeting for two days later. At the meeting, Trans Union's investment banker was not invited, no copies of the proposed merger were distributed, senior management was against it, and Romans said the price was too low. Van Gorkom presented the deal in 20 minutes, saying that the price might not be the highest that could be received, but it was fair. The outside lawyer told the board that they might be sued if they did not accept the offer and that they did not need to get an outside "fairness" opinion as a matter of law. Romans said he had not done a fairness study but that he thought $55 per share was on the low end. Discussion lasted two hours, and the merger offer was accepted.

Within 10 days, management of Trans Union was in an uproar. Pritzker and Van Gorkom agreed to some amendments, which the board approved. Trans Union retained Salomon Bros. to solicit other offers. Kohlberg, Kravis, Roberts & Co. made an offer at $60 per share. Van Gorkom discouraged the offer and spoke with management people who were participating in it. Hours before a board meeting to consider it, it was canceled, and was never presented to the board. General Electric Credit Corp. made a proposal at $60 per share, but wanted more time, which Pritzker refused to give, so it too was withdrawn.

On December 19, some shareholders began this suit. On February 10, 70% of the shareholders approved the deal. The trial court held that the board's actions from its first meeting on September 20 until January 26 were informed. Ps appeal.

Issue. Did the directors act in accordance with the requirements of the business judgment rule?

Held. No. Judgment reversed and case remanded.

- The business judgment rule presumes that directors act on an informed basis, in good faith, and in an honest belief that their actions are for the good of the company. Plaintiffs must rebut this presumption. There is no fraud here, or bad faith. The issue is whether the directors informed themselves properly. All reasonably material information available must be looked at prior to a decision. This is a duty of care. And the directors are liable if they were grossly negligent in failing to inform themselves.

- The directors were grossly negligent in the way they acted in the first board meeting that approved the merger: They did not know about Van Gorkom's role, and they did not gather information on the intrinsic value of the company. Receiving a premium price over market is not enough evidence of intrinsic value.
- An outside opinion is not always necessary, but here there was not even an opinion given by inside management. The Van Gorkom opinion of value could be relied on had it been based on sound factors; it was not and the board members did not check it. The post-September market test of value was insufficient to confirm the reasonableness of the board's decision.
- Although the 10 board members knew the company well and had outstanding business experience, this was not enough on which to base a finding that they reached an informed decision.
- There is no real evidence of what the outside lawyer said, and as he refused to testify, Ds cannot rely on the fact that they based their acts on his opinion.
- The actions taken by the board to review the proposal on October 9, 1980, and on January 26, 1981, did not cure the defects in the September 20 meeting.
- All directors take a unified position, so all are being treated the same way.
- The shareholder vote accepting the offer does not clear Ds because it was not based on full information.

Dissent. There were 10 directors; the five outside ones were chief executives of successful companies. The five inside directors had years of experience with Trans Union. All knew about the company in detail. No "fast shuffle" took place over these men. Considering this experience, the directors made an informed judgment.

---

3) *Van Gorkom* Distinguished

Cinerama, Inc. v. Technicolor, Inc., 663 A.2d 1156 (Del.Supr. 1995), is the culmination of twenty years of litigation. In 1983, Perelman offered to buy Technicolor from its shareholders for $23 a share, or $125 million, an amount far above the company's market price. Forman, an investor whose family controlled Cinerama, a Technicolor shareholder, filed a suit charging the price was not high enough. In 1986, Forman's lawyer filed a second suit claiming the deal had been tainted by gross negligence and conflicts of interest by the Technicolor directors. As in *Smith v. Van Gorkom*, *supra,* Technicolor's CEO had made the deal with Perelman before presenting it to the Board of Directors; the board approved quickly, without adequate information and deliberation, and without a "market check." However, the CEO had investigated thoroughly, had bargained hard, and had hired experts who had worked in support of the fairness of the deal for Technicolor. This, however, did not remove the Board's obligations. Forman wanted $40 million, plus interest, of the $750 million profit Perelman made when he sold Cinerama to Carlton Communications. When the second suit was filed, the court ruled that Cinerama had to choose to challenge the fairness of the price or the fairness of the process. On appeal, Cinerama won the right to pursue both. After trial in 1990, the court found Perelman's price was fair and generous; later, in 1991, the judge ruled that the directors might have been negligent, but that Cinerama had not proved it had been injured by any negligence, given the price. Cinerama appealed. The Delaware Supreme Court reversed Delaware's Court of Chancery and remanded; once the directors were found negligent, it ruled, the burden of proof shifted to Technicolor to prove that the deal involved both a fair price and a fair process. On remand, the Chancery Court found Technicolor had met its burden of proof and dismissed the action. On appeal, the Delaware Supreme Court stated that the fiduciary duties of care and loyalty are the bases for the requirement that a director must disclose to shareholders all material facts surrounding a merger vote. The court distinguished *Van Gorkom, supra,* where the court held that the *Van Gorkom*'s board of directors' failure to inform itself before recommending a merger was a breach of its duty of care and rebutted the presumptive protection of the business judgment rule. It also found that the directors had violated the duty of disclosure and held the directors liable for damages. Finally, noting the CEO's thoroughness and the high price he secured for the company, the court upheld the Chancery Court's finding for Technicolor.

4) Director Must Be Familiar with the Company and Business

Francis v. United Jersey Bank

432 A.2d 814 (N.J. 1981).

Facts. Francis and others (Ps) were trustees in bankruptcy for Pritchard & Baird Corp., a reinsurance broker run by members of the Pritchard family. The company arranged contracts between insurance companies seeking indemnification against losses under their own policies (ceding companies) and other insurance companies (the reinsurers). In accordance with industry custom, the reinsurance brokers collected premiums and loss payments from the ceding companies and reinsurers, respectively, then deducted their own commissions, and transmitted the funds to the proper parties. Industry practice was to segregate these insurance funds from the brokers' own general accounts.

Contrary to this custom, Pritchard & Baird commingled its own funds with its clients'. Beginning in 1970, Charles Pritchard, Jr. and William Pritchard, officers, directors, and shareholders of the company, withdrew funds from the commingled account and designated them as "shareholders' loans." These "loans" showed up as assets on the balance sheets, which were prepared internally. The loans increased annually, and left the company with insufficient funds with which to operate. Finally, an involuntary petition in bankruptcy was filed.

United Jersey Bank and Lillian Overcash (Ds) represented the estates of Charles Pritchard, Sr. and Lillian Pritchard. Pritchard, Sr. was chief executive of the company, but relinquished control to his sons in 1968. Mrs. Pritchard was a director of the corporation. She was not active in the business, was unfamiliar with its corporate affairs and with the industry in general, and never read the annual financial statements. After her husband's death, she was somewhat incapacitated.

Ps sued Mrs. Pritchard's estate, alleging that she was negligent in allowing her sons to withdraw corporate funds for their own use. The trial court held for Ps, characterizing the payments as fraudulent conveyances. Judgment for Ps was upheld on appeal, but the appellate court ruled that the payments were a conversion of trust funds. The New Jersey Supreme Court granted certification on the issue of Mrs. Pritchard's liability.

Issues.

(i) Was Mrs. Pritchard, as a corporate director, individually liable in negligence for the acts of the corporation?

(ii) If she was negligent, was her negligence the proximate cause of Ps' losses?

Held. (i) Yes. (ii) Yes. Judgment affirmed.

- Directors in this state are under a statutory duty to act in good faith as ordinarily prudent persons would under similar circumstances in like positions. This standard is a relative concept, depending on the kind of corporation, the director's corporate role, and the particular circumstances.

  Generally, a director should have a basic understanding of the corporation's business and knowledge about its ongoing activities, which require a general monitoring of its affairs and policies. The director has a responsibility to attend board meetings and regularly review financial statements. If there is illegal conduct, a director has the duty to object, and possibly either take reasonable means to prevent such conduct or resign. In this case, Mrs. Pritchard did not fulfill any of the director's obligations.

In determining Mrs. Pritchard's liability, we must also find that she had a duty to the corporate clients. A reinsurance broker, which holds funds in trust for its clients, greatly resembles a bank. Mrs. Pritchard's relationship to the corporation's clientele is similar to that of a bank director to depositors. She breached her duty to protect the clients, as a reading of the financial statements would have disclosed the misappropriation without requiring any special knowledge or expertise on her part.

- In cases involving nonfeasance, the causation issue requires determining what reasonable steps a director could have taken and whether those steps would have prevented the loss. The failure to act must be a substantial factor in producing the harm. Here, Mrs. Pritchard's inaction served to encourage the illegal conduct, as it is reasonable to infer that if her objections were not enough to stop it, seeking counsel and threatening legal action would have been sufficient. Causation is best decided on a case-by-case basis; there is ample evidence here that Mrs. Pritchard's failure to act proximately caused the misappropriation of trust funds.

B. DUTY OF LOYALTY

1. Directors and Managers

The directors owe a duty of loyalty to the corporation. This means that the directors must place the interests of the corporation above their own personal gains. But problems arise because directors have other business involvements, and it is often for this reason that they are placed on the board. Therefore, no rule of law that prevents a corporation from dealing with its directors is feasible, but it is difficult to develop rules that properly circumscribe these dealings.

The problems arise in a number of contexts: contracts between a corporation and one of its directors; transactions by a director (that result in profits) that the corporation might have engaged in; contracts for directors' compensation, etc.

2. Self-Interested Transactions

a. Introduction

Over time, there has been an evolution in the rules applied by the courts.

b. The Early Rule

The early common law rule was that any contract between a director and her corporation, whether fair or not, was voidable (*e.g.*, by means of a shareholder derivative suit). This rule applied not only to individual contracts with directors, but also to the situation of interlocking directorates (two or more corporations having common directors). It was even applied to the situation where one corporation owned the majority of the stock of another and appointed its directors (parent-subsidiary relationship).

c. Disinterested Majority Rule

Later, the courts began to hold (and many still do) that conflict of interest dealings were voidable only if the director had not made a full and complete disclosure of the transaction (its value, her interest, profit, etc.) to an "independent board" (quorum of disinterested directors), or the transaction was shown to be unfair and unreasonable to the corporation (if either condition was absent, the contract could be voided). The burden of proof as to the fairness of the transaction was on the director.

d. The Liberal Rule

Many courts now hold that it makes no difference whether the board is disinterested or not. The issue is whether the transaction is fair to the corporation. Part of the "fairness" requirement is that the director's interest be fully disclosed, however. If the board is not disinterested, the contract will be given very close scrutiny. Many states have adopted statutes that combine elements from all of the previous judicial positions.

1) Action Benefiting Corporate Officer's Relative

Bayer v. Beran

49 N.Y.S.2d 2 (N.Y. Sup. 1944).

Facts. Shareholders of Celanese Corporation of America (Ps) filed suit against the company's directors (Ds) charging them with negligence, waste and improvidence in engaging the company in a radio advertising campaign which cost about $1 million per year. The complaint also alleges that Ds were negligent in selecting the type of radio program during which to advertise, and that the directors were motivated by the noncorporate purpose of fostering the singing career of the company president's wife, who provided vocal talent for the radio commercials.

Issue. Did Ds breach any fiduciary duties to the corporation in connection with the radio advertising campaign?

Held. No. Complaint dismissed.

- Ps claim that the amount spent on radio advertisements was excessive, and that Ds were negligent in advertising during a classical music program because other programs, such as variety shows, have a wider popular appeal. There is nothing in the record to support these allegations. The amount expended here bears a fair relationship to the amount of sales and to the net earnings of the company. In addition, the record indicates that the directors chose the classical music hour because they felt it was dignified and in keeping with the beauty and superior quality of their product. The character of the advertising, the amount expended for advertisement, and the manner in which it should be used are all matters of business judgment. It was for the directors to decide whether or not to use radio advertisements, how much to spend, and the programs during which to run the advertisements. There is nothing to indicate any breach of fiduciary duty with regard to these matters.
- Ps' complaint also claims that Ds breached their fiduciary duty to the company by using the radio commercials to promote the career of the company president's wife, Ms. Tennyson. When a close relative of the chief executive officer of a company and one of its dominant shareholders take a position closely associated with a new and expensive field of activity, the motives of the directors are likely to be questioned. The burden is on the directors not only to show the good faith of the transaction, but also to show inherent fairness to the corporation. The record indicates that Ms. Tennyson was an experienced and competent singer. There is nothing in the record questioning her competence as a singer, and nothing to show that some other singer would have enhanced the quality of the advertisements. Ms. Tennyson was one of many singers used, and her compensation was in conformity with that normally paid for such work. In fact, she was paid less than any other singer on the show. The evidence fails to show that the radio commercials were designed to foster her career or for any purpose other than marketing the Celanese product. As long as the advertising served a legitimate and useful corporate purpose, the fact that Ms. Tennyson's participation may have helped advance her singing career is no ground for subjecting Ds to liability for breach of duty. The complaint is accordingly dismissed on the merits.

2) Director Negotiating with Corporation on Behalf of Another

Benihana of Tokyo, Inc. v. Benihana, Inc.

906 A.2d 114 (Del. 2006).

Facts. Aoki founded Benihana of Tokyo, Inc. (P), and its subsidiary, Benihana, Inc. (D), which owned and operated Benihana restaurants in the United States. Aoki was the sole shareholder of P, but when he pled guilty to charges of insider trading, he transferred his stock to a trust, with his children and family attorney as trustees. Later Aoki remarried, and against his children's wishes, he changed his will to give his new wife control over P upon his death. D's president was concerned about the situation and looked for a way to avoid this change in control. At the same time, many of D's restaurants were in need of renovating. The board's executive committee began discussing various ways to finance the renovations. D hired Morgan Joseph & Co. ("Joseph") to develop the financing options. Joseph recommended that D issue convertible preferred stock to provide the funds needed for the renovations. The buyer of the stock would get one or two seats on D's board, and the buyer's approval would be required for material corporate transactions. Joseph presented D's directors with a board book analyzing the proposed stock issuance. Among other things, the book contained a confidential term sheet outlining the terms D would require from a buyer. Shortly thereafter, one of D's directors, Abdo, contacted Joseph on behalf of BFC Financial Corporation ("BFC"). Abdo, who was a director and vice chairman of BFC, told Joseph that BFC was interested in buying the new convertible stock. They negotiated for several weeks and reached an agreement on terms. Abdo issued a memorandum to some, but not all, of D's board, listing the agreed upon terms of the transaction. The trial court found that the board was not informed that Abdo had negotiated the deal on behalf of BFC, but did know that Abdo was a principal of BFC. The board approved the transaction, subject to a fairness opinion. After the stock issuance was publically announced, Aoki's counsel sent a letter to the board asking it to abandon the transaction in favor of other financing. Joseph told the board that the transaction was fair, and the board approved the transaction. D later received three alternative financing proposals, but rejected these proposals as inferior. P filed an action against D's directors, alleging breach of fiduciary duty.

Issue. Was there a breach of fiduciary duty when the board approved a transaction that a director negotiated with the corporation on behalf of the other party?

Held. No.

- Delaware law provides a safe harbor for interested transactions if the material facts as to the director's interest are disclosed and the board in good faith authorizes the transaction by a vote of a majority of the disinterested directors. P argues that the safe harbor rule does not apply here because the disinterested directors did not know that Abdo had negotiated the terms for BFC. We agree that the board needed to know about Abdo's involvement in order to make an informed decision. However, the record establishes that the board possessed that information when it approved the transaction. They knew that BFC was the proposed buyer, and Abdo made the presentations on behalf of BFC. Even though no one explicitly said that Abdo was negotiating the deal for BFC, it was understood.
- The record does not support P's contention that Abdo used confidential information against D. For the most part, D got the terms it wanted in the transaction. The record does not support the claim that Abdo breached his duty of loyalty.
- Finally, P argues that the primary purpose of this transaction was to dilute P's voting control, but the trial court found that the primary purpose was to provide the best financing vehicle for the renovations. That conclusion has ample support in the record.

3. Corporate Opportunities

a. Introduction

The duty of loyalty of directors and officers to the corporation prevents them from taking opportunities for themselves that should belong to the corporation.

1) Use of Corporate Property

For example, clearly a director may not use corporate property or assets to develop her own business or for other personal uses.

2) Corporate Expectancies

Furthermore, a director or officer may not assume for herself properties or interests in which the corporation is "interested," or in which the corporation can be said to have a tangible "expectancy," or which are important to the corporation's business or purposes.

a) For example, if the corporation has leased a piece of property, a director cannot buy the property for herself.

b) If it is "reasonably foreseeable" that the corporation would be interested in the property, then there is the necessary expectancy. If opportunities relate very closely to the business of the corporation, there is also the necessary expectancy.

3) Defenses to the Charge of Usurping a Corporate Opportunity

a) Individual Capacity

Defendants may claim that the opportunity was presented to them in their individual capacities, and not as fiduciaries of the corporation.

b) Corporation Unable to Take Advantage of the Opportunity

The law is now that an officer or director may take advantage of a corporate opportunity if it is disclosed to the corporation first and the corporation is unable to take advantage of it.

(1) If Corporation Is Financially Unable to Act on Opportunity

Broz v. Cellular Information Systems, Inc.

673 A.2d 148 (Del. 1996).

Facts. Broz (D) was the president and sole stockholder of RFB Cellular, Inc. ("RFBC"), a company that provided cellular phone service in the Midwest. D was also a member of the board of directors of Cellular Information Systems, Inc. (P). RFBC owned an FCC license area known as Michigan-4, which provided service to certain parts of rural Michigan. Mackinac Cellular Corporation ("Mackinac") owned Michigan-2, the license area adjacent to D's. In April of 1994, Mackinac sought to sell the Michigan-2 license, and asked a brokerage firm to prepare a list of potential purchasers. RFBC was included as a likely candidate. P was not considered a likely candidate because it had recently emerged from a lengthy insolvency reorganization, during which it had been forced to sell 15 of its cellular licenses, and was continuing to have financial difficulties. In May of 1994, P sold four more of its licenses, leaving it with only five. RFBC was offered the Michigan-2 license. In June, 1994, D spoke to P's company president about the offer following a board meeting. P's president told D that P was not interested in acquiring the license. D submitted offers to Mackinac for the purchase of the Michigan-2 license. Also in June, PriCellular, another communications company, began organizing a tender offer for the acquisition of P. The closing date was ultimately delayed until November due to PriCellular's financial difficulties. In the meantime, PriCellular became aware of the Michigan-2 license and began negotiating with Mackinac for an option to purchase. PriCellular acquired the option for $6.7 million, with an agreement that Mackinac could sell the license to anyone who exceeded this amount by at least $500,000. On November 14, D agreed to pay $7.2 million for the Michigan-2 license, thus meeting the terms of the option agreement, and Mackinac sold the license to D. Nine days later, PriCellular closed its tender offer for P. Prior to that point, PriCellular owned no equity interest in P. P filed suit against D, alleging that D breached his fiduciary duty as a director of P by usurping a corporate opportunity. The lower court held for P, and D appeals.

Issue. Did D usurp a corporate opportunity?

Held. No. Judgment reversed.

- It should be noted first that D became aware of the Michigan-2 opportunity in his individual, not his corporate, capacity. In fact, Mackinac did not consider P a viable candidate for the acquisition of the license and did not offer it to P. This fact lessens the burden on D to show adherence of his fiduciary duties to P.
- At the time of the negotiations for Michigan-2, P was in a precarious financial state, and we find that it was financially incapable of exploiting the opportunity. In addition, it is not clear that P had a cognizable interest or expectancy in the license. At the time, P was in the process of divesting its cellular license holdings, and its business plan did not involve any new acquisitions. Further, P's entire board testified that the Michigan-2 license would not have been of interest to P even if it had been in a financial position to acquire it. We therefore find that P had no interest or expectancy in the Michigan license opportunity.
- In holding that D usurped a corporate opportunity, the lower court emphasized the fact that D did not formally present the matter to P's board of directors. However, formal presentation is not required under circumstances in which the corporation does not have an interest, expectancy, or financial ability to pursue. D did not usurp any opportunity that P was willing and able to pursue. He sought only to compete with an outside entity, PriCellular. D was not obligated to refrain from competition with PriCellular. We therefore reverse the lower court's decision on this issue.
- The lower court also held that PriCellular's proposed acquisition of P caused P's interests to merge with PriCellular's even before its tender offer for P stock. Based on this fact, the court found that D was required to consider PriCellular's interest in determining whether to forgo the opportunity. We disagree. D was under no duty to consider PriCellular's contingent and uncertain plans for acquisition of P. We find that D did not breach his fiduciary duties to P.

---

4) Corporation Refuses the Opportunity

If the corporation, by independent directors or shareholders, turns down an opportunity, then fiduciaries may take advantage of the opportunity.

5) Remedies

If the fiduciary has usurped a corporate opportunity, then the corporation has the following remedies:

a) Damages

When the opportunity has been resold, the profits made by the fiduciary may be recovered by the corporation.

b) Constructive Trust

The corporation may force the fiduciary to convey the property to the corporation at the fiduciary's cost.

6) Competition with the Corporation

Another area of conflict of interest arises when a director or officer enters into competition with the corporation.

a) Use of Corporate Assets, Property, Trade Secrets, etc.

Clearly, a fiduciary may not use corporate assets, property, materials, trade secrets, etc., to form a competing business.

b) Formation of a Competing Business

However, a fiduciary (without using corporate assets) may leave the corporation and form a competing business. In some instances, the conduct of the fiduciary while still with the corporation and preparing to leave to form the new business is questioned.

7) Collateral Investment Opportunities

In re eBay, Inc. Shareholders Litigation

2004 WL 253521 (Del. Ch. 2004).

Facts. In 1995, Omidyar and Skoll founded the online auction community, eBay, as a sole proprietorship. In 1998, eBay retained investment banks to underwrite an initial public offering of common stock. Goldman Sachs was the lead underwriter. The stock became immensely valuable. Goldman Sachs "rewarded" favored clients, including some directors and officers of eBay, by allocating to them thousands of IPO shares at the initial offering price, resulting in huge instant profits. Certain other shareholders of eBay stock (Ps) filed suit against those eBay directors and officers (Ds) for usurping a corporate opportunity. Ds move to dismiss these claims for failure to state a claim.

Issue. Did Ds usurp a corporate opportunity?

Held. Yes. Motion denied.

- Ps claim that Ds have usurped a corporate opportunity of eBay. Ds argue that Goldman Sachs's stock allocations to Ds were collateral investments and not a corporate opportunity within the corporation's line of business. This argument is not persuasive.
- First, eBay was financially able to exploit the opportunity in question. Second, eBay was in the business of investing in securities. Investment was, in fact, integral to eBay's cash management strategies and a significant part of its business. It does not matter that these could be considered risky investments; the fact remains that eBay was never given an opportunity to consider the risks.
- This does not mean that every advantageous investment opportunity that comes to a director will be considered a corporate opportunity. Here, a unique, below-market-price investment was offered as a direct reward for their dealings with Goldman Sachs. No one can seriously argue that this conduct did not place Ds in a position of conflict with their duties to the corporation.
- Finally, an agent is under a duty to account for profits obtained personally in connection with transactions related to the company. It is a reasonable inference that Ds accepted a commission or gratuity from Goldman Sachs that rightfully belonged to eBay.
- Ps have also stated an adequate claim against Goldman Sachs for aiding and abetting Ds' breach of fiduciary duty.

---

4. Dominant Shareholders

a. Introduction

Shareholders are not free in every instance to cast their votes as they want. They have responsibilities, in some cases, to the other shareholders. For example, a shareholder cannot sell his vote (*i.e.*, accept a cash bribe for voting his shares in a certain way). In addition, a majority vote is not always effective where it is "unfair" to the minority shareholders.

b. Duty of Loyalty and Good Faith

Thus, in effect, the majority shareholders have a fiduciary relationship to the corporation and the minority shareholders. This duty is manifest in several circumstances: For example, if a majority shareholder deals with the corporation (such as in a contractual relationship), the transaction will be closely scrutinized to see that minority shareholders are treated fairly. An example would be where a corporation loans a majority shareholder money. In addition, in various types of corporate transactions, where the majority has the voting power to effectuate a transaction, the effect on minority shareholders may be reviewed by the courts to see that the majority acted in "good faith" and not to the specific detriment of the minority shareholders.

1) The Standard to Be Applied

Sinclair Oil Corporation v. Levien

280 A.2d 717 (Del. 1971).

Facts. Sinclair Oil Corporation (D) owned 97% of the stock of a subsidiary, Sinven, involved in the crude oil business in South America; D appointed all board members and officers. Then, over a six-year period, D drained off dividends from Sinven to meet its own needs for cash. The dividends paid met the limitations of state law, but exceeded the current earnings of the same period. Levien (P) charged that this limited Sinven's ability to grow; also, that in a contract between D and Sinven for the purchase of crude oil, D had failed to pay on time and had not purchased the minimum amounts as required by the contract. The suit is a derivative action; P is a shareholder of Sinven.

Issue. Is the intrinsic fairness test the appropriate standard for defining the fiduciary duty of the parent corporation to its controlled subsidiary?

Held. Yes. Judgment for D on the dividend and expansion questions; judgment for P on the breach of contract issue.

- Where there is self-dealing, the intrinsic fairness test must be applied, which puts the burden on the majority shareholder to show that the transaction with the subsidiary was objectively fair. On the dividend issue, there was no self-dealing (because the parent did not receive something from the subsidiary to the exclusion or detriment of the minority shareholders; they shared pro rata in the dividend distributions). On the expansion issue, D did not usurp any opportunities that would normally have gone to the subsidiary. Thus, the business judgment rule applies; the court will not disturb a transaction under this rule unless there is a showing of fraud or gross overreaching, which there was not.
- Although a parent need not bind itself by a contract with its dominated subsidiary, D chose to operate in this manner. D received the benefits of this contract, and so must comply with the contractual duties. Under the intrinsic fairness standard, D must prove that its causing Sinven not to enforce the contract was intrinsically fair to the minority shareholders of Sinven. D has failed to meet this burden. D made its payments under the contract on a late basis and failed to purchase the required minimum amounts of crude oil.

Comment. This case is confusing. The court should have decided on one standard to apply in situations of transactions where the majority controls the corporation. If the standard is the intrinsic fairness test, then one factor is self-dealing. Where it is absent, there is no violation.

---

2) Liquidation

Zahn v. Transamerica Corporation

162 F.2d 36 (3d Cir. 1947).

Facts. Zahn (P) owned class A common stock; there were two other classes (class B common and preferred stock). Upon liquidation, the preferred received a set amount; then class A got $2 for each $1 paid to class B (the voting stock). The class A stock (convertible on a one-to-one basis into class B stock) was callable by the board for $60 per share plus any accrued dividends. Transamerica (D) bought both class A and B stock; it then converted its A stock into B and owned almost all of the B stock. It thus controlled the company; it also controlled the board. The inventory of the corporation was listed with a book value of $6 million but actually had a market value of $20 million (due to a recent rapid rise in the value of tobacco, which was the inventory). This was unknown to the shareholders. D called the class A shares. Then it liquidated the assets, paid off the preferred shares and paid itself (since it controlled almost all of the class B stock) the remainder. P claimed (in a class action of class A shareholders) that, had he been included in the liquidation, he would have received $240 per share rather than the $80 per share paid pursuant to the call ($60 plus accrued dividends). P's action was to recover this difference. The lower court found for D. P appeals.

Issue. May the majority shareholder use its control of the board of directors to gain at the expense of the minority shareholders in a transaction where each step is performed in accordance with state law?

Held. No. Judgment reversed.

- ♦ A majority shareholder may vote according to its own interests.
- ♦ But a majority shareholder also has a fiduciary duty to the corporation and the minority shareholders the same as the directors. Actions taken by the majority must, therefore, meet the standards of good faith and fairness.
- ♦ Disinterested directors could have called the class A stock. But here, the directors were controlled by the majority shareholder. Directors owe the duty of acting in the best interests of all of the shareholders; these directors acted only in the best interests of the majority shareholder.
- ♦ There was no business purpose for the call of class A stock and then liquidation, except to benefit the class B shareholders at the expense of the class A shareholders.

---

5. Ratification

a. Delaware Corporations Statute

Section 144 of the Delaware corporations statute provides that a contract or transaction between a corporation and one or more of its directors or officers will not be void or voidable solely for this reason ***if*** the contract or transaction is fair as to the corporation as of the time it is authorized, approved or ratified by the board of directors, a committee, or the shareholders.

b. Interested Directors Still Must Prove Transaction Was Fair

Fliegler v. Lawrence

361 A.2d 218 (Del. 1976).

Facts. Agau Mines ("Agau") was a gold and silver mining company. It had several properties, but lacked the capital to mine them. Lawrence, an officer and director of Agau, individually purchased some properties and offered them to Agau. Agau's board decided that the company could not possibly pursue the opportunity, so the individual board members (Ds) formed United States Antimony Corporation ("USAC"), a closely held corporation formed exclusively for this purpose and whose stock was owned by the individual directors. Ds gave Agau a long-term option to purchase USAC if the properties proved to be of commercial value. In 1970, the option agreement was executed between USAC and Agau. Upon its exercise and approval by Agau shareholders, Agau was to deliver 800,000 shares of its restricted investment stock for the authorized and issued shares of USAC. The exchange was calculated to reimburse USAC and its shareholders for their costs in determining whether the properties had commercial value. A shareholder of Agau (P) filed this derivative suit to recover the 800,000 shares, arguing that Ds usurped a corporate opportunity, and that the transaction was unfair to Agau. Ds argued that they did not need to prove the fairness of the transaction because Agau's shareholders ratified the board's decision to exercise the option. The lower court found the transaction to be fair and held for Ds. P appeals.

Issue. Are interested directors required to prove the fairness of a transaction even when the decision was ratified by shareholders?

Held. Yes. Judgment affirmed.

- In *Gottlieb v. Heyden Chemical Corp.*, 91 A.2d 57 (Del. 1952), this court held that shareholder ratification of an interested director transaction shifts the burden of proof to the plaintiff to demonstrate that the terms of the transaction are so unequal as to amount to a gift or waste of corporate assets. However, *Gottlieb* does not apply in a case where, as here, the majority of shares voted were cast by the defendants. Only one-third of the disinterested shareholders voted in this case, and Ds are not relieved of their burden of proving fairness.
- Ds also argue that the transaction in question is protected by 8 Del. C. § 144. However, this statute only provides that when a transaction is properly ratified by shareholders, the transaction is not voidable simply because interested directors participated. The statute does not relieve Ds of the burden of proving the fairness of the transaction.
- After reviewing the economics of the transaction, we conclude that Ds have proven that it was fair. Agau was in serious financial difficulty and by exercising the option to purchase, it received properties which were clearly of substantial value, and potentially profit-generating. The interest given to the USAC shareholders was a fair price to pay.

---

c. Ratification and the Business Judgment Rule

In re Wheelabrator Technologies, Inc. Shareholders Litigation

663 A.2d 1194 (Del. Ch. 1995).

Facts. Waste Management, Inc. ("Waste") and Wheelabrator Technologies, Inc. ("WTI") were both in the waste management business. In 1988, Waste bought 22% of WTI's stock and elected four of its own directors to WTI's 11-member board. In 1990, Waste and WTI began negotiating a merger in which Waste would acquire another 33% of WTI stock, and WTI shareholders would receive .574 WTI shares and .469 Waste shares for each WTI share they held. The board of directors held a meeting to consider the merger. During the meeting they reviewed reports and opinions from investment bankers and

WTI's attorneys, all of whom declared that the transaction was fair. Following the meeting, the seven non-Waste directors unanimously approved the merger. Then the full board voted to approve the merger. The directors prepared and distributed proxy statements explaining the merger to the WTI shareholders. A majority of WTI shareholders voted to approve the merger. A group of WTI shareholders (Ps) filed this action against the directors (Ds) alleging that the directors failed to use due care in reviewing the terms of the merger in that they were not fully informed, and that the proxy statements were materially misleading. Ps also claim that Ds breached their duty of loyalty to the company, and argue that Ds have the burden of proof on this issue under the entire fairness standard of review. Ds filed a motion to dismiss.

Issues.

(i) Are Ds entitled to summary judgment on the claims of failure to exercise due care?

(ii) Are Ds entitled to summary judgment on the disclosure claims?

(iii) Do Ds bear the burden of proof under the entire fairness standard of review?

Held. (i) Yes. (ii) Yes. (iii) No. Summary judgment granted in part and denied in part.

- Directors have a fiduciary duty to disclose fully and fairly all material facts that would have a significant effect on a shareholder's vote. Ps claim that Ds violated that duty in that the statement in the proxy materials that the board had "carefully considered the financial, business, and tax aspects" of the merger was materially misleading. Ps base this claim solely upon the fact that the board meeting to consider the merger lasted only three hours. We find that this argument lacks evidentiary support. WTI and Waste had a close business relationship for over 20 years. This fact would indicate that the WTI directors already had a substantial working knowledge of Waste long before the actual merger discussions. In addition, the proxy statement indicates that WTI's investment bankers and outside counsel attended the meeting, submitted reports, and made presentations regarding the terms and fairness of the merger. The proxy statement describes these considerations in detail, and Ps offer no evidence that the description was in any way inaccurate. We find no evidence that the proxy statement was materially misleading and grant Ds summary judgment on this issue.
- In rejecting the claim above, we necessarily have determined that the merger was approved by a fully informed vote of a majority of shareholders. Ps concede that if the shareholder vote was fully informed, the claim that the board failed to exercise due care in negotiating and approving the merger must be extinguished.
- Regarding the duty of loyalty claim, the parties disagree on the standard of review and burden of proof. When a board's action has been ratified by shareholders, the standard of review and burden of proof depends on the type of underlying transaction. The cases fall into two categories. In "interested director" transactions, approval by fully informed, disinterested shareholders invokes the business judgment rule which limits judicial review to issues of waste or gift. The burden of proof is on the party attacking the transaction. The second category of cases involves transactions between the corporation and a controlling shareholder. These cases usually involve parent-subsidiary mergers. In that situation, the standard of review is normally entire fairness, with the directors having the burden of proof. In this case, there is no evidence that Waste exercised de jure or de facto control over WTI. Waste was not a majority shareholder—it only owned 22%. Thus, the standard of review is business judgment, with Ps having the burden of proof. As no party has presented evidence as to business judgment, we must deny summary judgment on this issue.

C. THE OBLIGATION OF GOOD FAITH

1. Introduction

Directors and officers have a fiduciary duty to act in good faith in their relationships, dealings, and management of the corporation. Recall that under the business judgment rule, a director acting in good faith is only liable for gross negligence or worse.

2. Compensation

a. Executive Severance Payment

In re Walt Disney Co. Derivative Litigation

906 A.2d 27 (Del. 2006).

Facts. Michael Ovitz entered into an employment agreement with the Walt Disney Company ("Disney") to serve as the company president for five years. Prior to his contract with Disney, Ovitz was a founder and the leading partner of a major talent agency and was regarded as one of the most powerful figures in Hollywood. He earned between $20 and $25 million per year. Disney's chairman and chief executive officer, Michael Eisner, personally recruited Ovitz to join Disney. During negotiations, Ovitz made it clear that he would not enter into employment with Disney without "downside protection." Thus, the contract was negotiated to contain a clause that guaranteed Ovitz a severance payment if Disney fired him for any reason other than gross negligence or malfeasance. Ovitz and Eisner signed a letter agreement, outlining the terms of Ovitz's employment, and the Disney board of directors voted unanimously to elect Ovitz as president. During negotiations, Ovitz came to believe that he and Eisner would run Disney together as junior and senior partners. Eisner had a different view of their roles, and the two were unable to work well together. After Ovitz took office, there were also allegations of improper behavior on his part, but these were not proven. Eisner began to negotiate a "trade" with Sony, whereby Sony would take Ovitz from Disney and Disney would be relieved of its obligation to pay Ovitz based on the termination clause. This negotiation did not pan out. Eisner then explored terminating Ovitz for cause but was advised that there was not sufficient cause to do so. Eventually, Eisner terminated Ovitz without cause. Ovitz served as president of Disney for only 14 months, but received a severance payout of approximately $130 million under the contract. Several Disney shareholders (Ps) brought derivative actions against Ovitz and the Disney board of directors (Ds), claiming a breach of fiduciary duty and a waste of assets. The chancellor determined that Ds did not breach their fiduciary duties or commit waste. Ps appeal.

Issue. Did Ds violate their duty of good faith in approving and paying out on the contract?

Held. No. Judgment affirmed.

- First, Ovitz did not breach his fiduciary duties to Disney by entering into the hefty employment contract. He did not have a fiduciary duty to Disney until he formally assumed office, by which time the terms of the contract had already been negotiated. Nor was he a de facto officer before that time; he did not assume the duties of president until he was formally in office.

- Ps contend that the contract is not entitled to protection under the business judgment rule because approval of this contract was either grossly negligent or not performed in good faith. The law presumes that in making a business decision, the directors of a corporation act on an informed basis, in good faith, and with the honest belief that the action taken is in the best interests of the company. This can be rebutted if the plaintiffs showed that the directors breached their duty of care or of loyalty or acted in bad faith. Ps have failed to meet this burden.

- Contrary to Ps' claim, the full Disney board was not required to approve the employment agreement, because the company's governing instrument allocated that decision to the compensation committee. Under the best case scenario, the committee would have been provided with a spreadsheet explaining Ovitz's compensation under each possible scenario. That did not happen here. Instead, the committee considered a summary sheet of the terms of the employment agreement. Nonetheless, the committee clearly knew that in the event of non-fault termination, Ovitz would receive a significant severance payment. The committee knew that Ovitz was demanding "downside protection" to compensate him for leaving his very lucrative and secure position to come to Disney.
- Furthermore, in electing Ovitz as president, the directors were informed of all information reasonably available and were not grossly negligent. They knew of the pressing need to fill the role of president in the company, and they knew of Ovitz's background and qualifications. They also knew that Eisner had personally vouched for Ovitz. Ps failed to establish any lack of due care.
- The chancellor held that the business judgment rule presumptions protected Ds' decisions because they acted with due care and had not acted in bad faith. The chancellor opined that the concept of intentional dereliction of duty, a conscious disregard for one's responsibilities, is an appropriate, though not the only, standard for determining whether fiduciaries acted in good faith.
- Three different categories of fiduciary behavior are candidates for the "bad faith" label. The first is "subjective bad faith," where the conduct is motivated by an actual intent to do harm. Ps have not claimed that Ds acted in subjective bad faith. The second is at the opposite end of the spectrum and involves action taken solely through gross negligence, without any malevolent intent. Ps failed to establish gross negligence. Furthermore, gross negligence, without more, does not constitute bad faith. The third category falls in between the first two categories. This is what the chancellor's definition of bad faith was intended to capture. The chancellor's definition is a legally appropriate definition of fiduciary bad faith.
- Eisner had the power to terminate Ovitz. The board's failure to vote on the termination does not give rise to a breach of the duty of care or the duty to act in good faith. The board and Eisner both understood that Eisner had concurrent power with the board to terminate Ovitz.
- Ps attempted to show that Ovitz should have been fired for cause, but the chancellor determined independently that Ovitz had not engaged in any conduct that constituted gross negligence or malfeasance, the standard for termination under the employment agreement. Eisner was unable to work with Ovitz, and Eisner exercised his business judgment in terminating Ovitz. Ds' reliance on the advice that Ovitz could only be fired without cause was also in good faith.
- Finally, the claim that the payment to Ovitz constituted waste is meritless. To prove corporate waste, a plaintiff must prove that the exchange was so one-sided that no business person of ordinary, sound judgment would conclude that the corporation received adequate consideration. Here, Disney was contractually required to pay out on the contract, thus the payment cannot be considered waste.

---

3. Oversight

Directors have a duty to attempt in good faith to ensure that the corporation has adequate internal control systems that are reasonably designed to prevent employees from engaging in illegal acts. [*In re* Caremark International Inc. Derivative Litigation, 698 A.2d 959 (Del. Ch. 1996)]

a. Showing of Bad Faith Required

Stone v. Ritter

911 A.2d 362 (Del. 2006).

Facts. AmSouth Bancorporation ("AmSouth") operated numerous bank branches across the southeastern part of the United States. AmSouth was assessed millions of dollars in fines and civil penalties based on the failure of some bank employees to file suspicious activity reports as required by various anti-money-laundering regulations. No fines were imposed directly against AmSouth's directors. Certain shareholders of AmSouth filed a derivative complaint against 15 directors for their alleged lack of proper oversight. The court of chancery dismissed the complaint. Ps appeal.

Issue. Is a showing of bad faith necessary to establish director oversight liability?

Held. Yes. Judgment affirmed.

- ♦ A showing of bad faith conduct is essential to establish director oversight liability. Failure to act in good faith requires conduct that is different from, and more culpable than, conduct giving rise to a violation of the fiduciary duty of care. The obligation to act in good faith does not establish an independent fiduciary duty that stands on the same footing as the duties of care and loyalty. Only the duties of care and loyalty, where violated, may directly result in liability; a failure to act in good faith may do so, but indirectly. Where directors fail to act in the face of a known duty to act, thereby showing a conscious disregard for their responsibilities, they breach their duty of loyalty by failing to discharge that fiduciary obligation in good faith.
- ♦ In *Graham v. Allis-Chalmers Manufacturing Company*, 188 A.2d 125 (Del. 1963), a derivative action was brought against the corporation's directors for failure to prevent violations of federal anti-trust laws by employees. We held in that case that, absent cause for suspicion, there is no duty for directors to install a corporate system of espionage to ferret out wrongdoing.
- ♦ Later, in the case of *In re Caremark, supra*, the court narrowly construed *Graham* and found that a sustained or systematic failure of a board to exercise oversight over its employees will establish the lack of good faith that is a necessary condition to liability. *Caremark* established the necessary requirements for director oversight liability: (i) the directors utterly failed to implement any reporting system or controls, or (ii) having implemented such a system or controls, consciously failed to monitor the operations. Imposition of liability requires a showing that the directors knew they were not discharging their fiduciary obligations. By consciously disregarding their responsibilities, they breach their duty of loyalty.
- ♦ Here, the directors properly discharged their oversight responsibility by establishing an information and reporting system that was designed to permit the directors to periodically monitor AmSouth's compliance with the regulations. Ps' complaint seeks to equate a bad outcome with bad faith. However, a director's good faith exercise may not always prevent employees from violating criminal laws.

D. DISCLOSURE AND FAIRNESS

1. Introduction

The federal government and most, if not all, of the states regulate the dissemination of information by corporations, particularly publicly held ones. This regulatory regime mandates certain periodic and episodic disclosures and prohibits fraud and a variety of "misrepresentations." It also forbids "insiders" from trading shares in their corporations without disclosing "material, nonpublic" information in their possession. The Securities and Exchange Commission ("S.E.C.") may enforce these regulations, and in some instances, private individuals may, too.

a. The Disclosure System

1) The Securities Act of 1933

The 1933 Act primarily regulates the process of raising capital rather than trading in securities. The Act creates a scheme of mandatory disclosure for initial public distributions of securities by issuers, underwriters, and dealers (the "primary market"). Much of the scheme revolves around a disclosure document called a "registration statement," whose contents are prescribed by the S.E.C. The first part of a registration statement is called the "prospectus." The 1933 Act bars any effort to sell securities before the registration statement is filed with the S.E.C. From the time the registration statement is filed to the time the S.E.C. makes it "effective," the only written materials that an offeror may use are the registration statement and the prospectus. From the effective date to the completion of the distribution, usually a very short period, sellers may use other written materials, but only in conjunction with the registration statement or prospectus. The 1933 Act renders issuing corporations strictly liable for material "misrepresentations" or omissions in their registration statements. It also subjects to liability other participants in the distribution unless they can show that they exercised "due diligence." This costly and elaborate regulatory regime would apply to every sale of a security except that the 1933 Act exempts many securities and most securities transactions from its reach, including "transactions by any person other than an issuer, underwriter, or dealer."

2) The Securities Exchange Act of 1934

The 1934 Act primarily regulates securities trading among investors (the "secondary market"). It creates a scheme of mandatory continuous disclosure for corporations that: (i) list securities on a national exchange, (ii) own at least $5 million in assets and have at least 500 holders of any class of securities, or (iii) file a 1933 Act registration statement that becomes effective. These corporations must file with the S.E.C. annual, quarterly, and event-prompted reports. Investors do not receive these reports, although they may obtain them. Professional analysts use them, and through them, so do investors.

3) Integrated Disclosure: Meshing the 1933 and 1934 Acts

In 1977, the S.E.C. began prescribing disclosure documents responsive to both acts. Later, it promulgated regulations permitting some corporations to incorporate by reference material from their 1934 Act reports in their 1933 Act registration statements. Still later, the S.E.C. adopted Rule 415, permitting qualified corporations to register stock for future sale, "shelf registration." Once the corporation files a registration statement incorporating by reference subsequently filed 1934 Act reports, it may sell the registered securities at any time during the following two years. In promulgating these regulations, the S.E.C. relied on the "efficient capital market hypothesis" ("ECMH").

4) "Blue Sky" Regulation

The federal securities statutes explicitly provide for the simultaneous application of "blue sky" laws, state securities statutes. Many of these statutes subject brokers, dealers, and investment advisors to licensing regulations; most prohibit fraud; and most require securities registration with a state agency. Some of the state statutes authorize a state bureaucrat to bar sales of securities on "substantive" grounds, without regard to disclosure. The National Securities Markets Improvement Act of 1996 ("NSMIA") exempts all "covered securities" from state registration and other "blue sky" requirements. The Act defines "covered securities" as those traded on any S.E.C.-approved exchange. The Securities Litigation Uniform Standards Act of 1998 preempted class actions and other consolidated or multiple party proceedings resembling class actions brought under state law for securities fraud in connection with "covered securities."

5) Disclosure Requirements of Self-Regulatory Organizations

The New York Stock Exchange, the American Stock Exchange, and the National Association of Securities Dealers Quotation System regulate the dissemination of information by listed corporations as part of their listing agreements. Generally, these self-regulatory organizations require the prompt disclosure of material information except where delay would serve a legitimate business purpose. The organizations enforce these obligations, not private investors.

b. Definition of a Security

The initial question in securities litigation is whether or not the instrument or investment at issue is a ***security*** within the meaning of the Securities and Exchange Act. This determination is important for two reasons. First, it indicates whether the registration requirements of the Securities Act apply to the transaction. Second, plaintiffs generally have an easier time bringing suit under the federal securities laws than under the state common law fraud rules. The elements of federal securities fraud are easier to prove.

1) Application of the 1933 Act to "Securities"

In order to come within the registration requirement of section 5 of the 1933 Act, the offer or sale of a property interest must constitute the offer or sale of a "security."

2) Categories of Securities

Basically, the Act defines three categories of securities (*see* section 2(1) of the Act).

a) Any Interest or Instrument Commonly Known as a Security

These would include bonds, stocks, debentures, warrants, etc.

b) Types of Securities Specifically Mentioned in the Act

The Act specifically mentions the following as being "securities": (i) preorganization subscriptions for securities; and (ii) fractional, undivided interests in oil, gas, or other mineral rights.

c) Investment Contracts and Certificates of Participation

The two most important clauses of section 2(1) are its broad, catchall phrases—securities are "investment contracts" and "certificates of interest or participation in any profit-sharing agreement." The S.E.C. and the courts have defined these phrases so as to apply to a wide variety of financial schemes.

(1) The Traditional Test for a Security

The traditional test for whether a property interest constitutes a security under these two broad phrases is known as the "*Howey* test" (set forth by the Supreme Court in *S.E.C. v. W.J. Howey*, 328 U.S. 293 (1946)). In *Howey*, the Supreme Court held that an investment contract is any contract or scheme whereby a person invests his money in a common enterprise and expects to make a profit solely from the efforts of the promoter or a third party who is responsible for management. Thus, the elements of the test are:

(a) Is it a profitmaking venture?

(b) Is the investor passive in management?

(2) The Trend of Decisions

The trend of decisions is toward expanding the scope of what is regulated as a "security." Whereas, originally under the *Howey* test, the scheme had to have a profit objective and the investor had to be totally passive in management, the S.E.C. and the courts have expanded the test to cover situations where investors do participate in management and the form of benefit derived by the investor may be something other than cash profits.

(3) The Modern Tests

Modern courts are applying the following criteria to determine whether an interest is a "security" under the 1933 Act.

(a) Is the property interest one that is specifically mentioned in the Act?

(b) Is it the type of interest that is commonly thought to be a security?

(c) Is it an investment contract or a participation in a profitmaking venture?

  (i) Does the investor derive something of substantial benefit?

  (ii) Is the management principally provided by a third party other than the investors? Or, even if the investors are active in management, does the scheme involve the raising of capital and does control of this capital rest with a third party (the so-called "risk capital" test)?

(d) Is there a need for the protection of the Act? Is there an "investment" so that investors need the protection of full disclosure?

(4) Examples

The following are property interests that have been found to be "securities":

(a) Interests in Land

The Court found a "security" involved where small tracts of land were sold to investors to be used for growing fruit; the seller's company then managed the land for the investors and was responsible for growing the crops; the investors received a percentage of the net profits. [S.E.C. v. W.J. Howey, *supra*]

(b) Pyramid Sales Plans

A "pyramid plan" exists where a promoter takes a product (such as dish soap) and creates a type of franchise system where persons are sold (i) the right to distribute the product and (ii) the right to sell further distribution rights to others (on whom they receive an override on sales, or they are able to mark up the price of the product in sales to these "subdistributors"). In essence, the scheme is really one of everyone selling distributorships and subdistributorships, rather than trying to sell the product.

1] To get around the *Howey* test for a "security," these plans initially require the purchasers to perform some minor management duties (such as file reports), but the investors do not assume the major duties normally required of a person buying a franchise.

2] Many of these plans have been held to involve securities. Thus, the test for a "security" no longer requires total management passivity by the investor. The S.E.C. has indicated that it is enough if the promoter has "substantial control" over the investor's funds, even if other parts of management involve the investor.

3] These cases have also indicated that the benefit from the scheme need not necessarily be a share of the cash profits of the enterprise. Any "economic benefit" can constitute the property interest a "security." [SA Release No. 5211 (1971)]

(c) Sale of a Business

In the past, some courts had followed the doctrine that federal securities law did not apply to the sale of 100% of a corporation's stock because the economic realities of such a transaction involved the sale of a business, not the sale of securities. The Supreme Court has since held that the sale of all of the stock of a company ***is*** a securities transaction subject to the antifraud provisions of the federal securities law. [Landreth Timber Company v. Landreth, 471 U.S. 681 (1985)]

3) What Is a Security?

Robinson v. Glynn

349 F.3d 166 (4th Cir. 2003).

Facts. Glynn (D) founded GeoPhone Company, LLC, to develop and market telecommunications technology that he had purportedly developed. D contacted Robinson (P), a businessman with no telecommunications experience, in an effort to raise capital for GeoPhone. P invested heavily in the company, received shares, and was named GeoPhone's treasurer and appointed to the company's board of managers and the company's executive committee. It was later revealed that the technology on which P had based his investment had never actually been implemented. P filed suit alleging federal securities fraud. The district court found that P's membership interest was not a security within the meaning of federal securities law and dismissed P's claim. P appeals.

Issue. Was the membership interest a security within the meaning of the federal securities law?

Held. No. Judgment affirmed.

- ♦ P was an active and knowledgeable executive at GeoPhone, rather than a mere investor in the company. He had the power to appoint two members to the board, and he himself assumed one of the seats. He served as the company's treasurer. Even if P had no technological experience, there was nothing preventing him from seeking assistance in understanding the technology from outside parties. In fact, P reviewed GeoPhone's technology and financial records. P was a savvy and experienced businessman. Business ventures often have diverse contributors.
- ♦ Even though P and D labeled P's certificates as "shares" and "securities," this does not mean these laws applied. The characteristics of stocks include things such as the right to receive dividends, voting rights in proportion to shares owned, etc. P's interest lacked several of the classic stock characteristics. P did not receive profits in proportion to his "shares," and he could not transfer his interests freely. From the beginning, P and D viewed P's investment as a membership interest and not merely stock.
- ♦ We decline to extend this ruling broadly to all LLCs. LLCs can assume a variety of forms.

---

c. The Registration Process

Prior to the original public issuance of securities, the issuer must file a registration statement with the S.E.C. The purpose of the registration statement is to disclose all of the information needed to determine whether the securities offered are a good investment. The most important information in the registration statement is digested into a shorter document—the prospectus—which is the document actually given to a purchaser prior to purchase or at the same time as the purchased securities are delivered.

1) The Material Required in the Registration Statement

The S.E.C. does not approve or disapprove of the investment merits of the securities being registered (it is not supposed to protect the investor from this risk—it is only supposed to see that all material information is disclosed to the investor); but in performing its proper function, the S.E.C. in reality exercises broad discretion over what is put in the registration statement. Financial information about the issuer is a very important part of the information that must be disclosed in the registration statement.

2) Exemptions

The 1933 Act provides for certain exemptions from the registration requirements of section five. For example, securities issued by banks or issued or guaranteed by the United States, its territories, or the states are exempt from the registration requirements. Certain types of transactions are also exempt. Transactions by an issuer not involving a public offering (*i.e.*, a "private offering" of securities) are exempted from registration under section 4(2).

a) Private Offerings Under Section 4(2) of the Act

(1) Fact Question

Whether an offering is a "private offering" or a "public offering" is a question of fact. For the transaction to be exempt from registration under the Act, the offering must be "private."

(2) Primary Factors Considered

The following are the primary factors that are considered by the courts in making the determination whether an offering is a public or private one.

(a) Need for the Protection of the Act

Many courts have stated that the primary question is whether there appears, in the circumstances of the offering of securities, the need for the protection of the Act to be given to the purchasers.

(b) Access to Investment Information

Allied with the idea of the level of sophistication of the offerees is the idea of the investor's access to information material to an investment decision.

1] Courts have indicated that for the private offering exemption to apply, it must be shown that the offerees were given or had access to the same kind of information that would have been contained in a registration statement.

2] Allied with the concept of access to information is the concept that the offerees must be in, or have a close relationship to, the issuer and its management.

(c) Distribution of Material Information

Some courts have implied that the mere access to material information is not enough.

1] The issuer may have to actually distribute to its offerees the same type of material information as would be contained in a formal registration statement.

2] Also, the issuer may have to give the offerees access to any additional information that they request.

(d) The Number of Offerees

A "private offering" also seems to imply that the number of offerees will be few in number.

1] The Supreme Court has indicated that the number of offerees is not a major factor. However, the Court did suggest that the S.E.C. might adopt a rule of thumb for the purposes of administrative decisions. At one time, this rule of thumb was 25 persons (*i.e.*, if the offering was to more than 25 persons, it was a "public" offering).

2] But other courts and the S.E.C. have emphasized the aspect of the number of offerees. When they do, it is clear that the rationale is that the more offerees there are, the more the offering looks like a "public offering."

3] On the basis of this rationale, there is no question but that when the number of offerees gets very large, no matter how sophisticated the investors might be or how much information they might have, the offering would be a public one and registration would be required.

(3) Other Important Factors

In addition to the primary factors considered above, there are several other factors that courts have indicated are important in making the determination of whether the offering is a public or private one. Most of these factors are based on the rationale that if an offering looks like a public offering (*i.e.*, a large dispersed offering), then it is one for the purposes of the 1933 Act.

(a) The Size (Amount) of the Offering

The bigger in dollar amount that the offering is, the more public it looks.

(b) The Marketability of the Securities

If the issuer has created the type of security that tends to be readily marketable (such as many small units in small denominations; *i.e.*, $1 per share), then there is more reason to believe that the issue is made with the intent to distribute the securities to the public rather than to a few private persons.

(c) The Diverse Group Rule

The more unrelated to each other (*i.e.*, without knowledge of or relationship to each other) and diverse the group of investors is, the more the offering appears to be a public offering.

(d) The Manner of Offering

The manner in which the offering is made (*i.e.*, whether public advertising was used) may also be important.

b) Private Offerings Are Exempted

Doran v. Petroleum Management Corp.

545 F.2d 893 (5th Cir. 1997).

Facts. Petroleum Management Corporation (D) was a limited partnership engaged in drilling and operating oil wells. Doran (P) was advised by his securities broker, Kendrick, of an opportunity to become a "special participant" in the drilling program for an investment of $125,000. P put $25,000 down and was to pay the remaining amounts in installments under a note issued by Mid-Continent Supply Company ("Mid-Continent"). D periodically sent P production information throughout 1970 and 1971. However, during this period, the wells were deliberately overproduced in violation of the production allowances established by the Wyoming Oil and Gas Conservation Commission. As a result, the Commission ordered D's wells sealed for a period of 338 days. After this period, the wells yielded a production income level below that obtained before the shut-down order. P defaulted on his installment note, and Mid-Continent obtained a judgment against him for $50,000. P filed suit against D seeking damages for breach of contract, rescission of the contract based on violations of the Securities Acts of 1933 and 1934, and a judgment declaring D liable for the judgment obtained by Mid-Continent. P claimed that the offering and sale of the partnership interests violated the Securities Act because no registration statement was filed. The lower court found that the offer and sale of the "special participant" interest was a private offering which was exempt from the registration requirement of the Act. The court further found no evidence that D, its officers, or Kendrick made any misrepresentations or omissions of material facts to P, and that the initial overproduction of the wells was not a breach of the partnership agreement. P appeals.

Issue. Was the transaction a private offering within the meaning of the Securities Act?

Held. Probably. Judgment reversed and case remanded.

- It is a violation of the Securities and Exchange Act for any person to offer to sell a security unless a registration statement has been filed. D admits that no registration statement was filed in connection with its offering but contends that the transaction was a private offering and thus came within the exemption from registration found in section 4(2) of the Securities and Exchange Act.

- Section 4(2) exempts private offerings from the registration requirement. The term "private offering" is not defined in the Act, so the scope of the exemption must be determined by reference to the legislative purposes of the Act. Other courts have held that the applicability of the exemption should turn on whether the persons affected need the protection of the Act. An offering to sophisticated investors who are able to fend for themselves is a transaction not involving any public offering. Four factors must be considered: (i) the number of offerees and their relationship to the issuer; (ii) the number of units offered; (iii) the size of the financial stakes; and (iv) whether the offering was characterized by personal contact between the issuer and the offerees free of public advertising or intermediaries such as investment bankers. In this case, Ds have presented evidence of the latter three factors. The offer involved a small number of units. The financial stakes were relatively modest, and the offering was carried out by personal contact between the issuer and the offerees, without public advertising or intermediaries.

- We are not convinced that D has adequately demonstrated the first factor. The partnership interests were offered to eight individuals. This number is consistent with a finding that the offering was private. However, we find that a question remains regarding the relationship between the issuer and the offerees. Courts have sought to determine the need of offerees for the protections afforded by registration by focusing on the relationship between offerees and issuer and more particularly on the information available to the offerees by virtue of that relationship. The record clearly establishes that P was a sophisticated oil investor with a petroleum engineering degree and a net worth in excess of $1 million. The other offerees were also very sophisticated investors. However, a high degree of legal or business sophistication of all offerees does not satisfy the requirements for the exemption. If the investors do not possess the information requisite for a registration statement, they cannot bring their sophisticated knowledge to bear in deciding whether or not to invest. D must show that all offerees had available to them all information that a registration statement would have provided a prospective investor in a public offering.

♦ Availability of information means either disclosure or access to the relevant information. This is why the relationship between the issuer and offeree is important (such as if the relationship was such that it provided the offeree access to files and records). We remand the case for determination as to whether the offerees knew or had a realistic opportunity to learn facts essential to an investment judgment.

---

3) Other Exemptions

a) Regulation D

(1) Introduction

In a major initiative aimed at facilitating the capital formation needs of small business, the S.E.C. adopted regulation D, which contains rules 501–506. Rules 501 through 503 set forth definitions, terms, and conditions that apply generally throughout the regulation. Rules 504 and 505, respectively, replace prior rules 240 and 242 and provide exemptions from registration under section 3(b) of the 1933 Act. Rule 506 replaces prior rule 146 and relates to transactions that are deemed to be exempt from registration under section 4(2) of the 1933 Act. [*See* S.E.C. Release No. 33–6389 (1982)] These provisions apply only to the issuer; control persons may not use them. Regulation D is designed to: (i) simplify and clarify existing exemptions; (ii) expand the availability of existing exemptions; and (iii) achieve uniformity between federal and state exemptions.

(2) General Conditions to Be Met

There are several general conditions that apply to all offers and sales effected pursuant to rules 504 through 506 (under rule 502):

(a) Integration

All sales that are part of the same regulation D offering must be integrated. [*See* SA Rule 502(a)] The rule provides a safe harbor for all offers and sales that take place at least six months before the start of, or six months after the termination of, the regulation D offering, as long as there are no offers and sales (excluding those to employee benefit plans) of the same securities within either of these six-month periods.

(b) Information Requirements

The type of disclosure that must be furnished in regulation D offerings is specified. [*See* SA Rule 502(b)] If an issuer sells securities under rule 504 or only to accredited investors, then regulation D does not mandate any specific type of disclosure. But if securities are sold under rule 505 or 506 to any investors that are not accredited, then delivery of the information specified in rule 502(b)(2) to ***all*** purchasers is required. The type of information to be furnished varies depending on the size of the offering and the nature of the issuer (*i.e.*, whether the issuer is a reporting or nonreporting company under the 1934 Act). Reporting companies in essence can use the information they are already filing with the S.E.C. (*i.e.,* annual report, proxy statement, and Form 10-K). The issuer, in a rule 505 or 506 offering, must also give investors the opportunity to ask questions and to obtain any additional information that the issuer can acquire without unreasonable effort.

(c) Manner of the Offering

The use of general solicitation or general advertising in connection with regulation D offerings is prohibited, except in certain cases under rule 504. [*See* SA Rule 502(c)]

(d) Limitations on Resale

Securities acquired in a regulation D offering, with the exception of certain offerings under rule 504, have the status of securities acquired in a transaction under section 4(2) of the 1933 Act. [*See* SA Rule 502(d)] Issuers are required to exercise reasonable care to assure that purchasers of these securities are not underwriters and to make reasonable inquiry as to an investor's investment purpose. Also, a legend restricting transfer must be placed on the share certificates.

(3) Filing Notice of Sales

There is a uniform notice of sales form for use in offerings under both regulation D and section 4(6) of the 1933 Act. It is called "Form D." Issuers furnish information on Form D mainly by checking appropriate boxes. [*See* SA Rule 503] The notice is due 15 days after the first sale of securities in an offering under regulation D. Subsequent notices are due every six months after the first sale and 30 days after the last sale.

(4) Exemption for Offers and Sales Not Exceeding One Million Dollars

An exemption under section 3(b) of the 1933 Act is provided for certain offers and sales not exceeding an aggregate offering price of $1 million during any 12-month period. [*See* SA Rule 504] This exemption is not available to investment companies or to 1934 Act reporting companies. Commissions or similar remuneration ***may*** be paid to those selling the offering in a rule 504 offering.

(a) Rule 504 does not mandate specific disclosure requirements. However, an issuer proceeding pursuant to the rule is subject to the antifraud and civil liability provisions of the federal securities laws ***and must comply with any applicable state requirements.***

(b) If the entire offering is made exclusively in states that require the registration and the delivery of a disclosure document, and if the offering is in compliance with these requirements, then the general limitations of rule 502(c) (on the manner of the offering) and (d) (restrictions on transfer) do not apply.

(5) Exemption for Offers and Sales Not Exceeding Five Million Dollars

An exemption under section 3(b) of the 1933 Act is also provided for offers and sales to an unlimited number of accredited investors, and to no more than 35 nonaccredited investors, when the aggregate offering price in any 12-month period does not exceed $5 million. [*See* SA Rule 505] Rule 505 is available to any issuer that is not an investment company.

4) Securities Act Civil Liabilities

At common law, a defrauded purchaser of securities had to prove the same things to recover as any other purchaser of goods. Section 11 of the 1933 Act imposes liability on designated persons for ***material misstatements or omissions*** in an effective prospectus, unless the defendants can show that they had (after having made a reasonable investigation of the facts) reasonable grounds to believe and actually did believe that the statements made were accurate.

a) Material Misstatements or Omissions

The plaintiff must prove that any misstatement or omission was of a material fact.

b) Persons Subject to Liability

Section 11 indicates that the following persons can be held liable for material misstatements in the registration statement or prospectus:

(1) Every Person Who Signs the Registration Statement

The following persons must sign the registration statement: (i) the issuer; (ii) the principal executive officers of the issuer; (iii) the chief financial officer of the issuer; (iv) the principal accounting officer of the issuer; and (v) a majority of the members of the board of directors of the issuer. [SA § 6(a)]

(2) Every Person Who Was a Director of the Issuer

Every person who was a director of the issuer at the time the registration statement became effective can be held liable, even if such person did not sign the registration statement.

(3) Every Person Who Is Named (with His Consent) as About to Become a Director

(4) Every "Expert" Who Gives a Certificate That Part of the Registration Statement Was Prepared by Him

For example, accountants are "experts" as to the certified financial statements included in the registration statement.

(5) Every Underwriter Involved in the Distribution

(6) Control Persons

Persons who "control" any person liable under section 11 are also liable. [*See* SA § 15]

c) Elements Required in a Common Law Action Not Required in Section 11 Actions

Section 11 has eliminated some of the requirements that were included in common law fraud actions against sellers of securities.

(1) Privity of Contract Is Not Required

Any person acquiring a security that was the subject of a defective registration statement may sue under section 11. However, there is a tracing requirement. That is, the plaintiff must be able to trace the securities she purchased back to the defective registration statement.

(2) Reliance

The plaintiff need not prove that she purchased in reliance on the misstatement in order to recover. However, if the issuer sends out an earnings statement covering the period of one year after the effective date of the registration statement, then a person thereafter acquiring some of the registered securities must prove reliance to recover. [*See* SA § 11(a)]

d) Defenses—Standards of Diligence for Defendants to Avoid Liability

(1) The Issuer

The issuer has the following defenses to a section 11 action, all of which may also be claimed by any other defendant.

(a) The issuer can show that the statements made were actually true (and thus there was no misstatement).

(b) The issuer can also show that the misstatements or omissions were not of material facts.

(c) Finally, the issuer can show that the plaintiff purchaser knew of the misleading statements or omissions and invested in the securities anyway.

(2) Nonexperts

(a) Standard of Diligence Required

To avoid liability, a nonexpert must meet the following tests of due diligence regarding statements he has made in the registration statement: (i) the nonexpert must actually believe that the statements he made were true; and (ii) that belief must be a reasonable one. In order to have a reasonable belief, the nonexpert must have made a reasonable investigation into the facts. The courts look at each individual defendant and, based on his position, his responsibilities, his background, skills, training, and access to information, they determine what he should have done to fulfill the obligation to make a "reasonable investigation." In other words, the test is what kind of investigation a prudent person in the defendant's position, with the same responsibilities, skills, etc., would have made. [Escott v. BarChris Construction Corp., *infra*]

(b) Nonexpert Portions of the Registration Statement

It has been held that an attorney-director of the issuer who drafted the registration statement for the issuer is a "nonexpert" as to the registration statement in general. [*See* Escott v. BarChris Construction Corp., *infra*]

1] Due Diligence Test

In *BarChris*, the court indicated that each defendant would be looked at from the standpoint of his position, training, and responsibility in the registration process to determine what constitutes the reasonable investigation necessary to fulfill that party's due diligence responsibility.

2] Reasonable Investigation for the Attorney

The attorney-director does not have to conduct an independent audit of the issuer. But a reasonable investigation does go beyond merely trusting the opinions and responses of the issuer's officers as to material facts. [*See* Escott v. BarChris Construction Corp., *infra*]

a] A reasonable investigation, therefore, does include resort to original written records (such as written contracts to verify the fact that the issuer really did have the back orders it claimed) to verify statements in the registration statement. [Feit v. Leasco Data Processing Equipment Corp., 332 F. Supp. 544 (E.D.N.Y. 1971)]

b] A reasonable investigation would also probably have to include examination of the issuer's facilities, operations, material contracts, corporate minutes and other documents, and major items important to its financial condition, etc.

(c) Expert Portions of the Registration Statement

It is also conceivable that an attorney might be requested to certify, as an expert, some portion of the registration statement. In that case, the attorney would be held to the due diligence test of an expert (discussed below).

(d) Nonexperts Reviewing Statements in the Registration Statement Made by Other Nonexperts

A nonexpert (such as a member of the issuer's board of directors) may also have potential liability under the Act; to avoid liability, the nonexpert will have to show that the due diligence appropriate to his position has been exercised. Part of this responsibility must be exercised with regard to statements made in the registration statement by other nonexperts (*i.e.*, the director must review the registration statement written by the nonexpert lawyer).

(3) Standard of Diligence Required

The standard of diligence required is the same as for nonexperts concerning statements they make in the registration statement (*see* above).

(4) Inside Directors and the Principal Executive Officers

Directors who are also part of management, and all of the principal executive officers of the issuer, must also meet the standard of due diligence required of nonexperts.

(a) Note that, if there are misstatements made that relate to the issuer's financial condition, the issuer's chief financial officer will have a particularly difficult time sustaining his burden of showing that he really did not know of the misrepresentations.

(b) Not all of the individuals in this category will be required to do the same things to show due diligence, however. What is required of each depends on his position, access to information about the issuer, etc.

(5) Statements Made by Experts

Statements are also made in the registration statement by experts (for example, accountants may prepare and certify the issuer's financial statements).

(a) Standard of Diligence Required

As to the statements made by experts, they must meet the following test:

1] They must actually believe that the statements they made are true.

2] The belief must be reasonable.

3] In order for their belief to be reasonable, they must have made a reasonable investigation into the facts supporting the statements made. Normally, this means that the expert must perform up to at least the standards of his profession (for example, accountants in certifying that financial statements of the issuer are prepared according to "generally accepted principles" of accounting).

(b) Nonexperts Reviewing Statements Made by Experts

Nonexperts (such as an outside director; *see* above) are held to a lower standard of care with respect to statements made by experts than with respect to statements made by nonexperts; that is, nonexperts are entitled to rely to a greater extent on the statements made by experts (for example, an outside director, a nonexpert, relying on the certified financial statements of the accountants, who are experts).

1] The nonexpert must only show that he did not believe the statements made by the expert were untrue and he had no reasonable ground to believe they were untrue. No investigation need be made by the nonexpert in this case.

2] In most cases, nonexpert defendants will be able to meet this burden of proof (for example, most of the nonexperts in *BarChris* were not held for the misrepresentations of the issuer made by the expert accountants).

e) General Civil Liability Under the Act—Section 12(2)

The Act also prohibits fraud generally in the offer or sale of securities. It provides that any person who offers or sells a security (whether or not the sale is exempted from registration by the provisions of the Act) by the use of any means of interstate commerce and makes an untrue statement of material fact (or omits to state a material fact) in connection therewith (the purchaser not knowing of such untruth or omission), and who cannot sustain the burden of proof that he did not know and in the exercise of reasonable care could not have known of such untruth, is liable to the purchaser of such security. [*See* SA § 12(2)]

(1) Privity Requirement

There is a privity requirement.

(2) Persons Liable

See discussion of section 12(1) below.

(3) Liability Standard

The defendant is held liable for intentional or negligent violations. Note that the defendant has the burden of proof to show his nonnegligence.

f) The *BarChris* Case

Escott v. BarChris Construction Corp.

283 F. Supp. 643 (S.D.N.Y. 1968).

Facts. Ps were purchasers of BarChris Construction Corp.'s convertible debentures that were offered pursuant to a registration statement, which was claimed to have contained material misstatements and omissions; the action was brought under section 11. BarChris was building bowling alleys for a small down payment and an installment contract from the purchaser. The contract was either discounted (to give BarChris cash) or the alley was sold to a finance company and leased back (with BarChris guaranteeing the loan). BarChris was in a cash bind and the industry was overbuilt. At the time of registration, it overstated sales and earnings for 1960 by 15%, and various other items in the financial statements by even more significant margins (such as the backlog of orders, overstated by 75%, etc.). The action was against those who signed the registration statement, the underwriters, and the auditors (Ds). Within 18 months after the registration statement and the sale of the debentures, BarChris was bankrupt.

Issue. Did Ds meet the required standard of due diligence to avoid liability under section 11?

Held. No, most did not meet the due diligence standard.

- As a preliminary matter, I find that there was an abundance of misstatements pertaining to the company's financial state in the registration statement, and that these misstatements were material within the meaning of section 11.
- Nonexperts, with respect to parts of the registration statement not prepared by experts, must, after a reasonable investigation, have reasonable grounds to believe, and actually believe, that the statements made were true, and that there were no omissions of material fact. With respect to statements made by experts, nonexperts must show that they had no reasonable ground to believe, and did not believe, that the statements made were untrue or that there was a material omission. A reasonable investigation is one that a prudent person in the management of his own property would conduct.
- The only expert was the accounting firm as to their audited financial statements. Neither the lawyer for the company nor the lawyer for the underwriting firm (although participating in writing the registration statement) is an expert.
- The only expert parts of the registration statement are the certified financial statements; the statements in the body of the registration statement that purport to be based on the financial statements are not expert parts of the registration statement. Vitolo (president) and Pugliese (vice

president) were the founders of the business. Although they are both men of limited education such that the prospectus was likely difficult reading for them, the liability of a director who signs a registration statement does not depend on whether or not he read it or understood it. Vitolo and Pugliese were members of the executive committee and must have known of the company's financial situation. They knew of their own large advances to the company which remained unpaid. They could not have believed that the registration statement was wholly true. In any case, there is no evidence that they made any investigation of anything in the statement that they did not understand or did not know. Thus, they have not proved their due diligence defense.

- Kircher (treasurer, chief financial officer, and director) did not meet the standard of due diligence with respect to either the expert section or the nonexpert section of the statement. He knew all of the relevant facts; he was in a position to know of all of the misrepresentations and omissions; he worked on the registration statement; he lied to those checking on its accuracy. It is not a defense that he was never specifically asked for the information. He must show the necessary actual belief and reasonable belief in the accuracy of the statement, which he could not do.
- Birnbaum (secretary, house counsel, and director) met the burden with respect to the expert but not with respect to the nonexpert portion. His position gave him access to contracts, minutes, etc., and, while it appears that he did not actually know of the misstatements, he made no investigation into the facts but simply relied on statements of the other corporate officers.
- Auslander (outside director) joined the board a month before the offering; he read a draft of the statement but made no investigation of any of the facts. He could rely on the expert portion, but he breached his duty with respect to the nonexpert portion.
- More was required of Grant (director and outside lawyer, drafter of the registration statement) due to his unique position in drafting the registration statement. He did not know the statement was false, but he did not make a reasonable investigation (he need not have done an audit, but he could not accept the word of management; he had to check matters that were easily verifiable, such as contracts and agreements, the backlog figures, minutes of meetings, conflicts of interest by management, etc.). Here, he could rely on the expert portion, but he did not meet his burden with respect to the nonexpert portion of the statement.
- Coleman (a director and representative of one of the underwriters) met with BarChris management and asked several important questions; but once the offering was decided upon, he did not follow up and investigate any of these matters, but left the investigation to his underlings. A reasonable investigation would have discovered some of the misrepresentations. He is liable with respect to the nonexpert portion of the registration statement, but not with respect to the expert portion.
- The underwriters were represented by counsel, who made a cursory review of the important questions that had been asked initially, but essentially took management's word on answers to the question, rather than conducting an independent analysis or investigation (such as of the backlog figures, etc.). The underwriter is not the same as an outside director (who can rely to some extent on management); the underwriter has an adverse interest to the company and is responsible to the public. It must make an independent investigation, which the underwriters here did not do. Thus, the underwriters here did not meet the due diligence test with respect to the nonexpert portions of the statement.
- The accountants are experts with respect to the financial statements. They must conduct an investigation that meets the standards of their profession. Here, they had a young, relatively inexperienced accountant doing the audit for 1960 (and the subsequent investigation before the registration statement was filed). He should have discovered several important misrepresentations (such as the fact that BarChris had not sold one bowling alley that was included in income, but was still leasing and operating the alley). In the investigation after the audit (and prior to the filing of the registration statement), the accountants accepted the word of

management with respect to several important matters that should have been investigated (such as reading corporate minutes, reading the prospectus and checking its facts, etc.). The burden of proof is on the accountants, and they did not meet it.

---

5) Liability for Offers or Sales in Violation of Section 5—Section 12(1) of the Act

Section 12(1) provides that any person who offers or sells a security in violation of any of the provisions of section 5 of the 1933 Act shall be liable to the purchaser for (i) the consideration paid (with interest), less the amount of any income received on the securities, or (ii) for damages if the purchaser no longer owns the security.

a) Privity Requirement

Note that section 12(1) has a privity requirement. Thus, the purchaser may only sue the seller from whom she purchased the security.

b) Persons Liable

This section provides that only persons offering or selling the security can be held liable. Thus, issuers, dealers, and perhaps control persons (under section 15 of the 1934 Act) can be held liable (but probably others connected with the registration process, such as directors, accountants, etc., would not be).

c) Liability Standard

If the plaintiff proves that (i) there is privity with the defendant, and (ii) the defendant has violated one of the provisions of section 5, she can recover. Reliance, causation, and scienter are not required elements of a cause of action.

d) General Civil Liability Under the Act—Section 12(2)

The Act also prohibits fraud generally in the offer or sale of securities. It provides that any person who offers or sells a security (whether or not the sale is exempted from registration by the provisions of the Act) by the use of any means of interstate commerce and makes an untrue statement of material fact (or omits to state a material fact) in connection therewith (the purchaser not knowing of such untruth or omission), and who cannot sustain the burden of proof that he did not know and in the exercise of reasonable care could not have known of such untruth, is liable to the purchaser of such security. [*See* SA § 12(2)]

(1) Privity Requirement

There is a privity requirement.

(2) Persons Liable

See discussion of section 12(1) above.

(3) Liability Standard

The defendant is held liable for intentional or negligent violations. Note that the defendant has the burden of proof to show his nonnegligence.

d. Rule 10b–5

Rule 10b–5 makes it unlawful in connection with the purchase or sale of any security for any person, directly or indirectly by the use of any means or instrumentality of interstate commerce, or of the mails, or of any facility of any national securities exchange, to:

(i) Employ any device, scheme, or artifice to defraud.

(ii) Make any untrue statement of a material fact or to omit to state a material fact necessary in order to make the statements made, in the light of the circumstances under which they were made, not misleading.

(iii) Engage in any act, practice, or course of business conduct which operates or would operate as a fraud or deceit upon any person.

1) Transactions Covered by the Rule

a) Purchases and Sales

Rule 10b–5 applies to both purchases and sales in all contexts.

b) Remedies

The rule does not specifically give a private right of action, but the courts have implied such a cause of action. Thus, a private party may bring an action for an injunction, for damages, or for rescission. The S.E.C. may sue to enjoin fraudulent acts or for other appropriate remedies.

c) Securities

A "security" must be involved. The term is broadly defined. Note that the rule applies to all types of securities transactions (those on an exchange, etc.).

d) Jurisdiction

Interstate commerce must be involved (*i.e.*, some means of interstate commerce must be used).

e) Statute of Limitations

There is no specific statute of limitations; courts refer to the statute of a relevant state.

f) Liable Parties

The rule is extremely broad in its application. It applies to "any person" who is "connected with" a securities transaction. Thus, accountants and lawyers and others involved in some way with a securities transaction may be held liable.

2) The Elements of a 10b–5 Cause of Action

a) Fraud, Deception, Misrepresentation, etc.

There must be some fraudulent action or deception in connection with the purchase or sale of securities. An issue can arise concerning whether, in some situations, there has actually been such a "deception."

b) The Concept of an "Insider"

Obviously, rule 10b–5 has very broad applications to securities transactions. For example, even though rule 10b–5 does not mention "insiders" specifically, nor specifically require that one person having information not had by another disclose this in a securities transaction, nevertheless, the S.E.C. and the courts have used rule 10b–5 to cover such transactions. There are two elements that must be shown to designate someone an "insider":

(1) The person must have a relationship giving access, directly or indirectly, to information intended to be available only for a business purpose and not for the personal benefit of anyone.

(2) There must be the presence of an inherent unfairness where a party takes advantage of such information, knowing it is unavailable to those with whom he is dealing.

c) Materiality

The misrepresented or undisclosed fact must be a "material" one.

(1) The Reasonable Person Standard

In *List v. Fashion Park, Inc.*, 340 F.2d 457 (2d Cir. 1965), *cert. denied*, 382 U.S. 811 (1965), the court stated that the "basic test of materiality . . . is whether a reasonable person would attach importance (to the misrepresented fact) in determining his choice of action in the (securities) transaction in question." Note that in a situation where the impact of a fact is uncertain, it has also been suggested that in applying this materiality test, the probability that the event will occur must be balanced against the magnitude of the event if it did occur. For example, a high probability, high magnitude event is clearly material.

(2) Consider All of the Facts

Under whatever test is used, it is clear that the courts consider all of the facts to determine whether the undisclosed information might reasonably have influenced the plaintiff's conduct.

(3) Examples of Material Facts

Examples of material facts include the intention of company management to pay a dividend, or a significant drop in the profit level of the company.

(a) Preliminary Merger Negotiations

Basic, Inc. v. Levinson

485 U.S. 224 (1988).

Facts. Officers and directors of Basic, Inc., including Ds, opened merger discussions with Combustion Engineering in September 1976. During 1977 and 1978 Basic denied three times that it was conducting merger negotiations. On December 18, 1978, it halted trading on the New York Stock Exchange, saying it had been approached. On December 19, 1978, it announced that the board had approved Combustion's $46 per share tender offer. Levinson and others (Ps) are a class of shareholders who sold their stock after Basic's 1977 statement and before the trading halt on December 18, 1978. They sued under rule 10b–5. The district court, on the basis of a "fraud on the market theory," adopted a rebuttable presumption of reliance by members of the class. On a motion for summary judgment, the district court ruled for Ds, holding that at the time of the first announcement in 1977, no negotiations were actually going on, and that the negotiations conducted at the time of the second and third announcements were not destined with reasonable certainty to become a merger agreement. The court of appeals affirmed the holding about reliance, but reversed the summary judgment. It held that preliminary merger discussions could be material. Further, it held that once a statement is made denying the existence of discussions, then even discussions that might otherwise have been immaterial can be material. The Supreme Court granted certiorari.

Issues.

(i) Is the standard used to determine whether preliminary merger negotiations must be disclosed a materiality standard under rule 10b–5?

(ii) Is it appropriate to use a rebuttable presumption of reliance for all members of a class on the basis that there has been a fraud on the market?

Held. (i) Yes. (ii) Yes. Judgment vacated and case remanded.

- The *TSC Industries* test is the test of materiality for rule 10b–5 cases; that is, a fact is material if there is a substantial likelihood that a reasonable shareholder would consider it important. [*See* TSC Industries, Inc. v. Northway, Inc., 426 U.S. 438 (1976)]
- With contingent events like mergers (that may or may not happen), the probability that the merger will occur and the magnitude of the possible event are looked at. Because of the ever-present possibility that merger negotiations may not yield a merger, it is difficult to ascertain whether the reasonable investor would have considered the omitted information significant at the time. All relevant facts bearing on these two issues should be considered.
- An absolute rule (such as the one requiring that a preliminary agreement be arrived at before negotiations are material), while convenient, is not in accord with the *TSC Industries* test. Likewise, the circuit court was wrong also. A denial of merger negotiations cannot itself render them material because rule 10b–5 requires the plaintiff to show that "the statements were ***misleading*** as to a ***material*** fact," not just that they were false or incomplete. If a fact is immaterial, it makes no difference that Ds made misrepresentations about it.
- Thus, the case must be remanded to consider whether the lower court's grant of summary judgment for Ds was appropriate.
- Reliance is an element of a rule 10b–5 cause of action. It provides a causal connection between a defendant's misrepresentation and a plaintiff's injury. But this causal connection can be proved in a number of ways. In the case of face-to-face negotiations, the issue is whether the buyer subjectively considered the seller's representations. In the case of a securities market, the dissemination or withholding of information by the issuer affects the price of the stock in the market, and investors rely on the market price as a reflection of the stock's value.
- The presumption of reliance in this situation assists courts to manage a situation where direct proof of reliance would be unwieldy. The presumption serves to allocate the burden of proof to defendants in situations where the plaintiffs have relied on the integrity of the markets, which rule 10b–5 was enacted to protect. The presumption is supported by common sense. Most investors rely on market integrity in buying and selling securities.
- Ds can rebut the presumption. First, Ds could show that misrepresentation or omission did not distort the market price (for example, Ds could show that market makers knew the real facts and set prices based on these facts, despite any misrepresentations that might have been made). Or Ds could show that an individual plaintiff sold his shares for other reasons than the market price, knowing that Ds had probably misrepresented the status of merger negotiations.

Concurrence and dissent (White, O'Connor, JJ.).

- The fraud-on-the-market theory should not be applied in this case. The fraud-on-the-market theory is an economic doctrine, not a doctrine based on traditional legal fraud principles. If rule 10b–5 is to be changed, Congress should do it. It is not clear that investors rely on the "integrity" of the markets (*i.e.*, on the price of a stock reflecting its value). In rejecting the original version of section 18 of the Securities Exchange Act, Congress rejected a liability provision that allowed an investor recovery based solely on the fact that the price of the security bought or sold was affected by a misrepresentation. Congress altered section 18 to include a specific reliance requirement.

- The fraud-on-the-market theory is in opposition to the fundamental policy of disclosure, which is based on the idea of investors looking out for themselves by reading and relying on publicly disclosed information.
- This is a bad case in which to apply the fraud-on-the-market theory. Ps' sales occurred over a 14-month period. At the time the period began, Basic's stock sold for $20 per share; when it ended, the stock sold for $30 per share, so all Ps made money. Also, Basic did not withhold information to defraud anyone. And no one connected with Basic was trading in its securities. Finally, some Ps bought stock after Ds' first false statement in 1977, disbelieving the statement. They then made a profit, and can still recover under the fraud-on-the-market theory. These Ps are speculators. Their judgment comes from other, innocent shareholders who held the stock.

(b) False Nonpublic Information

West v. Prudential Securities, Inc.

282 F.3d 935 (7th Cir. 2002).

Facts. Hofman, a securities broker working for Prudential Securities, Inc. (D), told 11 of his customers that Jefferson Savings Bancorp ("Jefferson") was "certain" to be acquired in the near future at a big premium. In fact, no acquisition was impending. The district court certified a class action on behalf of everyone who bought Jefferson stock during the seven months that Hofman continuously made this statement, regardless of whether or not the purchaser had personally learned of Hofman's statement. D appealed the class certification.

Issue. Can a class action for fraud-on-the-market be maintained in a case involving nonpublic information?

Held. No. Order certifying a class is reversed.

- The district court's order marks a substantial extension of the fraud-on-the-market approach outlined in *Basic, Inc. v. Levinson.* The underlying basis of fraud-on-the-market cases is that public information reaches professional investors, whose evaluation of that information influences securities prices. In this case, however, Hofman did not release inaccurate information to the ***public.*** He only told a handful of investors. Therefore, this case presents a departure from *Basic.* It also presents a novelty in fraud cases as a class. Oral frauds have not been allowed to proceed as class actions because the details of the fraud differ from victim to victim.
- In addition to the above, causation is the shortcoming of this class action certification. Professional investors monitor public news about companies, and this information influences the values such investors place on any particular stock. With professional investors alert to news, markets are efficient in rapidly adjusting to public information. If some of this information is false, stock prices will reach an incorrect level, and remain there until the truth emerges. No similar mechanism exists to explain how market prices respond to nonpublic information, such as the statements Hofman made to a small number of clients. Thus, the district court could not identify any causal link between the nonpublic information and the price of Jefferson securities. Instead, the district court relied on the fact that each party's position has the support of a reputable financial economist, and decided that this was enough to support class certification and a trial on the merits.
- Because there is nothing in the record to indicate that nonpublic information affected the price of Jefferson stock, we must remand the case. The plaintiffs point out that the price of Jefferson stock did rise during the time Hofman was spreading the acquisition rumor. However, there is nothing

to indicate that Hofman's statement is the factor that caused the price increase. A statement that an acquisition was imminent might fool investors for a month, but after two or three months pass with no merger or tender offer, professional investors would likely draw on more astute inferences and negate the price effect. The fact that this did not occur in this case means that either Jefferson stock was not closely followed by professional investors (and that the market therefore does not satisfy *Basic's* efficiency requirement) or that something else explains the price change.

(c) Where Defendant Follows Procedures Permitted by State Law

Santa Fe Industries v. Green

430 U.S. 462 (1977).

Facts. Santa Fe Industries owned more than 90% of the stock of a subsidiary corporation and, desiring to eliminate the minority shareholders, used a Delaware short-form merger statute that allowed a corporation holding more than 90% of the stock of a subsidiary to merge the subsidiary corporation, paying cash to the subsidiary's minority shareholders, giving notice to them within 10 days of the merger, and restricting the minority shareholders to an appraisal action in the state courts if they were dissatisfied with the price they received. D adopted the merger plan, disclosed all material information relative to the value of the subsidiary's stock, offered the shareholders $150 per share (when it had been appraised by a brokerage firm at $125 per share), and notified the minority shareholders of their option to seek an appraisal in the state courts. A number of minority shareholders (Ps) sued in federal court to enjoin the merger or for damages from a violation of rule 10b–5. They alleged that rule 10b–5 was breached in that (i) there was no business purpose for the merger except to freeze out the minority, and (ii) a grossly inadequate price was offered. The district court dismissed. The Court of Appeals reversed. Although the court found Ps' complaint contained no evidence of material misrepresentation or nondisclosure with respect to the value of the stock, it nonetheless held that an action can be maintained under rule 10b–5 for breaches of fiduciary duty by a majority against minority shareholders without any charge of misrepresentation or lack of disclosure. D appeals.

Issue. Does rule 10b–5 provide a remedy for breach of a fiduciary duty by officers and directors and majority shareholders (*i.e.*, is there a fraud) in connection with a sale of the corporation's securities by its minority shareholders even if there is full disclosure of all the facts, no misrepresentations are made, and the transaction is permitted by state law?

Held. No. Judgment for Ps reversed.

- The states should be free to regulate the conduct of corporate officials except for the specific areas regulated by federal statute. Expansion of rule 10b–5 to cover this form of activity would be an unnecessary intrusion on the powers of the states.
- Section 10(b) was designed to protect investors by requiring full and truthful disclosure so that investors could make informed choices as to their course of action. The language of section 10(b) gives no indication that Congress intended to prohibit any conduct ***not*** involving manipulation or deception. This transaction was neither deceptive nor manipulative, and therefore did not violate either section 10(b) or rule 10b–5. The Supreme Court has repeatedly described the fundamental purpose of section 10(b) of the Securities Exchange Act as implementing a "philosophy of full disclosure." Once full and fair disclosure has occurred, the fairness of the transaction is at most a tangential concern of the statute. We are reluctant to recognize a cause of action here to serve what is at best a subsidiary purpose of the federal statute.
- Here the investors were fully informed of their rights and options and ***had an adequate state remedy (appraisal) for the wrong alleged*** in the complaint.

Comment. The rationale of conservative opinions like *Green* is that rule 10b–5 is meant to control only the securities markets and fraud in the purchase and sale of securities, primarily in situations in which there has been an affirmative misrepresentation or omission to state material facts. It was not meant to regulate all forms of corporate mismanagement—an area traditionally covered by state law. However, *Green* should be read narrowly since an adequate remedy was available to the minority shareholders (state law provided for court appraisal of the fair market value of their shares). In other situations, where the court considers the available state law remedies inadequate, rule 10b–5 might still apply. It also seems clear that based on *Green* (at a minimum in the future) all the plaintiffs who wish to state a rule 10b–5 cause of action will attempt to show that there has been a material misrepresentation or omission of fact, whatever other fraud or deception might be present.

---

d) Reliance

"Reliance" is a showing by the plaintiff that he personally actually relied on the material fact that was misrepresented. The early cases, involving a plaintiff and a defendant in a personal, face-to-face relationship, required that the plaintiff show that he actually relied on the defendant's misrepresentation. The modern trend of the cases is toward abolishing or limiting the reliance requirement. [*See* Basic, Inc. v. Levinson, *supra*]

(1) Affirmative Representations and Open-Market Transactions

In cases involving situations where there are affirmative misrepresentations and the plaintiffs purchase or sell securities on the open market, two types of cases arise:

(a) Actual Reliance

It is possible that the plaintiff could argue that he actually read and relied on the statements made by the defendant. If there is a reliance requirement, this pleading would fulfill it.

(b) Effect on the Market

The other alternative is simply for the plaintiff to allege that the defendant's statements affected the market price at which the plaintiff sold his stock. The plaintiff in this situation need not argue that he actually read or relied on the defendant's statements at all.

1] This issue is closely related to the concept that the defendant's actions must have "caused" the plaintiff's injury (*see* below).

2] It is also closely related to the "materiality" issue. If a representation is "material," then it is of the type that would influence the market and a reasonable investor's actions (if he had been aware of it).

(2) Nondisclosures

Another type of situation sometimes arising is where the defendant does not disclose material facts. The issue here is whether the plaintiff would have acted differently if he had known of the material facts.

e) Causation and Causation-in-Fact

(1) Introduction

Courts have consistently stated that "causation" is a necessary element in a private action for damages under rule 10b–5. That is, the defendant's action must have "caused" the plaintiff's injury (for example, the misrepresentation must have caused a drop in the price of the stock). But as with the reliance requirement, it appears that the necessity of showing this element is gradually disappearing in rule 10b–5 actions.

(2) Relationship to Other Elements

(a) Reliance

There is a relationship between causation and reliance. The reason for the reliance requirement is to insure that the conduct of the defendant caused the plaintiff's injury. [*See* Basic, Inc. v. Levinson, *supra*]

(b) Materiality

There is also a relationship between causation and materiality. Causation is, in practice, largely determined by the answer to the threshold question of materiality. Once it is shown that the defendant has misrepresented a material fact or omitted to state a material fact, then it is practically a foregone conclusion that the defendant's conduct will be held to have "caused" the plaintiff's injury. This result has been influenced by the discussion of causation in nondisclosure cases, where the courts have found "causation-in-fact" (*i.e.*, that the nondisclosed fact would have been material had it been disclosed).

(3) Failure-to-Disclose Cases

The difficult causation cases arise in the context of a failure to disclose. For example, in *Affiliated Ute Citizens of Utah v. United States*, 406 U.S. 128 (1927), Ute Indian tribe members had received shares of stock from the United States Government. Employees of the Utah bank that acted as the transfer agent encouraged tribe members to sell their shares to them. The employees then resold the shares for a much higher price. The Supreme Court held that the tribe members only had to show the existence of an undisclosed material fact to prove reliance. The Court found that the fact that the bank employees were making a market in the shares and buying and then reselling them at a greater price were material facts that they were under an obligation to disclose to the tribe members. Although *Ute* seems to eliminate the requirement of reliance in cases of nondisclosure, subsequent courts have interpreted the holding as establishing a presumption of reliance that makes it possible for the plaintiff to meet his burden. A defendant can rebut the presumption by showing that the plaintiff would have followed the same course of action even with full and honest disclosure.

f) The Purchase or Sale Requirement

(1) Definition of "Purchase" and "Sale"

Rule 10b–5 expressly covers only the "purchase" or "sale" of a security. "Purchase" and "sale" are defined to include "any contract" to purchase or sell.

This suggests that something beyond a mere offer to purchase must be involved before 10b–5 applies.

(2) Fraud in Connection with a Purchase or Sale

Clearly, the defendant's fraudulent activity must be in connection with the purchase or sale of a security.

(3) Purchase or Sale by the Plaintiff

The plaintiff must either be an ***actual*** "purchaser" or an ***actual*** "seller" of securities to have standing to maintain a 10b–5 cause of action.

(i) The issue has arisen in the context where the plaintiff has not sold his stock but argues that the stock has depreciated in value due to the misrepresentations made by the defendant. [*See* Greenstein v. Paul, 400 F.2d 580 (2d Cir. 1968)—no standing since no actual purchase or sale by the plaintiff had occurred]

(ii) The issue has also arisen where the plaintiff claims he would have purchased stock but for the negative statements made by the defendant. In *Blue Chip Stamps v. Manor Drug Stores*, 421 U.S. 723 (1975), the Supreme Court held that only a person who had actually purchased or sold stock had standing to bring a private action under rule l0b–5. The Court reasoned that policy considerations demand this result. It would be too easy for a plaintiff to make a claim that he "would have purchased" stock, and such claims cannot be independently verified.

(a) Derivative Actions

Normally, a plaintiff in an action to enforce a fiduciary responsibility of corporate management sues in a representative capacity on behalf of the corporation. In these situations, the courts have held that the individual plaintiff shareholder need not be an actual purchaser or seller; it is sufficient if there is a purchase or sale by the corporation. [*See* Superintendent of Insurance v. Bankers Life and Casualty Co., 404 U.S. 6 (1971)]

(b) Exception to the Need for a Purchase or Sale by the Plaintiff

An exception to the purchase or sale requirement has been held to exist where the plaintiff seeks an ***injunction*** against the continuance by the defendant of market manipulation violative of rule 10b–5; here, status as a shareholder (without an actual purchase or sale in connection with the defendant's activity) is sufficient for bringing the injunctive action. [*See* Mutual Shares Corporation v. Genesco, Inc., 384 F.2d 540 (2d Cir. 1967)]

(4) Trading in Stock Options

Deutschman v. Beneficial Corp.

841 F.2d 502 (3d Cir. 1988).

Facts. Deutschman (P) filed a class action suit against Beneficial Corporation ("Beneficial"), Caspersen (Beneficial's CEO and chairman), and Halvorsen (Beneficial's Chief Financial Officer) (Ds), alleging violations of section 10(b) of the Securities Exchange Act of 1934. Beneficial's insurance division had suffered severe losses which had caused a sharp decline in the market price of the company's stock. Ps' complaint alleges that Caspersen and Halvorsen, who held stock and stock options, issued public statements that they knew were false and misleading in an effort to prevent further decline in the stock price. The statements indicated that the problems in Beneficial's insurance department were resolved and were covered by sufficient financial reserves. The statements had the effect of temporarily stabilizing the stock price. P's complaint does not allege that Caspersen or Halvorsen traded in Beneficial stock at the time of these misrepresentations, or that P himself traded in Beneficial stock. It alleges that P suffered losses when, upon disclosure of the facts, call options on Beneficial's stock that he and others had purchased in reliance on the market price, created by Ds' misstatements, became worthless. The complaint was dismissed for lack of standing, and P appeals.

Issue. Does a plaintiff who traded in stock ***options*** in reliance on misstatements made by corporate management have standing to sue under section 10(b)?

Held. Yes. Judgment reversed.

- The district court held that option traders who suffer losses as a result of intentional misstatements by the management of a corporation lack standing to assert a cause of action for damages under rule 10b–5. The court held that in the absence of allegations that P bought or sold stock, or that Ds bought or sold options, there was no duty to P to refrain from misstatements that would affect the market price of Beneficial stock.
- Ds do not dispute that the affirmative misrepresentations alleged in P's complaint, if proven to be true, would subject them to liability in a suit by a ***purchaser*** of Beneficial stock. They argue, however, that P was not a purchaser of stock, and that purchasing of option contracts is essentially gambling, which is not protected under section 10(b). We disagree. The only standing limitation recognized by the Supreme Court with respect to section 10(b) damage actions is the requirement that the plaintiff be a purchaser or seller of a ***security.*** Congress specifically amended the Securities and Exchange Act of 1934 to explicitly include option contracts in the definition of a security. We hold that P has standing as a purchaser of an option contract to seek damages under section 10(b) for the affirmative misrepresentations he alleges Ds made.

---

g) Scienter

A major issue in actions brought under rule 10b–5 concerns the standard of care a defendant will be held to in a securities transaction. Historically, various jurisdictions disagreed about what the standard should be. The issue has been resolved by the Supreme Court, which has held that, in order for liability to exist under rule 10b–5, it must be shown that the defendant has "scienter." [*See* Ernst & Ernst v. Hochfelder, 425 U.S. 185 (1976)] In *Ernst & Ernst*, the Court defined scienter as a mental state embracing the "intent to deceive, manipulate, or defraud." Other courts have held that recklessness satisfies the scienter requirement. [*See* Sundstrand Corp. v. Sun Chemical Corp., 553 F.2d 1033 (7th Cir. 1977), *cert. denied*, 434 U.S. 875] The Supreme Court has also decided that scienter must be shown in injunctive actions brought by the S.E.C. [*See* Aaron v. S.E.C., 446 U.S. 680 (1980)] In both private damage and S.E.C. injunctive actions, ***reckless*** conduct may also qualify under rule 10b–5. The Supreme Court has not yet decided this issue.

h) Remedies

The rule itself says nothing about any remedies. It is clear, however, that both rescission and damages are available in 10b–5 actions.

(1) Rescission

A seller can recover his securities, and a buyer can recover the amount he paid for securities. There are limitations (such as waiver, laches, estoppel, etc.) on rescission actions. Or the remedy may just not be available (defendant purchaser has sold the securities purchased from the plaintiff).

(2) Damages

The basic formula for damages is to provide restitution—*i.e.*, to restore what the plaintiff has lost. But the formula has been applied differently by different courts: *Mitchell v. Texas Gulf Sulphur Co.*, 446 F.2d 90 (10th Cir. 1971), *cert. denied*, 404 U.S. 1004 (1971), represents one application. There, the court placed a time limitation on measuring damages. The court looked at what would be a reasonable period after discovery of the fraud and measured damages from that point. Thus, if the plaintiff is a defrauded seller, he has a reasonable period of time after discovery of the fraud in which to buy the stock back. Example: A sells for $10 per share; Company X has not disclosed very favorable news about its exploration activity; X discloses the news; the stock goes to $20 per share; A discovers the fraud; damages are measured from a reasonable time after the discovery ($20 – $10 = $10 per share). If the stock continues to appreciate to $30, A cannot get this amount. If the plaintiff is a defrauded buyer, then damages are calculated on the basis of what might have been a reasonable time for the plaintiff to have sold the stock after discovery of the fraud.

(3) Unlimited Liability

An unsettled issue is whether a defendant can be held for an unlimited amount of damages. For example, the individual defendant in *Mitchell* was a corporate officer who had also bought stock on the Exchange on the basis of inside information. He was held liable to the plaintiffs. But could all the other plaintiffs who had also purchased stock on the exchange during the period of the nondisclosure also sue and collect from this same defendant?

(4) Punitive Damages

There are no punitive damages under rule 10b–5.

E. INSIDE INFORMATION

1. Insider Trading

The typical problem involves the situation where someone related to the corporation (such as an officer or director or a shareholder owning a large amount of stock) is in a position to have inside information about how the corporation is doing, and, hence, what the corporation's stock is, or will be, worth. This person ("insider") then buys stock (with an advantage over the seller) or sells it (with the advantage over the buyer). The issue concerns what duty the corporate "insider" may owe to the other party.

a. Common Law Background

1) Majority Rule

The majority rule held that directors and officers owed no special duty to present or prospective shareholders and could deal with them at arm's length, with no duty of disclosure of inside information required.

a) No Duty to Disclose

Goodwin v. Agassiz

186 N.E. 659 (Mass. 1933).

Facts. Goodwin (P) saw an article in the newspaper that the company in which he had stock had discontinued copper exploration in certain fields. He sold his stock on the exchange. Agassiz (D), a director of the company, knew of a geologist's theory that he believed had value and that he planned to have the company test on company property. Without any disclosure, D bought P's stock in an exchange transaction. The theory later proved to be correct, and the company's stock went up in price. P sued for rescission of the sale.

Issue. Do those privy to "inside" information have a duty to disclose it in purchase and sale transactions over a stock exchange involving the corporation's stock?

Held. No. No right of recovery for P.

- In certain circumstances, a director with superior knowledge must act as a fiduciary to shareholders in buying and selling stock. For example, if a director personally seeks a stockholder for the purpose of buying his shares without making disclosure of material facts within his particular knowledge and not within the reach of the stockholder, the transaction will be closely scrutinized and relief may be granted. But here, the purchase was impersonal, on an exchange. There was no privity, relation, or personal connection.
- D had no duty of disclosure. The geologist's theory was only a hope, not a proven reality.
- P acted on his own judgment in selling his stock. He made no inquiries of D or of other officers of the company. D made no representations to anyone about the geologist's theory. D is not guilty of fraud on P.

---

2) Minority Rule

The minority rule held that directors or officers had a fiduciary duty to disclose facts to an outsider. For example, in *Hotchkiss v. Fischer*, 16 P.2d 531 (Kan. 1932), a widow shareholder asked a director before a board meeting whether the company was going to pay a dividend. He showed her the financial statements and told her he did not know. He then bought her stock for $1.25 per share. The board declared a $1 per share dividend three days later. The director was held liable.

3) Special Circumstances Rule

A number of courts took the position that a duty of disclosure is owed only if there are special facts or circumstances making nondisclosure unfair. For example, in *Strong v. Repide*, 213 U.S. 419 (1909), a director, president, and 75% shareholder used a strawman to purchase a minority interest, knowing that the United States Government was going to buy company property. Here, the Court held that the defendant had a duty of disclosure.

4) Modern Approach Under State Law

Many state courts have followed federal securities laws and developed a state cause of action for insider purchases and sales without disclosure. [*See, e.g.*, Diamond v. Oreamuno, 248 N.E.2d 910 (N.Y. 1969)]

a) Materiality Depends on Probability of Occurrence and Magnitude

Securities and Exchange Commission v. Texas Gulf Sulfur Company

401 F.2d 833 (2d Cir. 1968).

Facts. Texas Gulf Sulfur Company ("TGS"), a mining firm, detected a large, promising mineral deposit near Timmons, Ontario. TGS drilled a test hole, a sample of which contained an extraordinary level of mineral content. Several corporate officers who knew of the testing purchased TGS stock on the open market before public disclosure of the discovery. As geological testing of the area continued, rumors about the find began circulating in Canada. TGS then issued a press release that downplayed the significance of the preliminary findings, and stated that more testing was necessary to determine the commercial value of the find, if any. The S.E.C. (P) claimed that TGS, the corporate officers, and the geologist who purchased stock (Ds) violated rule 10b–5. The district court ruled that the test results were not material at the point where Ds purchased stock and issued the press release because extensive drilling would be required to establish the commercial value of the find. P appeals.

Issues.

(i) Was the information about the mineral find immaterial as a matter of law?

(ii) Did the issuance of the press release violate rule 10b–5?

Held. (i) No. (ii) Maybe. Judgment reversed and case remanded.

- The basic test of materiality is whether a reasonable person would attach importance to the information in making choices about the transaction. The test need not, as the trial court suggested, be a conservative one in the sense of assessing facts solely by measuring the effect that knowledge of them would have upon prudent and conservative investors. The test encompasses any fact that in reasonable and objective contemplation might affect the value of the securities.
- Whether the facts are material when they relate to a particular event will depend at any given time upon a balancing of both the indicated probability that the event will occur and the anticipated magnitude of the event in light of the totality of the company's activity. Here, the undisclosed facts might well have affected the price of TGS stock, and would certainly have been important to a reasonable, if speculative, investor in deciding whether to buy, sell, or hold the stock of D. It certainly would have affected the stock price and, as such, it was material.
- The results of the testing done on one test hole, known as K-55-1, yielded results that one trade publication called "one of the most impressive drill holes completed in modern times." Our survey of the facts conclusively establishes that knowledge of the results of test hole K-55-1 would have been important to a reasonable investor and might have affected the price of the stock. We therefore hold that all transactions in TGS stock or calls by individuals apprised of the drilling results of K-55-1 were made in violation of Rule 10b–5.
- The lower court held that although in retrospect, the press release may appear gloomy or incomplete in light of what was actually known at the time, the S.E.C. failed to demonstrate that the press release was false and misleading. We cannot definitively determine from the present record whether the statement was deceptive or misleading to the reasonable investor. There is evidence that some brokers considered this and other newspaper articles appearing at the time as favorable developments, so it is possible that a reasonable investor would have read between the lines of what appears to us to be a negative statement by TGS. However, there is also evidence that the price of TGS stock declined following the TGS press release. We therefore remand this issue to the district court for further determination.

Comment. The court's balancing test for materiality requires that the magnitude of an event be discounted by the probability of its occurrence and that the resulting expected value be compared to the company's financial posture.

b) Tippee Analyst's Duty to Disclose or Refrain from Trading

Dirks v. Securities and Exchange Commission

463 U.S. 646 (1983).

Facts. Dirks (D) was an officer of a broker-dealer firm that specialized in providing investment analyses of insurance company securities to institutional investors. He received information from a former officer of Equity Funding ("EF") that, due to fraudulent practices, EF's assets were grossly overstated. D investigated these charges, upon which several regulatory agencies had failed to act. The allegations were corroborated by other EF employees. D urged the *Wall Street Journal* to publish the story, but the *Journal* declined. Neither D nor his firm owned or traded any EF stock. However, D discussed his findings with a number of clients and investors, some of whom subsequently sold their EF stock. The price of EF stock dramatically declined. Trading on the stock was halted and other parties began looking into the situation. EF's fraudulent practices came to light and it went into receivership. The S.E.C. (P) investigated D's role in exposing the fraud, and ruled that D had aided and abetted violations of securities laws, including rule 10b–5. The appellate court upheld the ruling. D appeals.

Issue. Is a tippee always under an obligation to disclose inside information before trading or to refrain from trading?

Held. No. Judgment reversed; judgment for D.

- Tippees inherit the insider's duty to shareholders to disclose material, nonpublic information before trading or to refrain from trading only when the information has been ***improperly*** disclosed to them by the insider.
- Imposing this duty solely because a person knowingly receives material, nonpublic information from an insider and trades on it could have an inhibiting influence on the role of market analysts, which the S.E.C. itself recognizes is necessary to the preservation of a healthy market. The purpose of the tip will usually determine whether its disclosure constitutes a breach of the insider's fiduciary duty. The test is whether the insider will receive a direct or indirect personal benefit from the disclosure. If the insider does not stand to personally gain, he has not breached his duty to the shareholders, and there can be no derivative breach by the tippee.
- Here, those who provided D with the information about EF's conduct did not receive any personal benefit from the disclosures. The facts showed that they were motivated by a desire to expose the fraud. The insiders did not breach their duty, so D was not under any derivative obligation to EF's shareholders when he passed the nonpublic information to his clients.

Dissent (Blackmun, Brennan, Marshall, JJ.). The Court's ruling is another limitation placed on provisions intended to protect investors. The requirement of showing improper purpose has no basis in law, and results in excusing knowing and intentional violations of the insider's duty to shareholders. The Court justifies D's action because the benefits to society in general outweigh the harm caused shareholders when D's clients sold their EF stock before the fraud became public. This does not change the fact that D's clients profited from inside information, and that innocent parties paid for those gains. The insider gave D the information knowing that D would cause his clients to trade on it. Therefore, D was obligated to publicly disclose the information or to refrain from actions that he knew would lead to trading.

Comment. Under section 10(b), mere possession of material, nonpublic information does not give rise to a duty to disclose or abstain. A fiduciary relationship between the insider and the shareholders must already be in place before the tippee's role will be examined.

c) The Misappropriation Theory

United States v. O'Hagan

521 U.S. 642 (1997).

Facts. O'Hagan (D) was a partner in a law firm retained by Grand Metropolitan ("Grand Met") to represent it in a potential tender offer for the common stock of the Pillsbury Company. D personally did not work on the case. While his law firm was still representing Grand Met, D began buying Pillsbury stock options and common stock. When Grand Met announced its tender offer, the price of Pillsbury stock increased from $39 per share to $60 per share. At that time, D sold all of his Pillsbury stock, making a profit of $4.3 million. The S.E.C. began an investigation, which led to a 57-count indictment against D, including 17 counts of fraudulent trading in connection with a tender offer in violation of section 14(e) and rule 14e–3(a), and 17 counts of securities fraud in violation of section 10(b) and rule 10b–5. A jury convicted D on all 57 counts, but the court of appeals reversed all of the convictions. The appellate court held that liability under section 10(b) and rule 10b–5 could not be grounded on the "misappropriation theory." It also held that rule 14e–3(a) exceeds the S.E.C.'s rulemaking authority because it contains no breach of fiduciary duty requirement. The Supreme Court granted certiorari.

Issues.

(i) Is a person who trades in securities for personal profit, using confidential information misappropriated in breach of a fiduciary duty to the source of the information, guilty of violating section 10(b) and rule 10b–5?

(ii) Did the S.E.C. exceed its rulemaking authority by adopting rule 14e–3(a), which proscribes trading on undisclosed information in the tender offer setting, even in the absence of a duty to disclose?

Held. (i) Yes. (ii) No. Judgment reversed and case remanded.

- ♦ The "misappropriation theory" holds that a person commits fraud in connection with a securities transaction, and thereby violates section 10(b) and rule 10b–5, when he misappropriates confidential information for securities trading purposes, in breach of a duty owed to the source of the information. Instead of premising liability on a fiduciary relationship, the misappropriation theory premises liability on a trader's deception of those who entrusted him with access to confidential information. That is, the trader's duty is not owed to another trader, but to the source of the information.
- ♦ A section 10(b) violation requires "deceptive" conduct "in connection with" securities transactions. That is, the misappropriation of information first must involve some deceptive device or connivance. In this case, D's feigning fidelity to the source of the confidential information, while secretly converting the information for personal gain, constitutes deception. If D had disclosed to the source that he planned to trade on this nonpublic information, there would be no deceptive device and thus no 10(b) violation.
- ♦ We find that the "in connection with the purchase or sale of a security" requirement is also met in this case. D's fraud was consummated, not when he gained the confidential information, but when he used the information to purchase, and then sell, securities. The securities transaction and the breach of duty to the source of the information thus coincide. This is so even though the person or entity defrauded is not the other party to the transaction. The Act does not require deception of an identifiable individual. It requires only that the deception be "in connection with" a purchase or sale.
- ♦ We therefore find that the misappropriation theory can provide the basis for a section 10(b) violation. To hold otherwise would frustrate the congressional purposes of the Act. If such conduct were not held to be a violation, it could have the effect of inhibiting participation in the market.

- Section 14(e) prohibits fraudulent, deceptive, or manipulative acts in connection with a tender offer. For section 14(e) purposes, the S.E.C. is given authority to "by rules and regulations define, and prescribe means reasonably designed to prevent, such acts and practices as are fraudulent, deceptive, or manipulative."
- Under the authority of section 14(e), the S.E.C. promulgated rule 14e–3(a). Rule 14e–3(a) is violated if an individual trades on the basis of material nonpublic information concerning a pending tender offer that he "knows or has reason to know has been acquired directly or indirectly from an insider of the offeror or issuer, or someone working on their behalf."
- The lower court held that rule 14e–3(a) exceeds the S.E.C.'s rulemaking authority because it applies whether or not the trading in question breaches a fiduciary duty. The court reasoned that the S.E.C. does not have authority to create its own definition of fraud, but only to identify and regulate acts and practices that the law already defines as fraudulent. Thus the rule exceeds the S.E.C.'s authority.
- We disagree. Section 14(e)'s rulemaking authorization gives the S.E.C. latitude to regulate nondeceptive activities as a means of preventing manipulative acts. We therefore find that the S.E.C. may prohibit acts that are not themselves fraudulent under the common law or section 10(b) if the prohibition is "reasonably designed to prevent . . . acts and practices [that] are fraudulent."

F. SHORT-SWING PROFITS

1. Introduction

Section 16 of the 1934 Act is designed to prevent corporate insiders from unfairly using information about their company. The approach used by the statute to accomplish this is to make insiders report their transactions in securities of their own companies [SEA § 16(a)] and to forfeit to their companies any "profit" resulting from short-term trading (within a period of less than six months) in their company's securities [SEA § 16(b)]. Note that in some cases the statute deems a profit to exist when in fact the individual defendant lost money.

a. Rationale for Section 16

The rationale for section 16 is that insiders often possess valuable information about their companies, and this information might be used by them to gain an advantage over an "outside" seller or buyer. Section 16(b) makes it more difficult for an insider to use inside information. Section 16(c) makes it unlawful for insiders to engage in short sales of their company's equity securities. In other words, an insider may not sell shares he does not own, and then buy the shares for delivery later. The short seller sells at today's price, hoping that by the time he has to cover the sale by delivering the securities, the price will have gone down.

b. Distinguish Rule 10b–5 "Insider Trading"

Although both rule 10b–5 and section 16 are sometimes said to prohibit "insider trading," the provisions operate entirely differently. A rule 10b–5 case is based on a misrepresentation or failure to disclose. Section 16, on the other hand, is based on the amount of time elapsed between a purchase and sale (or a sale and purchase) of the issuer's securities by an insider. If the amount of time is too short, the insider must give up her "profits," regardless of whether information was misrepresented or withheld. The presence or absence of fraud is irrelevant to a section 16 case.

c. Strict Liability

The general rule is that there are no defenses to a section 16(b) action if all elements of the cause of action are present (*i.e.*, an "insider," registered equity securities, and a matching purchase and sale within the required time period). Thus, it makes no difference that the insider cannot be shown to have had access to any inside information, or to have used any inside information in effectuating the matching purchase and sale.

d. "Insiders" Defined

"Insiders" covered under section 16 are officers and directors of a corporation with a class of equity securities registered under section 12 of the 1934 Act, ***and*** all persons who beneficially own more than 10% of any class of the corporation's equity securities registered under section 12. Courts have generally refused to expand the class of potential defendants beyond the persons described in section 16 (*e.g.*, to other persons who possess the same inside information as officers and directors).

1) Officers and Directors

Whether a potential defendant was an officer or director at a particular point in time is in most cases readily established through the corporate minute book.

a) "Officer" Defined

An officer includes an issuer's president, principal financial officer, principal accounting officer, any vice president of the issuer in charge of a principal business unit, division or function (such as sales, administration, or finance), any other officer who performs a policymaking function, or any other person who performs similar policymaking functions for the issuer. [SEA Rule 16a–1(f)]

e. Elements of a Section 16(b) Cause of Action

The following elements must be shown to sustain a cause of action under section 16(b):

1) Transactions Involving Equity Securities

The transaction(s) for which the plaintiff seeks to hold the defendant liable must involve an "equity security." The 1934 Act defines "equity security" as "any stock or similar security; or any security convertible, with or without consideration, into such security"; as well as certain "acquisition rights" to such securities; and "any other security which the Commission shall deem to be of a similar nature and consider necessary or appropriate . . . to treat as an equity security." [SEA § 3(a)(11)]

2) Purchase and Sale Requirement

To establish liability under section 16(b), there must be a matching purchase and sale, or sale and purchase. The general rule is that for the purposes of section 16(b), a "purchase" occurs when the purchaser incurs an irrevocable liability to take and pay for the stock; and a "sale" occurs when the seller incurs an irrevocable liability to deliver and accept payment for the stock. Although these rules are easily stated, there are several types of stock transactions where it may not be clear if a "purchase" or "sale" has actually occurred. Many of these transactions involve the exchange of stock either for property or for other stock.

3) Time Requirement

For section 16(b) to apply, the matching purchase and sale must occur within a period of less than six months.

4) Damages

Generally, the measure of damages in a section 16(b) action is the "profit realized" in the matching transactions, which is the difference between the purchase price and the sale price.

a) Any Purchase or Sale

Section 16(b) may be applied to any matched purchase and sale or sale and purchase if the matched transactions occur within a period of less than six months.

(1) Example

A, a director, buys 100 shares of XYZ stock on June 1 for $10 per share. On July 1, A sells the stock for $9 per share; on August 1, she buys 100 shares for $8 per share; and on September 1, she sells the stock for $7 per share. In three months she has lost $300, but she is still liable under section 16(b) since the $9 sale can be matched with $8 purchases.

b) Profit Maximized

Whatever matching of purchase and sale transactions that will produce the maximum profit is the one used. For example, if 100 shares are purchased at $1 per share and 100 at $2 per share, and six months later 100 shares are sold at $10 per share, the profit is $9 per share.

5) Sales by Former 10% Holder Not Covered

Reliance Electric Co. v. Emerson Electric Co.

404 U.S. 418 (1972).

Facts. Emerson Electric Co. (D) acquired 13.2% of the outstanding common stock of Dodge Manufacturing Co. in an unsuccessful attempt to take over Dodge. The shareholders of Dodge approved a merger with Reliance Electric Co. (P). D realized that any further attempts to take over Dodge were certain to fail and decided to dispose of its shares. On the advice of counsel, D decided to sell enough stock to bring its holdings under 10% and thereby immunize the remainder of their shares from liability under section 16(b). D sold 37,000 shares, which brought its holding to 9.96%. D then sold the remainder of the shares. Both transactions took place within six months of the purchase. After P demanded the profits realized in the sale, D sought declaratory judgment as to its liability under section 16(b). The district court held D liable for the total amount of the profits. The court of appeals affirmed as to the first sale but reversed as to the second. P appeals.

Issue. May an owner of 10% of a company's stock sell off the stock in two separate transactions, within six months, in an attempt to immunize the second transaction from liability under section 16(b)?

Held. Yes. Judgment affirmed.

- Liability cannot be imposed on D merely because it sought to avoid liability under section 16(b). The only question is whether the method used to avoid liability was prohibited by the statute.
- The statute provides that the owner must have 10% at the time of the purchase and of the sale. Congress may have regarded one with a long-term investment of more than 10% as more likely to have access to inside information than one who moves in and out of the 10% at the time of the second sale; therefore it does not fall within section 16(b).
- If the two-step sale does give rise to a danger that the statute was intended to prevent, Congress should amend the statute to deter those transactions.

6) When Investor Becomes a 10% Owner as a Result of the Purchase

Foremost-McKesson, Inc. v. Provident Securities Company
423 U.S. 232 (1976).

Facts. Provident Securities Company (P) wanted to liquidate its assets and dissolve. Foremost-McKesson, Inc. (D) entered into an agreement with P under which D would purchase two-thirds of P's assets for $4.25 million in cash, and two of D's convertible subordinated debentures in the amounts of $25 million and $15 million. Under the agreement, P would then execute an underwriting agreement that provided for sale of the $25 million debenture. P's holdings in D's debentures were large enough to make it a beneficial owner of D within the meaning of section 16. Having acquired and disposed of these securities within a six-month period, P faced the prospect of a suit by D to recover any profits realized on the sale of the debenture to the underwriters. P therefore sued for a declaration that it was not liable to D under section 16. The district court granted summary judgment for P, and the court of appeals affirmed.

Issue. Is a person purchasing securities that put his holdings above the 10% level a beneficial owner at the time of the purchase such that he must account for profits realized on a sale of those securities within six months?

Held. No. Judgment affirmed.

- In a purchase-sale sequence, a beneficial owner must account for profits only if he was a beneficial owner ***before*** the purchase. The legislative history of section 16 supports this conclusion.
- This conclusion is also supported by the distinction Congress recognized between short-swing trading by mere stockholders and such trading by officers or directors. Congress thought that all short-swing trading by directors and officers was vulnerable because of their intimate involvement in corporate affairs. Trading by mere stockholders was viewed as being subject to abuse only when the size of their holdings afforded the potential for access to corporate information.

G. INDEMNIFICATION AND INSURANCE

1. Introduction

Statutes in most states govern the extent to which the corporation may properly indemnify its directors and officers for expenses incurred in defending suits against them for conduct undertaken in their official capacity. These statutes apply to derivative suits and direct actions by the corporation, its shareholders, or third parties (*i.e.*, the state for criminal violations, the S.E.C. for security law violations, an injured party for a tort, etc.). Most states provide that the statute is the exclusive basis on which indemnification is permitted. A few states, however, allow the matter to be regulated by the articles or bylaws, or by shareholder agreement.

a. When the Defendant Wins

As long as the director or officer wins on the merits, there is generally no problem; most states allow the corporation to reimburse the defendant for reasonable attorneys' fees and expenses. Section 145(c) of the Delaware General Corporation Code requires indemnification of expenses incurred in connection with the "defense of any action . . . " as to which the indemnification claimant is "successful on the merits or otherwise."

1) Rationale

The rationale is that public policy favors indemnification when the director or officer is vindicated, because it encourages people to serve in these capacities to resist unfounded charges against them and thus to preserve the corporate image. Moreover, it discourages minority shareholders from filing frivolous derivative suits, knowing that if they lose, the defendants' expenses will be paid from the corporation.

2) Indemnification as Discretionary or Mandatory

In most states, reimbursement is discretionary with the board; but under some statutes the corporation is required to indemnify a director or officer when he is successful on the merits in defense of a derivative suit. In other states, the right to indemnification is subject to a judicial finding "that his conduct fairly and equitably merits such indemnity." [Cal. Corp. Code § 830]

b. When the Defendant Settles or Loses

The statutes vary significantly as to the extent to which indemnification is permitted when the officer or director loses the lawsuit against him, or the suit is settled by his paying or incurring liability to pay. Many statutes distinguish between third-party suits and derivative suits.

1) Third-Party Suits

When the suit against the director or officer is by an outsider (*e.g.*, the state in a criminal action; an injured party in tort action), the statutes generally permit indemnification both for litigation expenses and for whatever civil or criminal liabilities are incurred (monies paid out in settlement, judgment, or fines), provided the directors or shareholders determine that he "acted in good faith, for a purpose which he reasonably believed to be in the best interests of the corporation and (where a criminal action was involved) that he had no reason to believe that his action was unlawful." [N.Y. Bus. Corp. Law § 723]

a) Indemnification Requires Good Faith

Waltuch v. Conticommodity Services, Inc.

88 F.3d 87 (2d Cir. 1996).

Facts. Waltuch (P) was a trader in silver futures and worked for Conticommodity Services, Inc. (D). In the 1980s, both P and D were the subjects of several lawsuits filed by silver speculators alleging fraud, market manipulation, and antitrust violations. These lawsuits were settled with D paying over $35 million in damages. P was dismissed from the suits with no settlement contribution. As a result of the litigation, P personally incurred $1.2 million in legal fees. P was also the subject of an enforcement proceeding brought by the Commodity Futures Trading Commission ("CFTC"), charging him with fraud and market manipulation. P was required to pay a fine and was banned from buying or selling futures for six months. P incurred another $1 million in legal fees in defending himself in the CFTC proceeding. P sued D for indemnification of his $2.2 million in legal fees. P claimed that D's articles of incorporation require D to indemnify him for his expenses in both actions. D argued that P's claim is barred because section 145 of Delaware's General Corporation Law permits indemnification only if the corporate officer acted in good faith. The district court agreed with D that P could recover only if he could demonstrate good faith. P appeals.

Issues.

(i) Does section 145 require a corporate officer to have acted in good faith in order to be reimbursed?

(ii) Must D reimburse P for legal fees P spent in defending both actions because he was "successful" on the merits?

Held. (i) Yes. (ii) No. Judgment affirmed in part and reversed in part.

- The relevant provision of D's articles of incorporation contains no requirement of good faith for indemnification. However, D correctly notes that section 145(a) of Delaware's General Corporation Law ***does*** contain a good faith requirement. D therefore argues that its article is invalid under Delaware law to the extent that it requires indemnification of officers who have acted in bad faith. P contends that section 145(f) expressly allows corporations to indemnify officers in a manner broader than that set out in section 145(a).
- Section 145(f) states that the indemnification "provided by, or granted pursuant to, the other subsections of this section shall not be deemed exclusive if any other rights to which those seeking indemnification . . . may be entitled under any bylaw, agreement, vote of stockholders. . . ." P argues that this subsection is a separate grant of indemnification power that is not limited by the good faith requirement of section 145(a).
- While no Delaware court has specifically decided the issue, related cases have supported D's contention that a corporation's grant of indemnification rights ***must be consistent*** with the substantive provisions of section 145. [*See* Hibbert v. Hollywood Park, Inc., 457 A.2d 339 (Del. 1983)] Our reading of the statute also supports this position. Section 145(a) gives a corporation the power to indemnify if the plaintiff acted in good faith and in a manner not opposed to the best interests of the corporation. This statutory limit must mean that there is no power to indemnify in the absence of good faith. To hold otherwise would render section 145(a) meaningless: a corporation could indemnify anyone in any manner it pleased, regardless of good faith.
- P's interpretation would also render section 145(g) unnecessary. Section 145(g) explicitly allows a corporation to circumvent the good faith requirement by purchasing a directors' and officers' liability insurance policy to cover situations in which the corporation could not indemnify its officers and directors directly. This section would be completely unnecessary if a corporation could indemnify anyone in any situation.
- Thus, we find that D's article that would require indemnification of P in the absence of good faith is inconsistent with section 145(a) and thus exceeds the scope of a Delaware corporation's power to indemnify. We therefore affirm the lower court's decision on this issue. However, we find that under section 145(c), D is required to indemnify P for the $1.2 million he expended from the private lawsuits.
- Section 145(c) requires corporations to indemnify officers and directors who are "successful" on the merits in defense of certain claims. P argued that he was successful in the private lawsuits because the suits were dismissed with prejudice and without any payment or assumption of liability by him. D argued that the claims against P were only dismissed because of D's $35 million in settlement payments, part of which was contributed on behalf of P, not because of P's innocence. The lower court agreed with D and held that section 145(c) mandates indemnification only when an officer or director is "vindicated," and here, P clearly was not.
- Courts have held that success or vindication under section 145(c) does not mean moral exoneration. [*See* Merritt-Chapman & Scott Corp. v. Wolfson, 321 A.2d 138 (Del. Super. Ct. 1974)]
- While P may not have been morally exonerated, he did escape liability. The reason for this outcome is irrelevant. Under *Merritt*, escape from an adverse judgment, for whatever reason, is determinative. Thus, D must indemnify P for his legal expenses in connection with the private lawsuits.

---

b) Advancement of Expenses

Citadel Holding Corporation v. Roven

603 A.2d 818 (Del. 1992).

Facts. Roven (P), a director of Citadel Holding Corporation (D), entered into a contract which required D to indemnify P and to reimburse him for costs he incurred in defending himself from certain claims that might arise by reason of his service as a director. Under the agreement, D was to advance P the costs of defending certain lawsuits. Later, D filed suit against P in federal court alleging that he violated section 16(b) of the Securities and Exchange Act by purchasing certain options to buy stock in D while he was a director. P denied the allegations and filed this action for breach of contract to enforce the advancement provision of the indemnification agreement. The lower court held that P was entitled to reimbursement in advance for sums he incurred for litigation costs in the federal action. D appeals.

Issue. Did the indemnity agreement require D to advance P expenses for defending himself against a section 16(b) suit?

Held. Yes. Judgment affirmed.

- ♦ D argues that P is not entitled to indemnification in this situation because the section 16(b) claim does not arise by reason of his service as a director. D is confusing the issue. The issue here is not whether P is entitled to indemnification, but whether he is entitled to obtain funds in advance to cover the expense of defending himself. The language of the contract in no way renders the right to advances dependent upon the right to indemnity.
- ♦ The relevant section of the agreement states that "costs and expenses (including attorneys' fees) incurred by the Agent in defending or investigating any action, suit, proceeding, or investigation shall be paid by the Corporation in advance of the final disposition of such matter. . . ." The contract requires the agent to execute a written promise to repay the company in the event that it is later determined that he is not entitled to indemnification.
- ♦ The parties may litigate their rights under the indemnification portion of the contract at an appropriate time in the future. Under the terms of the agreement, D is required to advance to P the reasonable expenses of defending suits. As written, the agreement makes this duty mandatory. Thus, the judgment of the lower court is affirmed.

---

2) Derivative Suits

When the suit against the director or officer is a derivative action, charging him with wrongdoing to the corporation, the statutes in most states are much stricter.

a) Suit Settled

If the derivative suit is settled prior to judgment, many statutes permit indemnification of the officer or director for his litigation expenses, including attorneys' fees, provided (i) the settlement was made with court approval, and (ii) the court finds that "his conduct fairly and equitably merits such indemnity." [Cal. Corp. Code § 830(a)]

(1) Such indemnification is often limited to litigation expenses. The corporation may not be permitted to reimburse or indemnify the director for any amounts paid out or liability incurred under such settlements. [*See* Cal. Corp. Code § 830(a)]

(2) The New York statute is substantially the same, but permits indemnification of litigation expenses, except that court approval is not required. It is sufficient if it is determined by the corporation that the director or officer had not violated his duty to the corporation. Such determination can be made either (i) by the board, acting through a quorum of directors who were not parties to the action; or (ii) if such a quorum is not available, by the board on the advice of independent legal counsel; or (iii) by a majority of the disinterested shareholders. [*See* N.Y. Bus. Corp. Law § 724]

b) Judgment Against Defendant

When a director or officer is adjudged to have breached his duty to the corporation in a derivative suit, most statutes prohibit indemnification by the corporation, and this applies both as to his litigation expenses and any liability imposed upon him. [Cal. Corp. Code § 830]

(1) It would destroy the purpose of the derivative suit if the corporation could make the errant director or officer "whole" for the consequences of his breach of duty to the corporation.

(2) Even so, a few states (notably Delaware) allow the corporation to indemnify the errant director or officer at least for his litigation expenses, including attorneys' fees (but not the damages assessed against him) in the derivative suit—if the court finds "such person is fairly and reasonably entitled to such indemnity." [Del. Gen. Corp. Law § 145]

c. Insurance Against Derivative Suit Liability

A number of states have statutes that authorize a corporation to purchase and maintain insurance (i) to protect the corporation against liability to its directors and officers for indemnification when otherwise authorized by law (above); and (ii) to protect the directors and officers against the expense of defending suits asserting such liability. (Sometimes, but not always, the directors and officers pay a portion of the insurance premium.)

1) Statutes

Several of the statutes are quite permissive as to such insurance and permit the corporation to maintain such insurance against any liability or expense incurred by a director or officer in his official capacity. [Del. Gen. Corp. Law § 145(g)]

a) Other statutes prohibit a corporation's insuring its officers or directors against liability for acts involving "deliberate dishonesty" or where the director "personally gained a financial profit or other advantage to which he was not legally entitled." [N.Y. Bus. Corp. Law § 727]

b) To the extent that such insurance is permitted, it may enable a corporation to do indirectly (by paying insurance premiums) that which it could not do directly (indemnifying officers and directors against liability for breach of duty to the corporation). This has been criticized as encouraging irresponsible conduct by management.

Chapter VI
Problems of Control

A. PROXY FIGHTS

In the large corporation with many shareholders, control of the corporation can be maintained with ownership of a minority percentage of the voting stock. This is done through installing management in the corporation and from this position soliciting voting proxies from the other shareholders. Because shareholders tend to vote with current management and proxy contests are expensive, control is normally easily maintained.

1. Shareholder Voting

The law regards shareholders as the owners of the corporation, the objects of management's fiduciary duty, and the ultimate sources of corporate power. Shareholders have two ways to exercise this power—the vote and the derivative suit. The right to vote may be allocated to others not owning the shares through a proxy or voting trust.

a. Proxy Regulation

A proxy is a power of attorney to vote shares owned by someone else. At common law such proxies were illegal, but statutes permit proxies. A proxy establishes an agency relationship. This relationship is generally revocable at any time (such as by the grant of a subsequent proxy, or by the shareholder personally attending the shareholder meeting and voting).

b. Proxy Regulation Under the Securities Exchange Act of 1934

1) Registration and Reporting Requirements

Section 12 of the 1934 Act requires a company to register its securities with the S.E.C. and thereafter to file periodic reports on the company's financial condition, if the company's securities are (i) traded on a regulated securities exchange or (ii) traded over the counter and the company has assets of at least $10 million ***and*** 500 or more shareholders of a class of equity securities (such as common stock). Companies that have so registered with the S.E.C. are called "registered companies."

2) Proxy Solicitation

Section 14 of the 1934 Act also regulates the solicitation of voting proxies from shareholders of companies registered under section 12.

3) Basic Provision of the 1934 Act

Section 14(a) of the 1934 Act provides:

> It shall be unlawful for any persons, by the use of the mails or by any means or instrumentality of interstate commerce or of any facility of a national securities

exchange or otherwise, in contravention of such rules and regulations as the Commission may prescribe as necessary or appropriate in the public interest or for the protection of investors, to solicit or to permit the use of his name to solicit any proxy or consent or authorization in respect of any security (other than an exempted security) registered pursuant to section 12.

4) Rules Adopted by the S.E.C.

Under the authority given by section 14 of the 1934 Act, the S.E.C. has adopted several rules for the regulation of proxy solicitation of registered securities. These rules are designed to accomplish three objectives.

a) Full Disclosure

Those soliciting proxies or attempting to prevent others from soliciting them must give full disclosure of all material information to the shareholders being solicited. [Rule 14a–3 to a–6]

b) Fraud

Resort to the use of fraud in the solicitation is made unlawful. [Rule 14a–9]

c) Shareholder Solicitation

Shareholders may solicit proxies from other shareholders, and management must include in its proxy statement proposals made by shareholders. [Rule 14a–8]

5) Remedies for Violation

a) Appropriate Remedies

If the proxy rules are violated, courts will fashion an appropriate remedy. The "fairness" of the transaction involved is taken into consideration in the type of remedy granted.

b) Actions by the S.E.C.

The S.E.C. may bring actions seeking administrative remedies, such as an injunction preventing solicitation of proxies, preventing the voting of shares obtained through improper proxy solicitation, or requiring resolicitation (and these actions may be enforced in the federal district courts).

c) Private Actions

The courts have held that a private cause of action is implied under section 14.

d) Materiality

It need not be shown that the violation (such as a misstatement or omission) caused the outcome of the voting on the matter. All that need be shown is that such statements were material and could have had a propensity to affect the voting.

e) Relief Granted

As stated above, the court will fashion whatever relief is appropriate to remedy the violation, whether damages or rescission of the transaction, etc.

2. Strategic Use of Proxies

a. Solicitation

Rule 14a–1 defines a "solicitation" as a "communication to security holders under circumstances reasonably calculated to result in the procurement, withholding, or revocation of a proxy."

b. Solicitation Methods Employed During Proxy Fight

Levin v. Metro-Goldwyn-Mayer, Inc.

264 F. Supp. 797 (S.D.N.Y. 1967).

Facts. Metro-Goldwyn-Mayer, Inc. ("MGM") was experiencing a conflict for control of the company between members of its management. The directors split into two camps, the "Levin group" and the "O'Brien group," and both groups intended to elect a slate of directors at the MGM annual stockholder meeting. The conflict was especially important because the two groups had extremely different ideas about the direction and future of the company. Each group actively solicited proxies in anticipation of the annual meeting. Six shareholders (Ps) filed this action against five members of the "O'Brien group" and MGM (Ds), alleging that Ds wrongfully committed MGM to pay for the services of specially retained attorneys, a public relations firm, and several proxy-soliciting organizations in connection with the proxy fight. Ps argued that the individual directors should be required to pay the expenses personally and requested an injunction to prevent Ds from further use of these solicitation methods.

Issue. Have Ds used any illegal or unfair methods in their proxy solicitation campaign?

Held. No. Injunction denied.

- Because the decision as to continuance of the present management rests solely with the stockholders, it is the concern of the court that they be fully and truthfully informed as to the merits and contentions of those soliciting their proxy. Because the business policies of the two groups involved here are so divergent, it is especially important that the shareholders are fully informed. The question is whether Ds have employed any illegal or unfair means in their proxy solicitation campaign. We find that they have not.
- The proxy statement indicates that MGM will bear all costs in connection with the management and solicitation of proxies. It discloses the employment of several proxy-solicitation firms, and the price for the services of each one. It further discloses that an estimated $125,000 will be spent in management's proxy solicitation campaign. We find the expenses are not excessive in light of the fact that MGM is a giant in the entertainment business, with total assets of over $251 million, and a gross income of $185 million last year. MGM management violated no federal statute or S.E.C. rule or regulation. Thus, we must deny Ps' motion for an injunction.

---

3. Reimbursement of Costs

The expenses for a proxy battle in a major corporation can be very substantial. Issues arise concerning who can be reimbursed for those expenses. Normally, courts hold that if management is successful in the proxy contest, it can recover its expenses from the corporation. The limitation is that the expenses must have been incurred in "good faith" for the benefit of the corporation.

a. Reimbursement Approved

Rosenfeld v. Fairchild Engine & Airplane Corp.

128 N.E.2d 291 (N.Y. 1995).

Facts. Rosenfeld (P), a shareholder of Fairchild Engine & Airplane Corporation, filed this derivative suit to compel the return of funds paid out of the corporate treasury to reimburse the expenses of both sides following a proxy contest. The old board of directors spent $106,000 in defense of their position while they were still in office. The new board then paid the old board $28,000 following the change in management to compensate the old directors for their remaining expenses which the new board found to be fair and reasonable. Another $127,000, which represented reimbursement of expenses to members of the new board, was ratified by a 16 to 1 vote of the shareholders. The lower court dismissed P's complaint, and the appellate court affirmed. P appeals.

Issue. May directors seek reimbursement from the corporation for the reasonable expenses they incurred in a proxy contest?

Held. Yes. Judgment affirmed.

- When directors act in good faith to defend their position in a bona fide proxy contest, they may recover the reasonable expenses of soliciting proxies from the corporate treasury. The court will disallow reimbursement only when it is shown that the funds have been used for personal power, individual gain, or private advantage and not in the best interest of the corporation. To hold otherwise would place directors at the mercy of anyone wishing to challenge them for control so long as such persons have ample funds to finance a proxy contest. Directors must have the right to incur reasonable expenses for proxy solicitation and in defense of their corporate policies.
- We further find that the members of the new board could be reimbursed by an affirmative vote of the shareholders. P admitted that the charges involved were fair and reasonable, and did not argue that they were fraudulently obtained from the corporation.

Dissent. The expenses incurred here went far beyond what was necessary to circulate information. The appellate division noted that the old management incurred a substantial amount of needless expense (such as expenses for entertainment, chartered jets, and limousines). The case should be remanded for the trial court to determine which expenses should be allowed in accordance with the rule that the directors have the burden of justifying their expenditures.

The majority emphasizes that the funds paid to the new management were ratified by a majority of the shareholders. However, reimbursement of these funds was arguably not for a corporate purpose. An act which is ultra vires cannot be ratified merely by a majority vote of the shareholders.

---

4. Private Actions for Proxy Rule Violations

Rule 14a–9 prohibits materially false or misleading statements or omissions in a proxy statement. Courts have held that a private cause of action is implied under section 14.

a. Implied Cause of Action to Further the Remedial Purposes of the Securities Laws

J.I. Case Co. v. Borak

377 U.S. 426 (1964).

Facts. J.I. Case Company (D) entered into a merger agreement with American Tractor Corporation. When the agreement was submitted to the shareholders for approval, D solicited proxies with a statement that allegedly contained false information. The shareholders approved by a narrow margin.

Borak (P), a shareholder in D, sought an injunction against the merger, damages, and other relief for violation of section 14a. The trial court held that it could not redress the alleged violations of section 14a except to grant declaratory relief under section 27 of the Act. The court of appeals reversed, and the Supreme Court granted certiorari.

Issue. Does section 27 of the Act authorize a federal cause of action for a shareholder seeking rescission or damages for a consummated merger authorized pursuant to a proxy solicitation allegedly containing false and misleading statements in contravention of section 14a?

Held. Yes. Judgment of court of appeals affirmed.

- Section 14a specifically grants district courts jurisdiction over all suits at equity or law. While section 14(a) makes no reference to a private right of action, among its chief purposes is the protection of investors. A section intended to protect investors would not deny them the right to adequate redress.
- The S.E.C. is not in a position to review every proxy statement for factual errors. Shareholders can assist the S.E.C. by policing this type of conduct. A private right of action provides additional deterrence.
- The courts may grant more than declaratory relief. They may fashion whatever remedy that they deem appropriate. To limit them would foreclose many shareholders from adequate reparations.

---

b. In Suit to Enjoin Voting of Proxies, Proof of Material Misstatement or Omission Was Sufficient Causation

Mills v. Electric Auto-Lite Co.

396 U.S. 375 (1970).

Facts. Shareholders (Ps) brought a derivative suit to enjoin Electric Auto-Lite Co. (D) from voting proxies it had solicited to approve a merger into Mergenthaler Linotype Co. ("M"). Proxy materials did not disclose that M controlled 54% of D and D's board of directors. The merger was already carried out; suit was to set it aside based on the false or misleading statements in the proxy materials. A two-thirds vote of the shareholders was necessary to approve the merger, so that to approve it the votes of shareholders other than M were required. The district court found that the proxy statements were deficient. The court of appeals agreed but reversed on the question of causation. The court of appeals agreed that the proxy statements were deficient. However, it reversed the lower court's decision and held that proof of whether the defect actually had a decisive effect on the voting was necessary. The Supreme Court granted certiorari.

Issue. If the plaintiff proves that the proxy solicitation contained materially misleading statements of fact, must the plaintiff also prove that he relied on the contents of the proxy statement and that such reliance caused his injury (*i.e.*, caused the plaintiff to vote as he did)?

Held. No. Judgment vacated and case remanded.

- The proxy solicitation omitted material information.
- The defect must be material—*i.e.*, it must have a significant propensity to affect the vote on the issue voted on (that is, it must be considered important by a reasonable shareholder). Where this is shown, it does not also have to be shown that the misleading statement was the cause of the shareholders' voting as they did (*i.e.*, that they relied on it). It must be shown, however, that the proxy solicitation was necessary to the transaction that resulted in the detriment to Ps.
- Section 29 of the Act makes void all contracts made in violation of the Act. But this does not mean that all such contracts are unenforceable. Courts of equity look at all of the circumstances in determining the appropriate remedy (and one factor in rescission is the fairness of the terms of

the merger). Recovering damages is also a possibility and depends on whether actual damage can be shown. The case must be remanded to the district court for findings on these issues.

- A successful plaintiff in a case of violation of section 14a is entitled to reasonable costs and attorneys' fees when the action is brought on behalf of a class and benefits all members of the class. This is a court-made rule. The class is all shareholders of the defendant. The benefit is the exposure of the deceit practiced on all of the shareholders.

Comment. The real issue here is whether a court will review the "fairness" of the transaction. The argument was made that to show causation the plaintiff had to show that the disclosure of the material fact would have changed the shareholder vote and therefore the court could look at the fairness of the merger transaction (since presumably if it was fair, then the shareholders would have approved it anyway, despite the nondisclosure). The court here held that it will not look into fairness—that even if a transaction is "fair," this does not excuse materially misleading statements in the proxy materials. Hence, "materially" misleading statements are enough for a violation where the proxy solicitation was necessary to approve the transaction. ***Actual causation need not be shown*** (D argued that since the transaction was fair, there was no causation). In effect, the court indicates that it will leave to the shareholders the issue of approving or disapproving the transaction. The "fairness" of the transaction, however, will be considered in determining the measure of damages for the violation.

---

c. Black-Scholes Calculations Not Material as a Matter of Law

Seinfeld v. Bartz

2002 WL 243597 (N.D. Cal. 2002).

Facts. A shareholder (P) of Cisco Systems, Inc. ("Cisco") brought this derivative suit against the corporation and its 10 directors (Ds), alleging that Ds violated section 14(a) of the Securities Exchange Act of 1934 and Rule 14a–9 by issuing a proxy statement that contained misleading statements and omissions of material fact. Ds prepared a proxy statement to solicit proxies in favor of an amendment to the company's option grant program for outside directors. The proxy statement states that Cisco pays each outside director an annual retainer between $32,000 and $40,000, and periodic option grants. P argues that Ds omitted material facts by failing to include the value of the option grants based on the theoretical Black-Scholes option pricing model. P argued that Cisco uses the Black-Scholes model to prepare annual financial statements, and therefore it would have been easy for Ds to include this information in the proxy statement. According to the Black-Scholes calculations, the value of the options granted to the outside directors was $1,020,600. P argues that Ds' statement that outside directors receive a $32,000 annual retainer plus stock options materially misrepresents the actual compensation of each outside director.

Issue. Did the failure to include the value of the option grants based on the Black-Scholes model constitute omission of material facts in violation of section 14(a) or Rule 14a–9?

Held. No.

- The four courts that have considered P's argument have held that Black-Scholes valuations are not material as a matter of law. We know of no court that has ever held to the contrary. P points to a Ninth Circuit case, *Custom Chrome, Inc. v. Commissioner of Internal Revenue*, 217 F.3d 1117 (9th Cir. 2000), in which the court noted in a footnote that Black-Scholes was a reliable method of determining the value of options at issue in that case. However, the court explicitly distinguished options issued as part of a loan transaction (as involved in *Custom Chrome*) from options granted for services rendered (as in the present case). We hold that as a matter of law, Black-Scholes valuations are not material for purposes of Rule 14(a) analysis.

---

5. Shareholder Proposals

As an alternative to an independent proxy solicitation, a shareholder may serve notice on management of his intention to propose action at the shareholders' meeting. The shareholder may only propose such action if (i) he would be entitled to vote at the shareholders' meeting to which the management's proxy statement relates and (ii) he is a shareholder at the time the proposal is submitted.

a. Inclusion in Management's Proxy Statement

If the shareholder's notice of proposed action conforms to the proxy rules, management must include the proposal in its own proxy statement and make provisions in its proxy form for an indication of shareholder preference with respect to the proposal—at no expense to the proposing shareholder. [SEA Rule 14a–8] If management opposes the proposal, then the shareholder may also include a 200-word statement in support of the proposal, which management must also send out with its own proxy statement if the proposal conforms to the proxy rules.

b. Management's Omission of Shareholder Proposals

If management opposes the shareholder proposal, it must file the proposal and the reasons for opposing it with the S.E.C. The S.E.C. will review the proposal and give an indication of whether it agrees or disagrees with management (*i.e.*, whether it would issue a "no action letter" if management omits the proposal from its proxy solicitation). Management may properly omit shareholder proposals in the following situations under SEA Rule 14a–8(c):

1) Proposal Not a "Proper Subject"

If the shareholder's proposal is not a "proper subject" for action by the shareholders, it may be omitted from management's proxy solicitation. The state law of the issuer's domicile is used for purposes of determining what is a "proper subject."

2) Proposal Relates to "Ordinary Business Operations"

Similarly, management may also omit proposals that relate to the "ordinary business operations" of the issuer. This rule prohibits shareholder intervention in the "minute" matters of the daily operation of corporate business.

3) Proposal Submitted for Noncorporate Purpose

If it "clearly appears" that the shareholder has submitted the proposal primarily for "noncorporate purposes," management may properly omit it. [SEA Rule 14a–8(c)] The following areas are deemed by the proxy rules to be "noncorporate purposes":

a) Personal Claims

Personal claims or grievances against the issuer or its management are not proper purposes. [*See* SEA Rule 14a–8(c)(4)]

b) Matters Outside Issuer's Control

Matters ***not within the control*** of the issuer are not appropriate for a proposal. [*See* SEA Rule 14(a)–8(c)(6)]

c) Matters Not Related to Business

Matters not significantly related to the issuer's business are also not appropriate. [*See* SEA Rule 14a–8(c)(5)]

(1) Amendments

Note that rule 14a–8(c)(5) used to include language to the effect that proposals promoting general economic, political, racial, religious, or other social causes not significantly related to the issuer's business could be omitted. The 1976 amendment to this section eliminated the "economic, political, racial, religious" language; the S.E.C. has indicated that this language was deleted as being "superfluous" but that the deletion "should not be construed as an implication that a different standard was contemplated." This provision was further amended with the addition of the 5% threshold for determining "significance."

d) Election of Directors

Rule 14a–8 does not apply to proposals by shareholders for election of directors.

e) Proposal Previously Submitted

The rules also permit management to turn down a shareholder proposal if it has been previously submitted and it failed to get a substantial number of votes. For example, if the proposal fails to get at least three percent of the votes cast when it is first submitted, it cannot be proposed at the next three annual meetings.

f) Burden of Proof

As noted above, management has the burden of proof to show that the shareholder proposal is not proper for any of the above reasons.

4) Operations Accounting for Less Than 5%

Lovenheim v. Iroqouis Brands, Ltd.

618 F. Supp. 554 (D.D.C. 1985).

Facts. Lovenheim (P), a shareholder of Iroqouis Brands, Ltd. (D), wanted D to include his proposal in proxy materials sent in preparation for the next annual shareholders meeting. The proposal called upon the directors to form a committee to study whether the method used by D's supplier in the production of a pâté caused undue distress, pain or suffering to animals. D refused to include the proposal because it related to operations that account for less than 5% of D's total assets, and less than 5% of its net earnings and gross sales. P requests injunctive relief to bar D from excluding his proposal.

Issue. Should D be enjoined from excluding the proposal?

Held. Yes. Preliminary injunction granted.

- Rule 14a–8([i])(5) would allow D to omit P's proposal if it relates to operations accounting for less than 5% of its total assets at the end of the most recent fiscal year, and for less than 5% of its net earnings and gross sales for the most recent fiscal year, and is not otherwise significantly related to D's business. D has sufficiently demonstrated that its operations involving pâté account for far less than the 5% thresholds in rule 14a–8. However, P argues that the exception is not applicable because his proposal involves a matter that is "otherwise significantly related" to D's business. P argues that when a proposal has ethical or social significance, rule 14a–8 does not permit its exclusion merely because it is not economically significant to the company.
- The Securities Exchange Commission has indicated that the monetary thresholds of economic significance were adopted to create a more objective standard. However, the Commission has stated that proposals should be included despite their failure to reach the specific economic thresholds if a significant relationship to the issuer's business is demonstrated on the face of the resolution or supporting statements. Thus the legislative history of the exception demonstrates that the meaning of "significantly related" is not limited to economic significance.

- In light of the ethical and social significance of P's proposal, P has shown a likelihood of prevailing on the merits. P has also demonstrated that he would be irreparably harmed if this injunction were denied because he would lose his opportunity to communicate with other shareholders. We therefore conclude that P's motion for a preliminary injunction should be granted.

---

5) Election Exclusion

AFSCME v. AIG, Inc.

462 F.3d 121 (2d Cir. 2006).

Facts. The American Federation of State, County & Municipal Employees (P) is one of the nation's largest public service employee unions. Through its pension plan, P holds stock in American International Group (D). P submitted to D for inclusion in its company proxy statement a shareholder proposal that, if adopted by a majority of D's shareholders, would amend D's bylaws to require D, under certain circumstances, to publish the names of shareholder-nominated candidates for director positions together with any candidates nominated by D's board of directors. D sought the input of the Division of Corporate Finance ("Division"), the group within the S.E.C. that handles investor disclosure matters, as to whether it could exclude the proposal from its proxy statement under the election exclusion on the basis that it "relates to an election." The Division issued a no-action letter, indicating that it would not recommend an enforcement action against D if it excluded the proposal from its proxy statement, and D excluded the proposal. P brought suit seeking a court order compelling D to include the proposal in the next proxy statement. The district court denied P's claim and dismissed P's complaint. P appeals.

Issue. Can a shareholder proposal requiring a company to include certain shareholder-nominated candidates for the board of directors on the corporate ballot be excluded from the corporate proxy materials on the basis that the proposal "relates to an election" under S.E.C. Rule 14a–8(i)(8)?

Held. No. Judgment reversed and case remanded.

- Rule 14a–8(i)(8), also known as the "town meeting rule," requires that eligible shareholder proposals be included in a proxy statement unless the proposal can be excluded based on one of 13 grounds enumerated in the regulations. One of these grounds provides that a corporation may exclude a shareholder proposal if it relates to an election for membership on the company's board of directors. P reads this exclusion to refer to proposals addressing a particular seat in a particular election, as opposed to the proposal here, which simply sets the background rules governing elections generally.
- The language of the rule is ambiguous, and the S.E.C. has itself offered two different informal interpretations of the rule's language. In its amicus brief, the S.E.C. contends that the election exclusion applies to proxy access bylaw proposals. However, in a statement published by the S.E.C. in 1976, the last time the S.E.C. revised the election exclusion, the S.E.C. expressed the view that the election exclusion is limited to shareholder proposals used to oppose solicitations dealing with an identified board seat in an upcoming election. The S.E.C. rejected the broader interpretation that the election exclusion applies to shareholder proposals that would institute procedures making such election contests more likely.
- An agency's interpretation of an ambiguous regulation made at the time the regulation was implemented or revised should control. Thus, we hold that a shareholder proposal that seeks to amend the corporate bylaws to establish a procedure by which shareholder nominated candidates may be included on the corporate ballot does not relate to an election and cannot be excluded from the corporate proxy materials unless the agency has offered sufficient reasons for its changed interpretation.

Comment. After this decision, the S.E.C. began the process of amending Rule 14a–8(i)(8). In November 2007, the S.E.C. released the amendment, which allows corporations to exclude shareholder proposals that relate to an immediate election contest or to a procedure for shareholders to carry out a future election contest by requiring that the corporation include shareholders' nominees for director in the corporation's proxy materials.

---

6) Reimbursement of Proxy Vote Expenses

CA, Inc. v. AFSCME Employees Pension Plan

953 A.2d 227 (Del.2008).

Facts. CA's (P's) (Appellant's) twelve board of directors ("board") serve one-year terms. AFSCME (D), a CA stockholder, is associated with the American Federation of State, County and Municipal Employees. D proposed a bylaw amendment ("Proposed bylaw") to be included in P's proxy materials for its 2008 annual meeting. If adopted, the new bylaws would provide that the board would cause the corporation to reimburse stockholders for reasonable expenses incurred in nominating candidates in a contested election of directors as long as the election was held, fewer than 50% of the directors up for election were contested and one or more of the nominated directors was elected. The company's current bylaws do not address reimbursement of proxy expenses. The decision whether to reimburse such expenses is currently vested in the discretion of the board, subject to their fiduciary duties and Delaware law. P notified the SEC's Division of Corporation Finance (the "Division") that it intended to exclude the proposed bylaw from its 2008 proxy materials and requested a "no-action letter" from the Division, stating that the Division would not recommend any enforcement action to the SEC if CA excluded the AFSCME proposal. The SEC certified two questions to us.

Issues.

1) Is the AFSCME Proposal a proper subject for action by shareholders as a matter of Delaware law?
2) Would the AFSCME Proposal, if adopted, cause CA to violate any Delaware law to which it is subject?

Held. 1) Yes. 2) Yes.

♦ State law empowers both directors and shareholders to adopt, amend, or repeal the corporation's bylaws. P's certificate of incorporation confers that power upon the directors. Under state law, it is possible that the shareholders have coextensive power with the directors, but the law has not allocated identical power to each group.

♦ State law vests in the shareholders the power to adopt, amend or repeal bylaws that cannot be eliminated or limited without consent by anyone other than the legislature. This would appear to make the shareholders' power identical and coextensive, but 8 Del. C. sect.141(a) confers on the directors the power to manage or direct the business and affairs of the corporation. No such power is allocated to the shareholders and it is well-established that shareholders subject to Delaware law may not directly manage the corporation's business affairs. Therefore, the shareholders' power regarding the bylaws is not coextensive with the board's concurrent power but is limited by the board's management prerogatives.

♦ P suggests that any bylaw that might be seen as limiting or lessening the board's power is outside of the scope of permissible bylaws. We do not agree. Such a view would eliminate the shareholders right to adopt, amend or repeal bylaws since bylaws by their nature generally set down rule and regulations that bind both the board and the shareholders and could be said to limit the board's otherwise discretionary power. Yet, the law has made the shareholders' power inviolate.

♦ In examining the scope of the shareholders' action that the law allows that does not improperly affect the directors' power to manage, we note that the law is well-established that the function of bylaws is not to lay down how the board should decide specific business decisions, but rather to define the process and procedures by which those decisions are made.

- Common examples of procedural, process-oriented bylaws those that fix the number of directors on the board, the number of directors required for a quorum (with certain limitations), and the vote requirements for board action. Procedural bylaws do not improperly encroach upon the board's managerial authority under state law. Where a bylaw requires that the full board be present at the corporation's headquarters, and the directors live in different states, such a bylaw would be process-related, but would require the corporation to spend funds to reimburse the board for travel.
- P claims that that proposed bylaw here intrudes upon the board's authority because it mandates reimbursement of proxy expenses, thereby limiting the board's discretionary authority.
- The wording of the proposed bylaw, *i.e.,* "The board of directors shall cause the corporation to reimburse a stockholder," is phrased as a command, but that does not mean it is not process-related. When viewed in context, the proposed bylaw addresses the process for electing directors to promote the integrity of that process by making it easier for stockholders to nominate director candidates. Delaware corporation shareholders have a legitimate and protected interest in that process.
- Under the current process only board-sponsored nominees are reimbursed for their expenses. Unless dissident candidates replace a majority of the board, they are not reimbursed. By encouraging the nomination of non-management board candidates the proposed bylaw would facilitate the shareholders' right to participate in selecting contestants for the election.
- Our courts have recognized that shareholders have a right to participate in selecting candidates for election to the board. Here, the shareholders have facilitated that right by proposing a means that would encourage candidates other than board-sponsored nominees. That the adoption of the bylaw would require corporate funds to be expended will not, alone, make such a bylaw an improper subject matter for shareholder action.
- We now address whether the proposed bylaw would violate any common law rule or precept. We invalidated a "no shop" provision in a merger agreement with a favored bidder that prevented the target company directors from communicating with a competing bidder the terms of the competing bid in an effort to secure the highest possible bid for the shareholders. We held that such a provision was invalid because it required the board to act or not act in a way as to limit the exercise of its fiduciary duties. The directors could not contract away their fiduciary obligations. See, *Paramount Communications, Inc. v. QVC Network, Inc.*, 637 A.2d 34 (Del. 1994) *infra.*
- The board of directors had voluntarily imposed binding contractual arrangements upon themselves. Here the shareholders seek to impose a binding bylaw involuntarily on the directors in the specific area of election expense reimbursement. In both cases, the internal governance contract would stop the directors from exercising their full managerial power in circumstances where their fiduciary duties would otherwise require them to deny reimbursement to a dissident slate. Whether this limitation is imposed by shareholders or the directors' themselves does not matter.
- Thus, under the proposed bylaw, the directors have full discretion to determine the amount of reimbursement, but they are not allowed to exercise their discretion as to whether or not it would be appropriate, in a specific case, to award reimbursement at all.
- Shareholders' recourse is to either seek to amend the Certificate of Incorporation to include the substance of the proposed bylaw or seek recourse from the Delaware General Assembly.

---

6. Shareholder Inspection Rights

a. Introduction

Pursuit of shareholder interests may practically require inspection of some corporate records, especially the list of shareholders. At common law a shareholder had a right to inspect his corporation's books and records if he had a "proper purpose." All corporation statutes regulate this matter. They may speak to the "proper purpose" requirement as well as to a number of other issues such as the type of books and records subject to inspection, shareholder qualification, the mechanics of demanding, court enforcement, and penalties for failure to permit.

b. Delaware Law

Section 220(b) of the Delaware Corporation Code provides in pertinent part: "Any stockholder, in person or by attorney or other agent, shall, upon written demand under oath stating the purpose thereof, have the right during the usual hours for business to inspect for any proper purpose the corporation's stock ledger, a list of its stockholders, and its other books and records, and to make copies or extracts therefrom. A proper purpose shall mean a purpose reasonably related to such person's interest as a stockholder." Section 220(c) provides that ". . . [t]he court may, in its discretion, prescribe any limitations or conditions with reference to the inspection. . . ."

c. List of Stockholders vs. Other Books and Records

Courts have received requests to inspect stockholder lists more hospitably than requests to inspect other books and records. Delaware shifts the burden of proof with respect to proper purpose. New York gives shareholders an unqualified right to inspect annual balance sheets and profit and loss statements, but it makes inspection of all other records conditional on a showing of good faith and proper purpose. Mandamus is the usual remedy for refusal to permit inspection.

d. Beneficial Owners

Some courts now honor requests for lists not only of shareholders, but also for beneficial owners known to the corporation. Courts have generally declined, however, to honor inspection requests from beneficial owners.

e. State Inspection Rights/Federal Proxy Rules

Under federal proxy rule 14a–7 a security holder, or tender offeror, may insist that the issuer either provide her with a list of security holders or mail her communications to them (at the holder's expense). Courts have rejected the claim that this rule preempts state inspection laws.

1) Informing Shareholders About Drawbacks of Corporate Exchange Offer as a "Proper Purpose"

Crane Co. v. Anaconda Co.

346 N.E.2d 507 (N.Y. 1976).

Facts. Crane Company (P) announced a proposed offer to exchange subordinated debentures for shares of common stock of Anaconda Company (D). D vigorously opposed the tender offer and sent four letters to its shareholders asserting that the offer was not in the best interests of the company. P requested a list of D's shareholders claiming that D had a fiduciary duty to present shareholders with all pertinent information regarding the pending tender offer. D refused to provide the list because it felt P's reasons for the request were not purposes relating to the business of D within the meaning of section 1315 of the Business Corporation Law. P filed this petition to compel D to produce its shareholder list. The lower court found that P did not have a proper purpose and dismissed P's petition. The appellate court reversed finding that the matter was proper because it was one of general interest to D's shareholders by virtue of their common interest in the corporation. D appeals.

Issue. May a shareholder access a shareholder list for the purpose of informing other shareholders of its exchange offer and soliciting tenders of stock?

Held. Yes. Judgment affirmed.

- Section 1315 of the Business Corporation Law states that access to corporate records such as shareholder lists must be permitted to qualified shareholders on written demand. The petitioner must furnish an affidavit that the inspection is not desired for a purpose other than the business of the corporation, and that the petitioner has not been involved in the sale of stock lists within the last five years.
- Although P complied with all statutory requirements, D argues that inspection should not be compelled when the petitioner only wants the list to convince other shareholders to sell their stock. We disagree. P wanted to communicate directly with shareholders to inform them of the offer, to reply to misleading statements issued by D, and to facilitate the further tender of shares. It cannot be said that a pending tender offer involving over one-fifth of the corporation's common stock is a purpose other than the business of the corporation. The pending tender offer may potentially affect the value of the shareholders' investment as well as the future direction of the company. Shareholders must be given the means to independently evaluate the situation.

---

2) Shareholder Must Demonstrate a Proper Purpose

State *ex rel.* Pillsbury v. Honeywell, Inc.

191 N.W.2d 406 (Minn. 1971).

Facts. A shareholder (P) bought 100 shares in Honeywell, Inc. (D) for the sole purpose of giving himself a voice in D's affairs so that he could persuade D to cease producing munitions used in the Vietnam War. P demanded access to D's shareholder list and all corporate records dealing with weapons and munitions manufacture, for the purpose of communicating with other shareholders to elect a new board of directors who would represent his viewpoint. D refused to provide the documents, and P filed suit to compel production. The lower court denied inspection, finding that P did not have a proper purpose germane to his interest as a shareholder. P appeals.

Issue. Must a shareholder demonstrate a proper purpose germane to his interest as a shareholder?

Held. Yes. Judgment affirmed.

- Under the Delaware Corporations Code, a shareholder must prove a proper purpose to inspect corporate records other than shareholder lists. P argues that a shareholder has an absolute right to inspect corporate records for the purpose of soliciting proxies. D argues that a "proper purpose" contemplates concern with investment return, and that P has no such interest. We agree. P admits that he sought inspection solely to adopt his social and political concerns, irrespective of any economic benefit to himself as a shareholder or to the corporation. P bought shares in D solely to protest its munitions production. He had utterly no interest in the business affairs of D, was not interested in D's profits, and would not have bought any shares in the company had he not learned of its munitions production. This purpose on the part of one buying into a corporation does not entitle P to inspect D's books and records.

---

3) Inspection of CEDE and NOBO Lists

Sadler v. NCR Corporation

928 F.2d 48 (2d Cir. 1991).

Facts. AT&T Corporation became a beneficial owner of 100 shares of stock in NCR Corporation (D), a large computer company. AT&T then began a tender offer for shares of D. D rejected the tender offer and declined to redeem a "poison pill" shareholders' rights plan. AT&T responded by soliciting D shareholders to convene a special meeting to replace a majority of D's directors. The meeting was set for March 28, 1991. The Sadlers owned more than 6,000 shares of D. On behalf of AT&T, the Sadlers tried to obtain shareholder lists from D. They also tried to acquire CEDE lists and NOBO lists. A CEDE list identifies brokerage firms and other record owners who bought shares for their customers and placed them in the custody of depository firms. A NOBO list contains the names of persons owning beneficial interest in shares who have consented to the disclosure of their identities. D refused to produce these lists, and the Sadlers (Ps) filed suit to compel production under section 1315 of the New York Business Corporation Law. The court ordered D to produce all materials sought by Ps. D appeals.

Issue. Must D produce its shareholder list, CEDE list, and NOBO list?

Held. Yes. Judgment affirmed.

- D challenges Ps' right to invoke section 1315 because of the arrangement Ps made with AT&T. AT&T could not make the requests itself because it had not held stock in D for six months. AT&T made an agreement with Ps under which Ps would make the demands for the lists, and AT&T would reimburse them for any expenses and indemnify them for any losses arising out of the demand. D argues that AT&T is using Ps as its agents for a demand that AT&T is not entitled to make. We see no reason to deny Ps the right to make the demands here because of their arrangement with AT&T. Section 1315 should be liberally construed in favor of the stockholder.
- D next argues that it is not required to produce the NOBO list because it does not have such a list in its possession. D admits that the list can be obtained, normally within 10 days, by requesting it from firms who offer this service. However, D argues that section 1315 is limited to production of lists that are in existence. We note that other courts have refused to order compilation of NOBO lists on the grounds that they, unlike CEDE lists which are easily compiled by computer, take time to compile and they play no central role in a proxy contest. However, we do not find these distinctions persuasive. The fact that compiling a NOBO list takes longer is an insufficient reason to distinguish it from a CEDE list. New York courts have made it clear that the statute is to be liberally construed to facilitate communication among shareholders on issues respecting corporate affairs. A narrow distinction such as this between NOBO and CEDE lists would not be in accord with New York law.
- In any event compilation of the NOBO list was properly ordered in this case because, under D's corporate charter, every share that is not voted at the special meeting is to be counted as a vote in favor of management. Thus, the shares of beneficial owners who might have sided against management if contacted by AT&T through the NOBO list would be counted in favor of management. Denying management opponents access to NOBO lists is inconsistent with the statute's objective of seeking to place shareholders on equal footing with management in gaining access to shareholders.

B. SHAREHOLDER VOTING CONTROL

1. Right to Vote

Shareholders vote annually to elect directors and on important corporate issues. In effect, the shareholders have indirect control over management. If the corporation is small and the number of shareholders relatively small, this control is meaningful. However, with larger corporations, this control may be illusory, since management really controls what happens and manipulates far-removed and disinterested shareholders to its wishes.

a. Who May Vote

1) The right to vote is held by the shareholders of record who hold shares with voting rights. Normally the right to vote follows legal title.
2) There must always be one class of shares with voting rights. If there is more than one class of shares, one or more of these classes may have restrictions on the right to vote. However, some states do not allow nonvoting common stock to be issued.
3) Only shareholders of record may vote. That is, management sets a date when all those holding shares with voting rights on that date will be able to vote at a future date.

b. Allocations of Voting Power

The right to vote may be allocated to others not owning the shares:

1) Proxies

A shareholder may give a proxy to another to vote the shares. Normally proxies are revocable.

2) Voting Trusts

A voting trust is another device to assure control of the corporation to some interested party. This device is often used because proxies are normally revocable.

a) Shareholders transfer legal title to their shares to a trustee and receive a "voting trust certificate." The trustee then has the right to vote the shares for the life of the trust.
b) Normally trusts are irrevocable by the shareholders, regardless of whether there was consideration given to the shareholder. But most states limit the permissible duration of such trusts.
c) An action for specific performance is available to compel the trust to perform according to its terms.
d) Shareholders receive all of the other usual benefits of being a shareholder (such as dividends).

3) Pooling Agreements

Shareholders may exchange promises to vote their shares in some specific way, or as some part of the group shall direct. In the absence of fraud or illegal motives, such pooling agreements are specifically enforceable.

4) Fiduciaries

Shares of stock may be held by a trustee, custodian, guardian, or other fiduciary.

5) Joint Ownership

Shares may be held by two or more persons—joint tenants, partners, etc.

6) Pledges

Shares may be pledged as security for a debt (and voting rights transferred).

7) Brokers

Brokers may hold stock in their names as agents for clients.

c. Other Limitations on the Voting Power of Shareholders

1) Introduction

Shareholders cannot make agreements relative to their voting power that will interfere unduly with the interests of minority shareholders or disrupt the normal operations of the corporate system.

2) Majority Approval

Matters requiring shareholder approval usually need only a majority of the shareholders. However, often those controlling the corporation at its formation attempt to provide in the articles and/or bylaws that a greater percentage is required. This assists those with a smaller percentage of the voting power to prevent change in the company.

a) Most courts have held that shareholder agreements that require unanimous shareholder approval for change are invalid. But many that require less than unanimous approval but more than a majority have been approved (such as a provision that 75% of the voting power must agree to a sale of the corporate assets).

3) Shareholder Agreements for Action as Directors

Most courts hold that shareholders cannot make agreements as to how they will vote as directors.

d. Shareholders' Meeting

Shareholders can only act at a meeting (although some states permit action based on unanimous written consent, or the consent of some specified percentage of shareholders), duly called, with notice, where a quorum (normally a majority) is present, and by resolution passed by the required percentage. The bylaws normally require an annual meeting and permit special meetings to be called by officers or shareholders holding a specified percentage of the voting shares.

e. Stock Must Have Voting Rights, Not Necessarily Dividends

Stroh v. Blackhawk Holding Corp.

272 N.E.2d 1 (Ill. 1971).

Facts. Blackhawk Holding Corporation (D) had two classes of stock. Each share of both class A stock and class B stock was entitled to one vote. According to D's articles of incorporation, class B stock was not entitled to dividends upon voluntary or involuntary liquidation, or otherwise. Stroh and other shareholders (Ps) contend that because this limitation deprives class B shareholders of the economic incidents of stock and the proportionate interest in the corporate assets, the class B shares do not constitute stock.

Issue. Do shares that carry voting rights but that are not entitled to share in the dividends or assets of the corporation constitute stock?

Held. Yes. Judgment affirmed.

- Under section 14 of the Illinois Business Corporation Act, shares of stock may be divided into classes with such preferences, limitations, and restrictions as shall be stated in the articles of incorporation. However, the articles must not limit or deny the voting power of the shares of any class. Under Illinois law a corporation may issue a class of stock that has preference over any other class as to the payment of dividends and as to the assets of the corporation upon the voluntary or involuntary liquidation of the corporation.
- Ps point to section 2.6 of the act which defines shares as "the units into which the proprietary interests in a corporation are divided." Ps argue that the word "proprietary" means a property right, and that thus shares must represent some economic interest or interest in the property or assets of the company. We disagree. Proprietary rights conferred by the ownership of stock are not limited to economic rights. Proprietary rights may consist of the right to participate in the control of the corporation (management rights), in its surplus profits, ***or*** in the distribution of its assets. A shareholder may have one or all of these rights attach to his stock.
- Section 14 of the Business Corporation Act indicates that a corporation may set any restrictions or limitations on its stock, with the exception of restricting voting rights. The Illinois constitution requires that a shareholder is guaranteed the right to vote based upon the number of shares he owns. It does not require that a shareholder have an economic interest. As class B stock has equal voting rights, we find nothing to invalidate the stock in this case.

Dissent. In my opinion, what is left after the economic rights are eliminated is not a share of stock under the law of Illinois.

C. CONTROL IN CLOSELY HELD CORPORATIONS

1. Introduction

Close corporations are those with very few shareholders. In effect, a close corporation is an incorporated partnership, since most often the few shareholders involved also assume roles as officers of the corporation. The chief problems associated with close corporations are discussed below.

a. Control Problems

1) The formal roles assigned by law to managers of the corporation may not be relevant—*i.e.*, the distinctions between the roles of shareholders, the board, officers, etc.
2) Formalities of notices, meetings, quorums, etc., may not be as relevant as in other situations, and yet there is little possibility of injury to outsiders—shareholders and creditors or the public—from internal deviations from formal corporate requirements.
3) Minority shareholders usually want more control in a close corporation, so voting requirements are usually set at higher percentages (often a unanimous vote is required). Alternatively, there may often be various types of voting agreements to give those in

management positions (but without stock interests) a greater voice and more control (such as by putting shares in a voting trust, etc.).

4) There are often agreements between the corporation and one or more founding members (directors and shareholders) who are not in day-to-day management, for services or supplies, etc., from the founder and his other businesses. These create conflict situations, but they are often the very reason for the formation of the corporation.

b. Provisions for Transfer

Public companies try to make their stock marketable. Close corporations try to control the transfer of stock, so that the nature of the partnership is preserved. Therefore, there are normally restrictions on transfers—buy-out arrangements in case of death or other contingencies, etc.

c. Provisions for Resolution of Disputes

Since there are normally provisions for higher percentages (sometimes unanimous) for voting and often buy-out arrangements for stock, disputes and disagreements can often arise and paralyze decisionmaking. Therefore, provisions for resolving such disputes often must be developed, such as arbitration proceedings.

d. Other Problems

Most of the other problems already discussed apply in equal measure to close corporations (piercing the corporate veil, promoters, stock issuance, etc.).

2. Voting Agreements

In a voting agreement, shareholders exchange promises to vote their shares in some specific way, or as some part of the group shall direct. In the absence of fraud or illegal motive, such agreements are generally held to be specifically enforceable.

a. Pooling Agreements

Ringling Brothers-Barnum & Bailey Combined Shows v. Ringling

53 A.2d 441 (Del. Super Ct. 1947).

Facts. Ringling (P) owned 315 shares of the Ringling Brothers corporation (D). Haley owned 315 shares, and North owned 370. P and Haley entered into an agreement for 10 years that they would act jointly in exercising their voting rights and if they could not agree, that the decision would be made by an arbitrator. One year, at a shareholder meeting, the parties could not agree on how to vote. Haley voted her shares rather than following the direction of an arbitrator. P sued for specific performance of the contract. The lower court held for P and ordered a new election to be held. D appeals, arguing that the agreement is illegal and against public policy.

Issue. May two of three shareholders of a corporation agree that they will jointly exercise their voting rights and that if they cannot agree, an arbitrator shall decide how they should vote?

Held. Yes. Order of the chancery court modified.

- D argues that under Delaware corporations law, there can be no agreement that operates to irrevocably separate the voting power of stock from the ownership of the stock except as provided in section 18, which authorizes transfer of stock in trust. D argues that here, the agreement illegally transfers voting power to an arbitrator, who has no ownership interest in the stock.
- However, various forms of pooling agreements have been held valid, and have been distinguished from voting trusts. The chancery court determined that this agreement to vote in accordance with

the decision of the arbitrator was valid as a "stock pooling agreement," and that it was not in violation of any public policy of this state. We agree.

- Power to vote the shares was in no way transferred to the arbitrator. The parties did not agree that either one could vote *the* shares of the other, or that the arbitrator could vote them. Rather, the parties promised to vote their own shares in accordance with the arbitrator's decision. The agreement is a valid contract, which has sufficient consideration in the mutual promises of the parties. Haley's refusal to exercise her voting rights in accordance with the decision of the arbitrator was a breach of her contract.
- The lower court declared the election invalid. However, we conclude that the proper remedy is to reject the votes representing Haley's shares, and to declare the election of the persons for whom P and the other shareholder voted.

---

b. Issues Associated with Pooling Agreements

The two major issues are (i) whether such agreements are void as against public policy, and (ii) if they are valid, how and against whom will they be enforced?

1) For example, pooling agreements have been upheld where shareholders get together and create a majority shareholder interest in voting to elect a certain slate of directors. This has been upheld even where cumulative voting has existed.
2) But note that whenever anything smacks of fraud, such agreements may be overturned. For example, if A agrees to vote with B if B releases A from a personal debt, this may be enough to cancel the agreement.
3) Courts have split in the situation represented by the *Ringling Brothers* case. Some have indicated that a vote cannot be split from its shares (in an arbitrator), and have refused to uphold such agreements. Did the court in *Ringling* really effectuate the intent of the parties? Other courts have specifically enforced such agreements.
4) The time period of the agreements is also an important factor, since voting trust statutes normally limit the duration (such as to 10 years).
5) Note that later the statutes of Delaware were amended so that voting agreements for a period of no longer than 10 years were approved. Irrevocable proxies were recognized as valid if there was the requisite interest (an interest in the stock or any interest in the corporation is sufficient). Thus, it appears that Delaware, by statute, avoided the difficult line-drawing problems created by the *Ringling Brothers* case.

3. Voting Trusts

The voting trust was developed to meet the limitations and problems associated with proxies and shareholder pooling agreements. The purpose of the trust is to assure control of the corporation to some interested party. It is often employed with public companies as well as with close corporations.

a. Shareholders transfer legal title to shares to a trustee and receive a "voting trust certificate." The trustee has the right to vote the shares for the life of the trust.

b. Normally, trusts are irrevocable by the shareholders regardless of whether there was consideration given the shareholder. But normally, most states limit the permissible duration of such trusts. Some states provide for revocation by a vote of a specified percentage of the shares subject to the trust.

4. Agreements Controlling Matters Within the Board's Discretion

a. Shareholder Agreements for Action as Directors

Most courts hold that shareholders cannot make agreements as to how they will vote as directors. Directors must be free to act independently in their roles as directors in order to faithfully execute their fiduciary duty to the corporation (part of which is to protect the interests of all shareholders, including minority shareholders). Of course, shareholders can agree on how they will vote as shareholders to elect directors, and then the directors may act as they choose. For the same reason, most courts hold that directors may not agree with other board members in advance of a vote as to how they will vote.

1) Less Than Unanimous Shareholder Agreements as to How They Will Act as Directors Are Invalid

McQuade v. Stoneham

189 N.E. 234 (N.Y. 1934).

Facts. The corporation had 2,500 shares outstanding. Stoneham and McGraw (Ds) had 1,306 shares and 70 shares, respectively; McQuade (P) had 70 shares. Ds and P agreed to use their best efforts to elect themselves directors and officers, to take salaries and to perpetuate themselves in office (and further, not to amend the articles, bylaws, etc., as long as any of the three owned stock). Stoneham appointed the other four directors. Three years later, at a directors' meeting, Ds refused to vote, thus allowing the other four directors to outvote P in removing him as an officer. At a later shareholder meeting, P was removed as a director (he had gotten into personal differences with Stoneham). P sued for specific performance of the shareholder agreement. The trial court found for P and Ds appeal.

Issue. May shareholders agree among themselves as to how they will act as directors in managing the affairs of the corporation?

Held. No. Judgment for P reversed.

- Shareholders may not agree to control the directors in the exercise of their independent judgment. They may combine to elect directors, but they must let the directors manage the business, which includes the election of officers.

Concurrence. I find the contract itself to be valid. A contract that provides that shareholders shall in combination use their power to achieve a legitimate purpose is not illegal. I concur in the judgment because the otherwise valid contract is unenforceable because it resulted in an employment which was itself illegal. P was a city magistrate at the time the contract was made and could not by law engage in any other business.

---

2) Unanimous Shareholder Agreements as to How They Will Act as Directors Generally Are Valid

Clark v. Dodge

199 N.E. 641 (N.Y. 1936).

Facts. Clark (P) owned 25% and Dodge (D) 75% of two corporations. P ran the business and knew the secret formula that was used. P and D agreed that P would be kept as a director and the general manager as long as he was "faithful and efficient." As compensation P would receive 25% of the net profits. D also agreed not to pay unreasonable salaries to other employees to reduce P's profits. P agreed to disclose the formula to D's son, which he did. P sues for specific performance of the contract on the basis that he was discharged without cause and unreasonable salaries were paid to reduce his income.

Issue. Where all of the shareholders agree on how certain matters of corporate business will be conducted, is the agreement enforceable?

Held. Yes. Judgment for P.

- ♦ This contract is not void on public policy grounds since there was no undue attempt to sterilize the board from its duty of managing the corporation.
- ♦ All the shareholders agreed.
- ♦ There is no injury to shareholders, creditors, or the public.
- ♦ This is a close corporation, like a partnership.

Comment. Compare the *McQuade* case (*supra*). The rationale (other than the factual difference that here all shareholders agreed) is different; *i.e.*, whether or not there is any injury to interested parties from such a mild interference with the management role of the board. In effect, this case represents the modern view of how to treat the close corporation; do not hold it to the statutory formalities of state corporation law, but do what makes sense in the factual context of a close corporation.

---

3) Shareholder Agreements Enforceable Even If They Deviate from State Corporation Law Practice

Galler v. Galler

203 N.E.2d 577 (Ill. 1964).

Facts. Emma Galler's (P's) deceased husband and his brother (D) owned 95% of the corporation's stock. An employee owned the remaining stock, which was repurchased by D after this suit began. P, her husband, D, and his wife all signed a shareholders' agreement that provided that the four of them would vote for themselves as the corporation's four directors, that an annual dividend of $50,000 would be paid as long as the corporation's accumulated earned surplus was $500,000 or more, and that upon the death of either brother, the corporation would give the widow a salary continuation contract for a five-year period. P demanded performance, and D refused. P sues for an accounting and specific performance.

Issue. When substantially all of the shareholders of a close corporation enter a shareholders' agreement that provides for actions to be taken by the corporation, will the court sustain such an agreement although it deviates from state corporation law practice?

Held. Yes. Judgment for P.

- ♦ Courts have allowed close corporations to deviate from corporate norms in order to give business effect to the intentions of the parties.
- ♦ Here, substantially all of the shareholders of the corporation entered the agreement. The agreement did not injure creditors, other shareholders, or the public. The duration of the agreement is until the death of P. This period is not too long. The purpose of the agreement (maintenance of the widow) is proper. The provision for a dividend is valid since a base surplus is required to be maintained.
- ♦ The terms of the agreement are upheld, to P's benefit.

---

4) Voting Agreements Enforceable

Ramos v. Estrada

10 Cal. Rptr. 2d 833 (Cal. Ct. App. 1992).

Facts. Two couples, Ramos and his wife, and Estrada and her husband, formed The Broadcast Group. The Broadcast Group ("TBG") and another group called Ventura 41 separately sought a permit to form a Spanish television station. Eventually the two groups combined in a corporation called Television, Inc. with 5,000 shares of the corporation being issued to members of TBG and 5,000 shares issued to members of Ventura 41. The board of directors was to have eight members (four from TBG and four from Ventura 41). After six months of operation, TBG was to acquire two additional shares and the power to elect an additional (ninth) member of the board. Members of TBG entered into an agreement to vote all of their shares of Television, Inc. in a manner determined by the majority of them. The agreement states that failure to vote with the majority constitutes an election by the shareholder to sell his shares to the rest of the group. Estrada later defected from TBG and at a special directors' meeting in 1998, voted with the Ventura 41 group to remove Ramos as president. Ramos (P) sued the Estradas (Ds) for breach of the voting agreement. The lower court ruled that Ds breached the valid voting agreement and ordered their shares sold in accordance with the specific terms of the agreement. Ds appeal, arguing that the agreement is void because it constitutes an expired proxy which Ds validly revoked.

Issue. Is the voting agreement valid and enforceable?

Held. Yes. Judgment affirmed.

- The shareholders entered into this agreement for purposes of limiting the transferability of their stock, ensuring that the company does not pass into control of persons with interests incompatible to theirs, establishing their mutual rights and obligations in the event of death, and establishing a mechanism for determining how the voting rights of the company shall be exercised. They agreed to vote their shares in accordance with the decision of the majority of the group. The agreement has the characteristics of a shareholders' voting agreement which is expressly authorized by section 706 of the California Corporations Code for close corporations. Section 706(a) states that two or more shareholders of a close corporation may agree in writing that they will consult each other and vote their own stock in accordance with the majority of the group.
- Although Television, Inc. does not qualify as a close corporation, section 706(d) states that this section shall not invalidate any voting or other agreement that is not otherwise illegal. The Legislative Committee comment to this section states that "this subdivision is intended to preserve any agreements which would be upheld under court decisions even though they do not comply with one or more of the requirements of this section, including voting agreements of corporations other than close corporations." Thus, we find the voting agreement to be valid, enforceable, and supported by consideration.
- Ds contend that the forced sale provision is unconscionable and oppressive. The evidence shows that Ds are extremely experienced in business and contracts, having operated a real estate brokerage business and managed investment property. Ds discussed the agreement with an attorney before signing it. They had full and fair opportunity to consider the agreement, and their consent was not obtained by fraud, duress, or other wrongful conduct. Ds breached the agreement and their breach constituted an election to sell their shares in accordance with the agreement.

D. ABUSE OF CONTROL

1. Fiduciary Obligations of Shareholders in Close Corporations

It is clear in the law that partners in a partnership have a fiduciary duty to each other. There is, therefore, also an implied-in-law fiduciary duty of shareholders to each other in a close corporation.

a. Breach of Duty

Wilkes v. Springside Nursing Home, Inc.

353 N.E.2d 657 (Mass. 1976).

Facts. Wilkes (P) had an option to purchase a building and lot where a hospital had once been located. Riche (D), Quinn (D), and Pipkin joined with Wilkes in forming a close corporation to run a nursing home on the property. Each invested an equal amount of cash and purchased an equal number of shares. It was understood that each would be a director and receive money from the corporation in equal amounts as long as each actively assumed his share of the burdens of operating the business.

Pipkin sold his shares to Connor (D), now deceased. Quinn (D) wanted to buy part of the corporate property. Wilkes (P) convinced the other shareholder-directors to sell the property at a higher price than Quinn had anticipated paying. From this point, the relationship between Quinn and Wilkes deteriorated.

Quinn and the other shareholders voted to put themselves on salary from the corporation. They did not give Wilkes a salary. Later, they voted Wilkes out of his office and his directorship.

Wilkes brought an action for a declaratory judgment against the other shareholders for breach of the incorporation agreement and breach of their fiduciary duty. The trial court found for Ds, and P appeals.

Issue. Did the majority shareholders breach their duty of utmost good faith and loyalty to P when they cut P out of the position of director and denied him a salary?

Held. Yes. Judgment reversed and case remanded for a determination of the damages P has suffered.

- ♦ The rule in the state is that shareholders in a close corporation have the same duty toward each other that partners have; that is, the utmost good faith and loyalty. If several shareholders combine to "freeze out" another shareholder by removing him from all decisionmaking roles and denying him a return on his investment, they have breached their fiduciary duty to him.
- ♦ We recognize that an untempered application of the strict good faith standard would hamper the ability of the controlling group to manage the corporation for the good of all concerned. The rights of this group must be balanced against its duty to minority shareholders. Therefore, when the control group can show a legitimate business purpose for its actions, no breach will be found.
- ♦ In this case, there was no valid business purpose in taking Wilkes's directorship, management position, and salary from him. He was at all times ready to perform his responsibilities to the corporation. His damages will not be diminished by Ds' claim that they performed his duties during the time they had refused to let him perform them.

---

b. Minority Shareholder Employment Not Guaranteed

Ingle v. Glamore Motor Sales, Inc.

535 N.E.2d 1311 (NY. 1989).

Facts. Glamore was the sole shareholder of Glamore Motor Sales, Incorporated ("GMS"). In 1964, Ingle (P) was hired as a sales manager for GMS. Two years later, P and Glamore entered into an agreement under which P would purchase 22 shares of Glamore's stock, P would have a five-year option to purchase 18 more shares, and Glamore would make P the director and secretary of the corporation. The agreement gave Glamore the right to repurchase all of P's stock if P ceased to be an employee of GMS for any reason. In 1982, GMS issued 60 additional shares of stock. Glamore purchased 22 shares, and each of his two sons purchased 19 shares. At that time, Glamore, his two sons, and P entered into another shareholder agreement. This agreement provided that if any stockholder ceased to be an employee for any reason, Glamore would have the option, for a period of 30 days after termination of employment, to purchase all of the shares of stock the former employee owned. At the 1983 directors' meeting, P was voted out of his corporate position and fired. Glamore notified P that he was exercising his option to repurchase P's stock, and paid him $96,000 for his shares. P filed suit against Glamore, his sons, and GMS (Ds) alleging that in terminating him, Ds breached the corporate fiduciary duties of loyalty and good faith they owed him as a minority shareholder in a closely held corporation. Ds argued that P was an at-will employee who could be terminated for any reason, and the lower court agreed. P appeals.

Issue. Does an at-will employee acquire fiduciary-rooted protection against being fired simply because he is a minority shareholder in a close corporation?

Held. No. Judgment affirmed.

- P argues that his status as a minority shareholder in a close corporation requires him to be treated as a co-owner or partner, whose employment rights flow from a special duty of loyalty and good faith. This case requires us to keep separate the duty a corporation owes to a minority shareholder ***as a shareholder*** from any duty it might owe him ***as an employee***. In this case, P was an at-will employee serving without an employment contract. Thus, the corporation owed him no duty as an employee. The shareholder agreement provided P no employment security. An employee who also happens to be a minority shareholder acquires no right from the corporation or majority shareholders against at-will discharge.
- P argues that he was discharged because Glamore wanted to buy back his stock. But P does not assert that the corporation undervalued his shares, or that the amount he received was not fair. He accepted payment from Glamore without reservation.

Dissent. The relationship of a minority shareholder to a close corporation cannot possibly be equated with an ordinary hiring and is regarded as nothing more than employment at will. A person who buys a minority interest in a close corporation does so not only in the hope of an increase in the value of his shares, but also for the assurance of employment in the business in a managerial position. By categorizing this case as a claim for breach of employment contract rather than an unfair squeeze out of a minority shareholder in a close corporation, the court concludes that P has no rights at all.

---

c. Remedy for a Freeze-Out

Brodie v. Jordan

857 N.E.2d 1076 (Mass. 2006).

Facts. Brodie, Barbuto, and Jordan each held one-third of the shares and served as directors of Malden Company, which operated a machine shop and produced ball bearings. Brodie served as president of the company for several years. Barbuto served as the company's treasurer. Jordan was in charge of the day-to-day operation of the business. The parties began to disagree over management issues, and Brodie asked that the company purchase his shares, but his requests were denied. The corporation did not pay any dividends to the shareholders for many years. Jordan received a salary from the corporation, participated in a profit-sharing plan made available by the corporation, and had the use of a company vehicle. Barbuto received director's fees and rent from a building that he owned that Malden used as its corporate office. Brodie received compensation for a time, but eventually was voted out as president and director. He died about five years later. After Brodie's death, his widow (P) attended a Malden shareholders' meeting, where she nominated herself as a director, but Barbuto and Jordan (Ds) voted against her. P filed suit against Ds, claiming that Ds failed to provide her with various financial and operational information on the company, failed to hold an annual shareholders' meeting for five years, and prevented her from participating in any company decisionmaking. The trial court found that Ds interfered with P's reasonable expectations of benefit from the ownership of shares by excluding her from corporate decisionmaking, denying her access to company information, and hindering her ability to sell her shares in the open market. Ds were the only ones receiving any financial benefit from the corporation. The appellate court affirmed. Ds have not sought further review with respect to liability. The only issue before the court is the remedy.

Issue. Is P entitled to a forced buyout of her shares by the majority?

Held. No. Judgment affirmed in part, reversed in part, and case remanded.

- Malden is a close corporation. Shareholders in a close corporation owe one another a fiduciary duty substantially the same as partners owe each other—the duty of utmost good faith and loyalty. Majority shareholders violate this duty when they act to "freeze out" the minority by frustrating the minority's reasonable expectations of benefit from their ownership of shares.
- The proper remedy for a freeze-out is to restore the minority shareholder, as nearly as possible, to the position she would have been in had there been no wrongdoing. Here, the superior court judge ordered Ds to buy out P, a remedy that no Massachusetts appellate court has previously authorized. The problem with this remedy is that it placed P in a better position than she would have enjoyed absent the wrongdoing and exceeded her reasonable expectations of benefit from her shares. Neither the articles of organization nor any corporate bylaw obligates Malden or Ds to purchase P's shares. The judge's order created an artificial market for P's shares, an asset that really has little or no market value.
- On remand, the court should determine P's reasonable expectations of ownership, whether those expectations have been frustrated, and, if so, the means of vindicating P's interests. Money damages may be an appropriate remedy, and prospective injunctive relief may also be granted to ensure that P is allowed to participate in company governance and enjoy financial or other benefits.

---

d. Unreasonable Exercise of Veto Power

Smith v. Atlantic Properties, Inc.

422 N.E.2d 798 (Mass. App. Ct. 1981).

Facts. Atlantic Properties (D) was a corporation organized to buy and manage real estate. Smith (P), Zimble (P), Burke (P), and Wolfson (D) invested equal sums and were the only stockholders. Atlantic's bylaws provided that corporate decisions must be approved by 80% of the stock eligible to vote, effectively giving any one stockholder veto power.

Atlantic showed a profit for 16 years but dividends were paid in only two of those years, due to Wolfson's refusal to declare dividends. Wolfson wanted Atlantic's earnings spent on repairs and improvements to its properties. However, only the most basic repairs were made, and Wolfson did not develop any plans or schedule for improvements. Because of the failure to declare sufficient dividends over the years, the IRS assessed penalty taxes against Atlantic, as Ps had warned Wolfson.

Ps, alleging breach of fiduciary duty, sued for a court determination of dividends, Wolfson's removal as a director, and for reimbursement by Wolfson of the penalty taxes and related expenses. The trial court held for Ps (the issue of Wolfson's removal was not addressed). Ds appeal.

Issue. Did Wolfson breach his fiduciary duty to the other stockholders by repeatedly exercising the veto power provided for in the bylaws?

Held. Yes. Judgment affirmed.

- The 80% provision is a reasonable means of protecting minority stockholders. But sometimes its exercise may violate the fiduciary duty stockholders in a close corporation owe each other. In determining this issue, the court must weigh the business interest each side presents as a reason for its action.
- Here, Wolfson's refusal to declare dividends was inconsistent with any reasonable interpretation of his duty of utmost good faith and loyalty to Ps. He was aware of the dangers of IRS penalties, but continued to cause them to be assessed against Atlantic. Ps' desire to avoid the assessments outweighed Wolfson's reasons for refusing to vote to declare dividends.

---

e. Duty to Disclose Merger Negotiations

Jordan v. Duff and Phelps, Inc.

815 F.2d 429 (7th Cir. 1987), *cert. dismissed*, 485 U.S. 901 (1988).

Facts. In 1977, Jordan (P) began working for Duff and Phelps, Inc. (D) as a securities analyst. In 1981, D offered P the opportunity to buy some stock. P eventually purchased 188 shares and was making installment payments on another 62 shares. Before selling him stock, D required P to sign the company's "Stock Restriction and Purchase Agreement," which stated in part that upon a shareholder's termination of employment, the shareholder will sell his shares back to the company for their book value on the December 31st preceding the date of termination. In November of 1983, unbeknownst to P, D's board began a search for a buyer for the company. D became involved in merger discussions with Security Pacific Corporation, but the negotiations eventually broke down. In 1983, P accepted another job and notified D of his resignation. On December 31, 1983, P delivered his stock certificates to the company in accordance with the agreement, and D mailed him a check for $23,000. Before he cashed the check, P saw an article in the newspaper announcing a merger of D with another company. If P had been an employee at the time of the merger, his stock would have been worth $452,000. P demanded his stock back, and D refused. P filed this suit based on section 10(b), and Rule 10b–5, and breach of fiduciary duty. P seeks damages and rescission of the sale. The district court granted summary judgment for D, holding that rescission is unavailable as a matter of law, and that P could not prove damages. P appeals.

Issue. Did D have a duty to inform P of the merger negotiations?

Held. Maybe. Judgment reversed and case remanded.

- Close corporations that purchase their own stock must disclose to the sellers all information that meets the standard of materiality set forth in *TSC Industries, Inc. v. Northway, Inc.*, 426 U.S. 438 (1976). A jury could reasonably conclude that the board's November 1983 decision to seek a buyer for the company was material. Although he gave his notice in November, P continued to work at D for the rest of the year to take advantage of the December 31, 1983 book value calculation which would have been higher than the December 31, 1982 value. D allowed P to exercise choice about the date on which he would leave. He could have decided to stay longer had he known that the company was involved in merger negotiations.

- ♦ The dissent argues that this does not matter because P was an at-will employee and could have been fired the day before the merger. We disagree. One term implied even in at-will employment situations is that neither party will try to take opportunistic advantage of the other. Had the firm terminated P the day before the merger, it would have broken the implied pledge to avoid opportunistic conduct. The timing of the sale and the materiality of the information D withheld are for the jury to decide. Thus summary judgment was not appropriate.
- ♦ We agree with the district court that rescission of the sale is not an available remedy. Employment at D is a condition of stock ownership. P could not own stock after December 31. We disagree, however, with the district court's finding that P could not show damages as a matter of law because the initial merger fell through. Security Pacific was willing to pay $50 million because it concluded that D was worth that much. If it was worth that much to Security Pacific, it was worth that much or more to someone else. The end of Security Pacific's bid therefore does not show that P was uninjured. Thus the problem in this case is not establishing damages, but showing causation. Even if the stock was worth much more than book value, P could only receive that price by holding on. So to recover, P would have to show that upon learning of the negotiations with Security Pacific, he would have dropped his plans to go to Houston, and that even after the deal fell through he would have remained until the end of 1985. The lower court denied D's motion for summary judgment finding that causation is a question for the jury. We agree. A jury could find that had he known of the initial merger proposal, P could have assumed there would be subsequent proposals and may have continued his employment at D.

Dissent. P was an at-will employee who quit owning shares that he had agreed to sell back to the company at book value according to the stockholder agreement. The agreement was specific that his status as a shareholder conferred no job rights. Nevertheless, the court holds that the corporation had a duty enforceable under rule 10b–5 to volunteer information about the company's prospects that might have led him to change his mind about quitting, although as an at-will employee he had no right to.

E. CONTROL, DURATION, AND STATUTORY DISSOLUTION

1. Introduction

Dissatisfied shareholders in publicly traded corporations may sell their shares on the open market. Because shareholders in close corporations cannot readily turn to a market to extract the value of what they have put into and expect from the business, internal disputes may threaten the wealth and livelihood of these holders, the profitability of the business, or both. Minority shareholders in a close corporation are particularly at risk of being "frozen out." The best remedy they can seek is for the corporation to buy back their shares at a fair price. This can occur in four different circumstances:

a. Articles or Bylaws

The corporation's articles of incorporation or the bylaws may contain such a provision allowing buyout at a stated price.

b. Involuntary Dissolution

A shareholder may petition the court for involuntary dissolution of the corporation. Many modern statutes authorize courts to order dissolution of a close corporation on petition of those owning less than a majority of a corporation's shares. Many courts take the position that, even in the absence of an authorizing statute, they may remedy abuse, dissention, or deadlock by appointing a receiver and winding up a corporation. However, there is generally a judicial reluctance to order dissolution, probably because of a desire to protect the interests of employees, creditors, and shareholders. Because of this reluctance, some states have begun to provide alternative forms of relief including appointing independent directors and compelling buyouts of minority shares at the fair market value.

c. Significant Change

Upon some significant change in corporate structure, such as a merger, the shareholder may demand a statutory right of appraisal. Where it applies, the appraisal remedy allows a dissenting shareholder in a merger or sale of the corporation's assets to get the value of his shares in cash (rather than accept the consideration otherwise received as part of the major corporate change).

d. Breach of Duty

A buyout may be used as an equitable remedy upon a finding of a breach of fiduciary duty.

1) Mandatory Buyout Denied

Alaska Plastics, Inc. v. Coppock

621 P.2d 270 (Alaska 1980).

Facts. Stefano, Gillam, and Crow formed Alaska Plastics, Inc., a company that produced foam insulation, in 1961. Each of the three owned 300 shares of stock in the company and were the only directors and officers. In 1970, Crow was divorced and as part of the property settlement gave his former wife (P) 150 shares or a one-sixth interest in the company. It is undisputed that P was not notified of annual shareholders' meetings in 1971, 1972, and 1974. She was given three hours' notice of the annual meeting in 1973. The directors have never authorized the company to pay dividends, and P has never received any money from the corporation. At the 1974 shareholders' meeting, Stefano, Gillam and Crow decided to offer P $15,000 for her shares. P rejected the offer as too low and demanded to inspect the corporation's books and records. An accountant who investigated the books estimated P's stock to be worth between $23,000 and $40,000. At the 1975 meeting, P offered to sell her shares to the company for $40,000. The board rejected her offer, but offered her $20,000, which she refused. A short time later, Alaska Plastics's plant, which was not insured, was completely destroyed in a fire. P filed suit requesting that the company buy her shares for a fair and equitable price. The trial court entered judgment against the individual directors and the company (Ds) for $52,314, which represented $32,000 for the value of the shares, $5,200 for attorney's fees, and $15,144 for interest and costs. Both sides appeal.

Issue. Did the trial court err in obligating the corporation to purchase P's shares?

Held. Yes. Case remanded.

- In publicly traded corporations shareholders can sell their shares on the open market. In a close corporation such as this, however, there is not likely to be a market for the corporation's shares, and the corporation itself or the other shareholders may not be interested in purchasing the shares. Thus majority shareholders in a close corporation are in a unique position to squeeze out a minority shareholder. The lower court concluded that the corporation was obligated to purchase P's shares for their fair value. We find that remedy unavailable on this record as a matter of law and remand the case to determine whether a more appropriate remedy is available.

- Of course, the most successful remedy for a shareholder such as P is to have the corporation buy out her shares for their fair value. There are four ways that this can occur:

  First, the articles of incorporation or the bylaws may contain a buyout provision. However, since P has not alleged any such provision in the articles or bylaws, we do not consider the availability of this method.

  Under the second method, Alaska's Corporations Code provides that a shareholder may bring an action for liquidation or dissolution upon a showing that the acts of those in control of the corporation are illegal, oppressive or fraudulent, or that corporate assets are being wasted. Because liquidation is such an extreme remedy, courts have recognized less drastic alternative remedies, such as requiring the corporation to purchase the minority shareholder's shares for a fair and reasonable price. The lower court did not reach this issue. We therefore remand the case for a determination as to whether P can show that the acts of Stefano, Gillam, and Crow were illegal, oppressive or fraudulent, or constituted waste of corporate assets.

  The third method of forced purchase of shares is not available in this case. There has been no fundamental corporate change such as a merger or sale of substantially all of the corporation's assets.

  The fourth possibility is a remedy for breach of duty. We note that other jurisdictions have held that transactions by one group of shareholders that enable it to derive some special benefit not shared by all should be subject to close judicial scrutiny. In this case, the directors received benefits that P did not. The corporation paid them "director's fees," Gillam received a substantial salary, and the corporation apparently paid some of the personal expenses of the directors' wives. These expenditures could be considered constructive dividends that were not shared with P. However, we note that none of the other shareholders ever sold stock back to the company. Thus this was not a benefit others enjoyed that P should have shared equally. We make no finding on this fourth possibility, but remand the case to the trial court to make the appropriate finding on this issue.

Comment. Upon remand, the trial court entered judgment for P for $32,000 after finding that the directors committed oppressive or fraudulent conduct sufficient to warrant a remedy as drastic as involuntary dissolution or a forced buyout of P's shares. The Alaska Supreme Court affirmed.

---

2) Dissolution More Equitable Than Buyout

Haley v. Talcott

864 A.2d 86 (Del. Ch. 2004).

Facts. Haley (P) and Talcott (D) were longtime friends. P found a location for a seafood restaurant ("the Redfin Grill"). D contributed substantial start-up money to the Redfin Grill and P managed the Grill without drawing a salary for the first year. Although the parties were operating the business as a joint venture, they structured the business so that the Redfin Grill was an entity solely owned by D, and P was an employee, with a series of elaborate employment contracts. One such contract limited D's ability to remove P from his active role and established a relationship more similar to a partnership than a typical employer-employee relationship. An opportunity arose to purchase the property that the Redfin Grill had been leasing. P and D formed Matt and Greg Real Estate, LLC ("the LLC") to purchase the property together. The Redfin Grill continued to operate at the site, paying the LLC rent. P and D's personal relationship deteriorated. D terminated P and forbade him from entering the premises of the Redfin Grill. P responded that this was a breach of the employment contract and that he intended to take legal action. Furthermore, as a 50% member in the LLC, P voted to reject the proposed new lease for the Redfin Grill on the LLC's property, to revoke the Redfin Grill's right of possession to the property, and to put the property for sale on the open market. D rejected these proposals, and a stalemate was reached. The Redfin Grill's lease has expired and it continues to occupy the property on a month-to-month arrangement. With each having only 50% ownership in the LLC, P cannot force the termination of the lease and evict the Redfin Grill, and D cannot renew the lease. An exit mechanism in the LLC agreement allows either member to quit the company and allows the other member to purchase the departing member's interest for fair market value. P does not believe he is obligated to exit by the agreement and instead moves for summary judgment seeking dissolution of the LLC.

Issue. Should dissolution of the LLC be granted?

Held. Yes. The parties should submit a plan for dissolution of the LLC and sale of the property. Either party may bid on the property.

- Under corporate law, there are three prerequisites for a judicial order of dissolution: (i) the corporation has two 50% stockholders; (ii) those stockholders are engaged in a joint venture; and (iii) they are unable to agree upon whether to discontinue the business and how to dispose of the assets. Each of these provisions is indisputably met. If the LLC were a corporation, there would be no question about P's request to dissolve.
- Here, the LLC has a detailed exit provision. However, it is an insufficient alternative to dissolution. Neither party has an obvious priority of interest, as P and D created this LLC together. The LLC agreement does not address what should happen if both parties prefer to buy the other party out and neither party desires to leave. To force P to follow the exit mechanism would permit D to penalize P. P would still be obligated under his personal guaranty for the mortgage on the property. It would not be equitable to force P to use the exit mechanism.

---

3) Expectations of Continuing Employment

Pedro v. Pedro

489 N.W.2d 798 (Minn. Ct. App. 1992).

Facts. Alfred, Carl, and Eugene Pedro were brothers who each owned a one-third interest in The Pedro Companies ("TPC"), a closely held corporation. The shareholders entered into a stock retirement agreement ("SRA") designed to facilitate the purchase of the shareholder's stock upon death, or when a living shareholder desired to sell his interest. The SRA stated that the shares would be sold at 75% of their net book value at the end of the preceding calendar year. Alfred (P) discovered a $270,000 discrepancy in the company's books and urged his brothers to hire an independent accountant to investigate. Carl and Eugene (Ds) resisted the idea, but Alfred insisted. After several months, a hired accountant could not explain the discrepancy, and Ds told P to forget about it or he would be fired. P claims that during this time, Ds interfered with his responsibilities in the company and undermined his authority with employees. A second independent auditor was hired and could not explain the discrepancy. The auditor testified that throughout his investigation he was refused access to numerous documents. When P later received written notice that his employment and benefits were terminated, he filed suit. The trial court awarded P $766,000 for his interest in the company, as calculated by the SRA. The court also awarded P an additional $563,000 after finding that Ds breached their fiduciary duties to him. The court further found that P had a contract of lifetime employment, and that he was wrongfully terminated. P was awarded $256,000 as compensation for lost wages. Finally, the trial court awarded P $200,000 in attorneys' fees based on its finding that Ds acted in a manner that was arbitrary, vexatious, and otherwise not in good faith. Ds appeal.

Issues.

(i) Did the trial court err in finding that Ds breached their fiduciary duties to P?

(ii) Did the trial court properly find that P had a reasonable expectation of lifetime employment and calculate damages appropriately?

Held. (i) No. (ii) Yes. Judgment affirmed.

- Shareholders in a close corporation owe each other a fiduciary duty that includes dealing openly, honestly and fairly with other shareholders. The record contains many examples where Ds did not act openly, honestly and fairly with P. Ds interfered with P's responsibilities at TPC, had him followed by a private investigator, and fabricated allegations of malfeasance and neglect against him. Ds told P that if he did not forget about TPC's financial discrepancies, he would be fired. Following his termination, Ds told TPC employees that P had a nervous breakdown. A finding of breach of fiduciary duty is supported on this record. Moreover, the measure of damages was proper. The court awarded P the difference between the market value of P's shares ($1,330,000) and the price TPC would pay to buy P out under the terms of the SRA ($766,000). The difference ($563,000) is the measure of P's damages from being forced to sell his shares to the company due to Ds' breach of fiduciary duty.
- Ds argue there was insufficient evidence to find that P had a contract for lifetime employment. Trial courts have broad equitable powers of fashioning relief for the buyout of shareholders in a closely held corporation, and the court may look to the minority shareholder's reasonable expectations when awarding damages. Other courts have held that the reasonable expectations of shareholders such as P include a job, a salary, a significant place in management, and economic security for his family. In a closely held corporation, the nature of the employment of a shareholder may create a reasonable expectation that his employment is not terminable at will. P had been employed at TPC for 45 years. His father had worked at the family-owned company until his death. The evidence suggested that Ds also expected to work at TPC as long as they wanted. It was reasonable for P to assume that he had lifetime employment, and reasonable for the trial court to find that the parties had a contract that was not terminable at will.
- Ds argue that P's award of damages for both lost wages and breach of contract affords P a double recovery. However, P has two separate interests—as owner and as employee—and recovery for both is appropriate. P's award of lost wages is also consistent with the court's equitable powers and is warranted by the finding of a contract for lifetime employment. Finally, Ds' challenge of the award of attorneys' fees is without merit. If a court finds that a party to a proceeding of this type has acted arbitrarily, vexatiously, or otherwise not in good faith, the court may in its discretion award reasonable expenses including attorneys' fees.

---

4) Involuntary Dissolution

Stuparich v. Harbor Furniture Mfg., Inc.

100 Cal. Rptr. 2d 313 (Cal. Ct. App. 2000).

Facts. Harbor Furniture Manufacturing, Inc. (D), a closely held corporation, was owned by Ilo and Malcolm Tuttleton, Sr. In addition to furniture manufacturing and sales, the company owned and operated a mobile home park. In 1982, Malcolm, Sr. turned over the position of CEO to his son, Malcolm, Jr. Malcolm, Jr.'s wife and son were both employed by D. His two sisters, Ann and Candi (Ps), obtained shares of the company through gifts and inheritance. Ps each owned 19% of the voting shares and 33.33% of the non-voting shares of the company. Other than attending board meetings, Ps were never involved in the operation of the company. In 1996, Malcolm, Sr. sold his voting stock to Malcolm, Jr., giving him 51.56% of the voting shares and 33.33% of the non-voting shares. When Ilo died, Ps, who were unaware of Malcolm, Sr.'s sale of stock to Malcolm, Jr., believed that they had acquired a controlling interest in the corporation. Ps proposed formally separating the mobile home park from the furniture business because the mobile home park had been very profitable and the furniture store was incurring losses. Malcolm, Jr. refused to hold a meeting on the restructuring and informed Ps that they did not have a controlling interest in the company. The relationship between Ps and their brother deteriorated severely to the point that a physical altercation occurred between Malcolm, Jr. and Candi. Ps then filed this suit seeking involuntary dissolution of the corporation under section 1800(b)(5) of the California Corporations Code. D was granted summary judgment, and Ps appeal.

Issue. Have Ps raised a triable issue of fact as to their right to involuntary dissolution of the corporation?

Held. No. Judgment affirmed.

- Section 1800(b)(5) applies when liquidation is reasonably necessary for the protection of the rights or interests of the complaining shareholders. Because this section permits a going concern to be involuntarily terminated, the application of such a drastic remedy should be limited. The power of minority shareholders to obtain involuntary dissolution carries the danger of abuse. Thus to survive summary judgment, Ps had to show that dissolution is reasonably necessary to protect their rights and interests. We agree with the trial court that Ps have not met this burden.
- As evidence that dissolution is reasonably necessary to protect their rights and interests, Ps presented the following evidence: (i) Malcolm has voting control of the company which he obtained through a "clandestine" purchase of stock from their father; (ii) Ps are not allowed meaningful participation in the corporation's affairs; (iii) the dispute gave rise to a violent confrontation between Malcolm and Candi; and (iv) Ps have an economic interest in reducing or ending the significant losses that the furniture business has suffered over the last 10 years.
- The distribution of voting shares is consistent with state law and does not by itself present a reasonable necessity for dissolution. Malcolm, Sr. was free to sell his shares to whomever he chose at whatever price he chose. There is no evidence of bad faith conduct by Malcolm, Jr. In fact, the record is clear that Ps have been paid significant dividends over the years, and that they received a significant payment in the period prior to the filing of this action. This is so despite the fact that their personal relationships had broken down. D argues that as minority shareholders, Ps' only right and interest is in continuing to receive dividend payments. D argues that since the dividend payments have continued, it is entitled to summary judgment.
- The evidence shows that Malcolm, Jr. has been instrumental in the daily operation of the corporation, and that Ps have played no role in these matters. Despite Ps' argument that the furniture store has lost money, the mobile home park has continued to generate significant profits which have been paid to Ps as dividends. Malcolm, Jr. asserts that the downward turn of furniture sales has ceased, and the furniture business is recovering. Ps presented no evidence to dispute this assertion.
- On this record we cannot say that the trial court erred in finding that the drastic remedy of dissolution was not reasonably necessary for the protection of the rights or interests of Ps. As holders of a minority of voting shares, Ps are not entitled to substitute their business judgment for D's with respect to the viability of the furniture business.

F. TRANSFER OF CONTROL

1. Introduction

The most complex problem involving the sale of corporate stock is the situation where a shareholder owning a majority interest (or a controlling minority interest) of the shares sells that control in a transaction from which the other shareholders are excluded (the controlling shareholder receiving a premium price per share on the stock over book or market value); or where all sell, but the owner of the control shares receives more per share than the other shareholders. Since a person purchasing "control" can dictate the affairs of the corporation, "control" is something of value.

2. The General Rule

The general rule is that a shareholder may sell his stock to whomever he wants to at the best price he can get.

a. Majority Shareholder

Most courts would say that a majority shareholder has the same right.

b. Agreement on Directors

If the majority shareholder agrees to have a majority of the board of directors resign and the purchaser's appointees elected (if this would naturally occur anyway), this is also not illegal per se.

3. Types of Purchase Transactions

Purchase of control may occur in several ways:

a. Direct from Shareholders—Purchase of Stock

The purchaser may approach the shareholders directly to purchase their shares. Here, the purchaser may buy all or only a controlling portion of the outstanding stock. If all of the outstanding stock is purchased, one price may be offered to controlling shareholders and a lower price may be offered to the minority shareholders.

b. Purchase of Assets

Here, the purchaser offers to buy the corporation's assets; the corporation itself holds a vote of its shareholders on the offer (normally, a majority vote is required to sell). If the necessary majority vote is secured, then the purchaser deposits *the* purchase price with the corporation, and this price is distributed pro rata to all the shareholders.

c. Merger or Consolidation

Here, the purchaser offers to merge the company to be acquired into it; a vote of the shareholders of the company to be merged is required. If it is secured (normally, a majority vote is required), then this company is merged into the acquiring company. Shareholders of the merged company receive a pro rata interest in the purchase price.

4. Exceptions to the General Rule

There are many exceptions to the general rule that a shareholder may sell to whomever he wishes for whatever price. In fact, it may be that, despite the general rule, sale of control is not possible unless all minority shareholders are given exactly the same terms as the majority shareholders. In other words, the courts apply the theory that one share owned by a majority shareholder ought to be worth the same as one share owned by a minority shareholder.

a. Theory of Corporate Action

In situations where the purchaser has first approached a majority shareholder and bought his stock and then either merged the corporation or bought its assets (giving the remaining shareholders in this transaction less than what the majority shareholders had previously been paid), some courts hold that the entire acquisition was really a "corporate action" and that the premium received by the majority should be placed in a pool and distributed pro rata to all shareholders.

b. Sale of a Corporate Office

Normally, in a purchase transaction, the majority also agrees to assist the purchaser in the accomplishment of some corporate action requiring the exercise of its corporate office. For example, the majority (having representation on the board of directors) may agree that, in connection with the sale of their shares, they will have the board resign and replaced with the purchaser's nominees. Some courts have held that any premium paid to majority shareholders must be distributed pro rata to all shareholders when a premium price has been paid based on the majority's exercise of its "corporate office" (on the basis that this belongs to the corporation as a whole, not to the majority exclusively).

c. Theory of Misrepresentation

Sometimes the majority will be involved in misrepresentation. For example, the majority shareholders may know that the purchaser is willing to pay $10 per share. It may buy the minority stock for $8 and then sell it and their own stock for $10 to the purchaser.

d. Looting Theory

In a situation where the purchaser buys only the controlling stock, the controlling shareholders may be liable to the minority when the purchaser later "loots" the corporation (if the majority shareholders knew or had reason to know that the purchaser intended to loot the corporation). Paying a "premium" is one indication or notice of possibly intended "looting."

e. Sale of a Corporate Asset

Where the purchaser buys only the majority stock, the majority may be liable for any premium received if the corporation has some particular "corporate asset" that creates this premium. But what constitutes a "corporate asset"? Is this not involved in every corporate sale, so that whenever a purchaser offers to buy control he must give this same offer to the minority shareholders?

1) Merger Versus Sale of Assets

Frandsen v. Jensen-Sundquist Agency, Inc.

802 F.2d 941 (7th Cir. 1986).

Facts. Jensen owned all of the stock of Jensen-Sundquist Agency, Inc., a holding company whose principal asset was a majority of the stock of the First Bank of Grantsburg. Jensen-Sundquist also owned an insurance company. Jensen sold 52% of his stock to members of his family (the "majority bloc"), 8% to Frandsen (P), and the rest to other non-family members. The stockholder agreement contained a provision stating that if the majority bloc wanted to sell their stock, they would first offer it to P at the same price, and that they would not sell their stock to any other person, firm, or organization without first offering it to the minority shareholders at the same price and upon the same terms. In 1984, First Wisconsin Corporation entered into negotiations with the president of Jensen-Sundquist to acquire First Bank of Grantsburg. First Wisconsin was to buy Jensen-Sundquist for cash, followed by a merger of First Bank of Grantsburg into a subsidiary of First Wisconsin. Under the proposed agreement, each stockholder of Jensen-Sundquist would receive $62 per share, which would translate into $88 per share of the bank. P announced that he was exercising his right of first refusal and would buy the majority's shares for $62 per share. The majority refused to sell its shares to P, and the deal was restructured so that Jensen-Sundquist would sell its shares in First Bank to First

Wisconsin at $88 per share and then liquidate. P brought suit against the majority bloc claiming breach of the shareholder agreement and against First Wisconsin claiming tortious interference with his contract rights. The district judge granted summary judgment for the defendants, and P appeals.

Issue. Was P's right of first refusal triggered by the merger transaction?

Held. No. Judgment affirmed.

- This case would be simple if Jensen-Sundquist had simply sold its principal asset, the bank, to First Wisconsin. Nothing in the shareholder agreement suggests that a minority shareholder has the right to block the sale of any corporate asset. The case is complicated because the deal was originally structured as a purchase of the holding company itself rather than just an asset of the holding company. P argues that his right of first refusal was triggered by the offer for the sale of the holding company, and that the fact that the offer was later withdrawn and restructured does not affect his right once he had already tried to exercise it. Even if P's argument is correct, we agree with the lower court that there was never an offer within the scope of the agreement.
- P's right of first refusal would be triggered by sale of the majority bloc's shares to First Wisconsin. This transaction was not a sale of stock but a merger of Jensen-Sundquist into First Wisconsin. First Wisconsin was not interested in becoming a majority shareholder of Jensen-Sundquist through the purchase of shares from the majority bloc. It only wanted the bank. The shareholders of a merged firm yield up all of the assets of the firm, and the firm dissolves. The majority bloc's shares would disappear, but not by sale because in a merger, the shares of the acquired firm are not bought but extinguished.
- P argues that the transaction completed here has the same practical effect as a sale of the majority bloc's shares, and the agreement was designed to protect P from such an occurrence. We note first that rights of first refusal are to be interpreted narrowly. This agreement was apparently designed to protect P from finding himself confronted with a new majority bloc made up of strangers. The sale of the assets of a company does not result in the substitution of a new majority bloc, and that is the possibility at which the protective provisions of the agreement are aimed. The agreement did not provide P with protection against a sale of the company.
- Because we find that no contractual right of P's was violated by this transaction, we cannot find that First Wisconsin was guilty of tortious interference with P's contractual rights.

---

2) Special Price for Control

Zetlin v. Hanson Holdings, Inc.

397 N.E.2d 387 (NY. 1979).

Facts. Zetlin (P) owned *2%* of Gable Industries. A group of shareholders (Ds) including Hanson sold their interest in Gable (44.6%, which was effective control) to another party for $15 a share when the market price was $7.38 a share. P wanted to be paid the same price as Ds and to share a proportionate amount of his stock. The trial court found for Ds; P appeals.

Issue. Absent fraud, can a controlling shareholder sell control for a premium price?

Held. Yes. Judgment affirmed.

- A majority interest can control the affairs of the company. Absent looting, conversion of a corporate opportunity, or other acts of bad faith, a controlling shareholder can sell the right to control the affairs of the corporation for a premium price.

---

3) Sale of a Corporate Asset

Perlman v. Feldmann

219 F.2d 173 (2d Cir. 1955), *cert. denied*, 349 U.S. 952 (1955).

Facts. This case involves a derivative shareholder action by minority shareholders of Newport Steel (Ps) against Feldmann (D) (president, chairman of the board, and owner of 37% of the common stock of the company) for selling his shares at $20 per share to Wilport Company, a syndicate of the company's customers who manufactured steel products (who thereby gained control of the company's steel output in a Korean War shortage market). After the sale, the directors of the company (who were the appointees of D) resigned, and the new purchasers were appointed as the board. The market price of the stock at the time of sale was $12 per share; the book value was $17. Ps claimed that the compensation received by D included compensation for the sale of a "corporate asset" held in trust by D as fiduciary for all the shareholders (the asset being the power to control allocation of the company's steel output in a tight market). The trial court found the price paid was "fair" (although it did not indicate what the price would have been if the power to control steel distribution had not been included; Ps had the burden of proof to show that the value of the stock was lower than what was paid). It was alleged by Ps that, due to the shortage, the company might have been able to use its supplies to get interest-free advances from customers to build new plant facilities, as well as to build up patronage in the area where it then could have competed successfully in normal markets. The trial court found that it had not been proved that these advantages existed. Ps appeal the judgment of the lower court.

Issue. Has there been a breach of fiduciary duty by the officer, director, and majority shareholder in selling majority control in these factual circumstances?

Held. Yes. Judgment for Ps. Remanded to the lower court for a finding of the value of the premium received for the stock of D. Premium to be distributed among all of the remaining shareholders.

- The director, officer, and majority shareholders all have a fiduciary duty to the corporation and to the minority shareholders.
- Normally, a majority shareholder may sell his stock, even to his customers. But here, there was an element of corporate goodwill that belonged to all shareholders. In a time of market shortage where a corporation's product commands an unusually large premium, a fiduciary may not appropriate to himself the value of that premium. Except in times of extreme shortage, Newport Steel was not able to compete profitably with other steel mills due in part to its aging facilities. Newport could have used the period of short supply to build up patronage in the area, and, as Ps argue, obtain interest-free funds from purchasers to update its facilities. These actions could have made Newport profitable even after the period of short supply ended. As a fiduciary, D could not take this profit for himself in the form of a premium price for his stock.
- The goodwill consisted of the opportunity to get interest-free money from customers, etc., which was created by a wartime shortage market. D had the burden to show that these advantages did not exist.

Dissent. The majority's opinion fails to specify what fiduciary duty D violated, and whether it was a duty imposed upon him as the dominant shareholder or as a director. There is no evidence that D knew or had reason to know that Wilport intended to use its power of management to the detriment of the corporation. Had that been the case, D would have been under a duty not to make the transfer. However, this duty appears to be more akin to the duty we all have not to assist another in committing a tort rather than a fiduciary duty. Wilport may have been able to purchase more steel than it would otherwise have been able to obtain due to its ownership of the company. However, there is nothing illegal about a dominant shareholder purchasing from its own company at the same prices it offers to others. There is no evidence that Newport was harmed.

4) Sale of Corporate Office

Essex Universal Corp. v. Yates

305 F.2d 572 (2d Cir. 1962).

Facts. Essex Universal Corp. (P) contracted to buy 28.3% of the stock of a company traded on the stock exchange from Yates (D). Provision was included giving P an option to require a majority of the existing directors to resign and be replaced by the purchaser's nominees (board of 14; equal number elected in each of three years). Summary judgment was granted in the trial court for D. Stock was sold at $8 per share; the market price was $6 per share. D refused to close the transaction on the basis that the contract for sale of control was invalid as against public policy.

Issue. Is a contract for sale of control, which provides for resignation and election of new directors, invalid?

Held. No. Summary judgment reversed and case remanded for trial.

- It is illegal to sell a corporate office or management control by itself.
- But a majority of the stock may be sold with an agreement to replace directors immediately in some instances, even at a premium over market price. This may not be done, however, if sellers should reasonably know that buyers will loot the company, or if the transfer also has with it the transfer of a unique corporate asset, as in *Feldmann (supra)*, but there is no implication of this here.
- The next issue is whether less than a majority of the stock may be sold with a promise to replace a majority of the board. In public companies, a substantial block normally amounts to control; inevitably, the purchaser will control the board. Here, 28% of the stock was sold; normally, this is control of the corporation in a public company. The burden of proof is on D to show that the interest transferred did not carry actual control, and thus the promise to transfer it was improper.

Concurrence. A clause where the sale of less than the majority promises to transfer control of the board should be void by public policy. Judge Lombard's test is too difficult to apply. It could never be known, short of an actual vote, whether directors could actually be elected. Directors can fill vacancies, but must abide by fiduciary duties in doing so. To permit mass resignation and replacement (except where 50% or more of the stock is transferred), and only hold directors liable for "reasonable notice" of subsequent looting, is to exceed what shareholders expect in the protection of their interests.

Chapter VII

Mergers, Acquisitions, and Takeovers

A. Mergers and Acquisitions

1. Introduction

Corporation law balances the right of directors to manage with the power of shareholders to veto fundamental changes—*i.e.*, mergers into another firm, amendment of the articles, dissolution of the corporation, sales of substantially all of the company's assets to another firm, etc. In most states, specific statutory provisions apply to all of these fundamental changes. In addition, the fiduciary concepts of fairness, the prohibition against self-dealing, etc., also apply. Also, in many situations, federal law may apply (such as the proxy rules when shareholder proxies are solicited).

2. Ways of Gaining Control

There are many alternative ways to gain control of a company:

a. **Buy Stock of Company A from the Shareholders of A for Cash** (*i.e.*, a "Cash Tender Offer")

b. **Buy the Stock of Company A from Its Shareholders with Stock of Another Company (B)** (*i.e.*, a "Stock Tender Offer")

c. **Merge One Company into Another** (*i.e.*, Combine the Two Companies)

In a statutory merger, state law rules are followed and A takes title to the assets of B and assumes B's liabilities, B dissolves, and B's shareholders receive A's stock. In a consolidation, a new firm, C, is formed. It gets title to the assets of both A and B; they dissolve and A and B shareholders receive C stock.

d. Buy the Assets of One Company (A) with Cash

e. Buy the Assets of One Company (A) with the Stock of Another (B)

f. Gain Voting Control Through a Proxy Contest

3. Mergers and Consolidations

a. Introduction

A "merger" occurs when one or more corporations are absorbed into another existing corporation. A "consolidation" involves the formation of a new corporation that takes over the assets and liabilities of one or more existing corporations. A merger and a consolidation are, in effect, the same thing (they reach a similar result). The surviving corporation issues its stock for the stock of the absorbed corporations and has the assets of all of the combined companies.

b. Statutory Requirements

State statutes always indicate the exact steps that must be taken to effectuate a merger or consolidation.

1) Shareholder Consent

The shareholders of all of the corporations involved must consent. Most states require a two-thirds majority, but some states require less; and at least one state has eliminated the need for shareholder approval of the surviving corporation (at least where the number of shares issued represents a small minority of the total shares outstanding).

2) Directors' Approval

Majority approval of the directors of all companies is required.

c. The Effect

1) Assets

The assets of the merged or consolidated corporations become the assets of the survivor.

2) Liabilities

The liabilities of all of the corporations involved become the liabilities of the survivor. All liens on the assets of the absorbed corporations remain in effect on the assets in the hands of the survivor corporation.

d. Dissenters' Rights

Most states permit shareholders who vote against the merger to elect to have their shares appraised and purchased by the corporation. In order to preserve this right, the shareholder must follow a specific set of steps. However, some states have limited dissenters' rights. Delaware does not allow such a right if the stock the dissenter would receive in the merger is listed on a national securities exchange or is held by 2,000 or more shareholders.

4. The De Facto Merger Doctrine

a. Introduction

The state law requirements for a merger or consolidation are more stringent than for a sale of assets or stock. Also, the rights of minority shareholders in the selling company receive greater protection (appraisal rights) in a merger. Therefore, in seeking to acquire another company, the acquiring company normally attempts to follow a method other than the merger route. On the other hand, courts sometimes treat an acquisition as a merger even if it has apparently followed another route (if the result is substantially the same as a merger). This is the "de facto merger" doctrine.

1) Treatment as De Facto Merge

Farris v. Glen Alden Corp.

143 A.2d 25 (Pa. 1958).

Facts. A shareholder (P) of Glen Alden Corp. sued to get the right of a dissenting shareholder (as in a merger) to have his shares appraised and purchased by the corporation for cash. Glen Alden (D) was principally in the coal business (and had a huge $14 million tax loss carry-forward). List was a holding company in many different businesses (through its subsidiaries). One of List's subsidiaries had bought 40% of D's common stock off the market a year earlier. At that time, three of List's directors became members of D's board of directors.

D's reorganization agreement provided for D to issue its shares to purchase the assets of List; but List was much larger than D and would control the board of the new company, and its shareholders would own 75% of the stock of the combined companies after the transaction was over. D assumed all of List's liabilities, including all of List's outstanding stock options. The new company would be named List Alden; the board was to be a combination of the boards of the two companies. A disinterested majority of the shareholders of D approved the deal. The List corporation would be dissolved after its assets were acquired.

P sued for an injunction based on the fact that the notice of the Glen Alden shareholders meeting was not proper for a ***merger*** transaction. D moved for judgment on the pleadings on the basis that the transaction was a "purchase" of assets, which gave no dissenters' rights by state law. The trial court found for P and the injunction was issued. D appeals.

Issue. Is the transaction a de facto merger, such that D corporation must comply with state law applicable to mergers, including giving dissenting shareholders the right of appraisal of their shares?

Held. Yes. Judgment affirmed.

- The different forms of combination came into being due to the tax laws and the efforts of lawyers to create forms of combination that would give the desired tax benefits. Thus, it is no longer a simple matter to determine which form is really being used (and it is not enough that a transaction meet the stated statutory requisites of state law). Rather, the agreement will be examined, as well as the consequences of the transaction and the purpose behind the state corporation laws.
- The rationale of the state statute permitting dissenters' rights in a merger is that the corporation loses its "essential character" in a combination with another company. The fundamental relationship of the shareholders to the corporation is altered.
- Such a fundamental change occurred here: (i) D is primarily a coal company, so the combined companies will be diverse; (ii) the combination would be more than twice the size of D and has seven times the debt of D; (iii) control is in the hands of List's directors (11 of the 17 directors); (iv) 75% of the stock would be in the hands of List's shareholders; and (v) the book value of D's stock will go from $38 per share to $21 per share in the combined company.

- The state law provision that in a purchase of assets the corporation's shareholders do not have dissenters' rights means only that these rights are not given in situations where there is a purchase of assets without the incidents of a merger, as is the case here.
- Even if state law does provide that, in a purchase of assets, there should be no dissenters' rights, we would not overlook the reality of the situation—this is really a merger (List is merging with D).
- Hence, the shareholder approval of the transaction is invalid, and the state merger statute (requiring notice and appraisal rights to dissenting shareholders) must be complied with.

---

2) Sale of Assets

Hariton v. Arco Electronics, Inc.

188 A.2d 123 (Del. 1963).

Facts. Arco Electronics, Inc. (D) entered into an agreement with Loral Electronics ("Loral") whereby D would sell all of its assets to Loral in exchange for 283,000 shares of Loral stock. The Loral stock was to be distributed to D's shareholders, and D would be completely liquidated. The agreement was put to a shareholder vote and approved. An Arco shareholder who did not vote (P) challenged the validity of the sale of Arco's assets for stock on the basis that the transaction is illegal and unfair. The lower court granted summary judgment for D. P appeals, alleging that this plan is not a true sale of assets, but a de facto merger.

Issue. Is the sale of D's assets for Loral stock really a de facto merger?

Held. No. Judgment affirmed.

- A sale of assets for stock, followed by dissolution, has the effect of a merger. In this case, however, D is being absorbed into Loral and the business will continue in an altered form. P concedes that if the two steps taken in this case were undertaken separately, they would have been legal. That is, a sale of assets, followed by a separate proceeding to dissolve and distribute, would be legal even though it accomplishes the same result.
- We hold that the reorganization here accomplished through the sale of assets and a mandatory plan of dissolution and distribution is legal. Although it achieves the same results as a de facto merger, it is not one.

---

5. Freeze-Out Mergers

a. "Freeze-Out" Mergers and the Appraisal Remedy

Controlling shareholders may find it advantageous to "freeze out" minority holders through a merger in which these holders must accept cash for their shares. Most corporation statutes provide that holders who vote against a merger may insist that their corporation buy their shares at a price set by a court. (In most states, this same right belongs to shareholders who vote against the sale of all or substantially all of their corporation's assets, and in some states, it also belongs to shareholders who vote against certain important amendments to the articles of incorporation. Many states have repealed the legislation granting such rights insofar as it applies to corporations with publicly traded shares, leaving shareholders in these corporations to the market.)

Minority holders have challenged the legality of freeze-out mergers, putting into question whether "appraisal" is their exclusive remedy. In *Singer v. Magnavox*, 380 A.2d 969 (1977), the Delaware Supreme Court ruled that (i) a merger "for the sole purpose of freezing out minority shareholders is an abuse of the corporate process" and (ii) even if the merger had a legitimate purpose, the controlling shareholders bore the burden to demonstrate its "entire fairness." The legitimate purpose requirement came to mean little because the Delaware Supreme Court held that a controlling shareholder's legitimate purpose would suffice. But "entire fairness" proved significant because it meant that the minority holder's lawyer could use the class action procedure (instead of the appraisal procedure, which required each shareholder to notify the corporation prior to the vote, cast a "no" vote, and petition the court for an appraisal) and perhaps obtain a more favorable measure of damages.

1) "Entire Fairness"

Weinberger v. UOP, Inc.

457 A.2d 701 (Del. Super. Ct. 1983).

Facts. In 1975, Signal Companies, Inc. ("Signal") proposed to acquire a controlling interest in UOP for $19 per share. UOP's shares were then trading on the NYSE for $14 per share. UOP's board sought $25 per share, but after arm's length bargaining, accepted $21 per share. At that price Signal acquired 50.5% of UOP, although many more shares were tendered. Signal nominated and elected six of UOP's 13 directors. When UOP's CEO retired later that year, Signal arranged to replace him with one of its longtime employees. This new CEO succeeded his predecessor on the UOP board and joined Signal's board, too.

In 1978, Signal's management directed two Signal officers to study the feasibility of acquiring the balance of UOP's outstanding shares. The two officers were also directors of both Signal and UOP. They concluded that the acquisition would be a good investment at any price up to $24 per share. At $24, the report projected a 15.5% return on investment. At $21—paying $17 million less—the report projected a 15.7% return. Neither the two officers nor anyone else ever disclosed this conclusion or their feasibility study to any non-Signal UOP director or shareholder.

At a meeting of Signal's executive committee on February 28, 1978, senior management proposed to offer $20 to $21 per share. UOP's CEO, who attended the meeting, labeled such an offer "generous." The executive committee authorized management to negotiate with UOP with the intention of presenting a proposal to Signal's board on March 6.

Between February 28 and March 6, UOP's CEO consulted by phone with all of UOP's outside directors and retained Lehman Brothers to render a fairness opinion about the $20 to $21 price. He picked Lehman, the CEO testified, because, having served as UOP's investment banker for many years, it could best meet the deadline, then three business days away. UOP's CEO advised Signal's management that it should offer $21 per share in order to obtain the approval of UOP outside directors. Meanwhile, Lehman conducted a hurried investigation and submitted a letter opining that a price in the $20 to $21 range would be "fair" to the minority shareholders.

On March 6, both the Signal and UOP boards met to consider the proposed merger. All board members had a copy of the proposal, UOP's most recent financial statements and financial data for 1974 to 1977, market price information, and Lehman's "fairness opinion letter." The outside directors resolved to accept the offer.

UOP's management submitted the merger to the shareholders at the May 26 annual meeting. Minority shareholders cast more than enough votes for approval to make the merger effective.

Weinberger (P), a former shareholder of UOP, brought a class action suit against UOP and Signal, challenging the cash-out merger as unfair to the minority shareholders. A chartered investment analyst called by P testified that both a discounted cash flow analysis and a comparative analysis of the premium paid over market in 10 other tender offer-merger combinations showed that UOP's stock was worth $26 per share. The chancellor rejected this testimony as inconsistent with the "Delaware block" or weighted average method of valuation, which assigns a particular weight to assets, market price, earnings, and other "elements of value." The chancellor held that Signal had dealt fairly with UOP's minority shareholders and paid them a fair price, and so entered judgment against P. P appeals. The Delaware Supreme Court reheard the appeal en banc.

Issues.

(i) Did Signal bear the burden of showing that the merger was "fair" to the minority shareholders?

(ii) Did the evidence show that Signal dealt fairly with UOP's minority shareholders?

(iii) In evaluating the fairness of the price that Signal paid for UOP's shares, must the court use the so-called "Delaware block" method of valuation?

(iv) Did the evidence show that Signal paid a fair price?

(v) When minority shareholders challenge a freeze-out merger, must the controlling shareholder(s) demonstrate that the merger serves a legitimate business purpose?

Held. (i) Yes. (ii) No. (iii) No. (iv) No. (v) No. Judgment reversed.

- Signal had to show that the transaction was "fair" to the minority shareholders—that they received what an independent board would have secured for them—because directors who sat on both company's boards participated in the UOP board's decisionmaking about the merger without disclosing all material information in their possession.
- Signal failed to show that it dealt fairly with the minority shareholders or that it paid them a fair price. With respect to its dealings, Signal failed to disclose: (i) the feasibility study, which was derived from UOP information, or that Signal considered a purchase at $24 per share a good investment; or (ii) the cursory nature of the Lehman investigation or the serious time constraints set by Signal that caused it to be cursory. The negotiations were modest at best. Crawford (UOP's CEO), Signal's man at UOP, never really talked price with Signal. The minority stockholders were denied critical information—such as that Signal considered a price of $24 to be a good investment. Since this would have meant over $17 million to the minority, we cannot find that the vote was informed.
- In evaluating the "fairness" of the price, a court need not use the "Delaware block" method exclusively. A court may use any valuation technique generally acceptable in the financial community, otherwise admissible in court, and consistent with section 262(h) of the Delaware Corporation Code, which governs the appraisal remedy. Section 262(h) provides that, in ascertaining "fair" price, a court should consider "all relevant factors," excluding "[o]nly the speculative elements of value that may arise from the 'accomplishment or expectation' of the merger." This eliminates the use only of "pro forma" data and projections of a speculative variety, not elements of future value, including the nature of the enterprise, which are known or susceptible of proof as of the date of the merger, or damages resulting from the taking. The chancellor may grant other relief if this appraisal remedy proves inadequate because of fraud, misrepresentation, self-dealing, deliberate waste of corporate assets, or gross and palpable overreaching. Except for this case and other designated cases in which a plaintiff shareholder relied on the formerly prevailing interpretation of section 262(h), that section now governs the financial remedy available to minority shareholders in a cash-out merger.
- In evaluating the fairness of a nonfraudulent transaction, price may be the preponderant consideration. In light of the testimony of P's chartered investment analyst that UOP shares were worth at least $26 per share, Signal failed to show that it paid a fair price (particularly since paying UOP's minority shareholders $24 would have had relatively little long-term effect on Signal given that the returns projected by Signal's officers at $21 and $24 per share differed by only .2%).

- When minority shareholders challenge a freeze-out merger, the controlling shareholder(s) need no longer demonstrate that the merger serves a legitimate business purpose. Requiring such a demonstration adds no meaningful protection now that the expanded appraisal remedy is available to shareholders and the chancellor has broad discretion to fashion such relief as the facts of a given case may dictate.

---

2) Eliminating Public Ownership

Coggins v. New England Patriots Football Club, Inc.

492 N.E.2d 1112 (Mass. 1986).

Facts. In 1959, Sullivan purchased a franchise for one of the eight original football teams in the American Football League and formed the New England Patriots Football Club, Inc. ("Old Patriots") with nine other investors. Later, shares of nonvoting stock were sold to the public. Sullivan had effective control of the corporation and served as president until 1974, when the other shareholders voted him out. In 1975, after purchasing all 100,000 voting shares of the corporation, Sullivan again gained control of the corporation. He then voted out all of the hostile directors, and elected a friendly board. In 1976, Sullivan organized a new corporation called the New Patriots Football Club, Inc. ("New Patriots"). The boards of both the New Patriots and the Old Patriots executed an agreement to merge the two corporations. After the merger, the voting stock of the Old Patriots would be extinguished and the nonvoting stock of the Old Patriots would be exchanged for $15 per share. Coggins owned nonvoting stock and opposed the merger. He filed this class action on behalf of nonvoting shareholders (Ps), alleging that the merger was unfair and illegal. The trial judge held for Ps but did not undo the merger. Instead, the judge held Ps were entitled to rescissory damages.

Issue. Was this merger fair and legal?

Held. No. Judgment affirmed.

- This transaction is a cash freeze-out merger. The dangers of self-dealing and abuse of fiduciary duties are greatest in situations like this, where a controlling stockholder and corporate director choose to eliminate public ownership in the corporation. The corporate directors who benefit from this transfer of ownership must demonstrate how the legitimate goals of the corporation are furthered by the merger. The defendant bears the burden of showing that the elimination of public ownership was in furtherance of a business purpose, and that the transaction was fair considering the totality of the circumstances.

- The trial judge found, and we agree, that the defendants have failed to demonstrate that the merger served any valid corporate purpose. In fact, it appears that the sole reason for the merger was to benefit Sullivan. In his campaign to win back control of the corporation, Sullivan borrowed over $5 million. It appears that the sole reason for the merger was to enable Sullivan to pay off his personal loans. Because no valid corporate purpose can be demonstrated, there is no need to consider the elements of fairness of the transaction.

- The normal remedy for an impermissible freeze-out merger is rescission. However, the merger is now 10 years old, and an effective and orderly rescission is not feasible. Ps are entitled to damages based on the present value of the Patriots, not the value in 1976. Ps are entitled to what they would have if the merger had not gone through—*i.e.*, what their stock would be worth today plus interest. Finally, we reinstate Ps' claim for waste against the individual defendants. This claim was dismissed by the lower court, but we reverse the dismissal and remand the issue for trial.

---

3) Remedies

Rabkin v. Philip A. Hunt Chemical Corporation

498 A.2d 1099 (Del. 1985).

Facts. Turner & Newall Industries, Inc. ("Turner & Newall") was the majority shareholder of Hunt Chemical Corporation ("Hunt"). Turner & Newall agreed to sell its 63.4% interest in Hunt to Olin Corporation ("Olin") at $25 per share pursuant to a stock purchase agreement. The agreement stated that if Olin acquired the remaining Hunt stock within one year, Olin would have to pay $25 per share for that stock as well. Apparently, there was no discussion between the boards of Hunt and Olin during the one-year period regarding the purchase of the remaining Hunt stock. However, it is clear from Olin's interoffice memoranda that Olin at all times anticipated owning 100% of Hunt. Shortly after the expiration of the one-year period, Olin's board unanimously voted to acquire the remaining Hunt stock, and commissioned an investment banking firm to determine if $20 per share was a fair price. The investment firm, along with Olin's financial advisors and counsel, found the price to be fair, and Olin's board issued a proxy statement favoring the proposal. The minority stockholders of Hunt (Ps) filed suit, alleging that the stock price was grossly inadequate because Olin had unfairly manipulated the timing of the merger to avoid the one-year commitment that would have forced it to pay $25 per share. The lower court dismissed the claim, finding that under *Weinberger v. UOP, Inc., supra*, absent allegations of fraud or deception, a minority stockholder's rights in a cash-out merger are limited to an appraisal. Ps appeal.

Issue. Did the trial court err in dismissing the claim on the ground that absent deception, Ps' sole remedy under *Weinberger* is an appraisal?

Held. Yes. Judgment reversed and case remanded.

- The trial court's narrow interpretation of *Weinberger* was erroneous. In that case, we made clear that appraisal is not a stockholder's sole remedy. We specifically noted that this remedy may not be adequate in certain cases, such as when there is possible fraud, misrepresentation, self-dealing, waste, or gross overreaching. *Weinberger* requires fair dealing which we defined as embracing questions of when the transaction was timed, how it was initiated, structured, negotiated, and disclosed to the directors, and how the approvals of the directors and the stockholders were obtained. This case does not turn on deception, but involves broader concerns regarding procedural fairness. Ps are not challenging the valuation itself, which is the traditional subject of an appraisal. In this case, Ps are seeking to enforce a contractual right to receive $25 per share, which they claim was unfairly destroyed by Olin's manipulative conduct.
- There were interoffice memoranda discussing the disadvantages of paying $25 under the one-year agreement. Three Hunt directors received this memorandum. This is indicative of manipulative activity.
- The complaint does not simply allege that the price was unfair. It asserts a conscious intent by Olin, as the majority shareholder of Hunt, to deprive the Hunt minority (Ps) of the same $25 deal it received in its stock purchase from Turner & Newall. The memorandum received by the three Hunt directors raises issues regarding their duty of loyalty to Hunt and the minority shareholders. We find that the facts alleged by Ps regarding the avoidance of the one-year commitment support a claim of unfair dealing sufficient to survive dismissal.

6. De Facto Non-Merger

a. Introduction

As discussed in section 4 *supra*, courts will sometimes treat an acquisition as a merger (if the result is substantially the same as a merger) even if the transaction has apparently followed another route. This is known as the "de facto merger" doctrine. In the case below, the plaintiff attempts to argue the opposite—that is, that the transaction is ***not*** a merger—and asks the court to adopt a "de facto non-merger" doctrine.

1) De Facto Non-Merger Argument Rejected

Rauch v. RCA Corporation

861 F.2d 29 (2d Cir. 1988).

Facts. General Electric Company entered into a merger agreement with RCA Corporation (D) under which all common shares of D would be converted to cash. Under the agreement, holders of preferred stock would receive $40 per share. Rauch (P), a holder of preferred stock, filed this class action arguing that the transaction constituted a liquidation or winding up of D, as a result of which holders of preferred stock were entitled to $100 per share in accordance with the redemption provisions of D's certificate of incorporation. The district court dismissed the complaint after finding that the transaction was a bona fide merger. P appeals.

Issue. Was the transaction a bona fide merger?

Held. Yes. Judgment affirmed.

- ♦ Delaware corporations law clearly states that a conversion of shares to cash that is carried out in order to accomplish a merger is legally distinct from a redemption of shares by a corporation. The RCA-GE merger agreement complied fully with the merger provisions in question. D chose to convert its stock to cash to accomplish the merger, and in the process chose not to redeem the preferred stock. It had every right to do so under Delaware law.
- ♦ Delaware law provides specific protection to shareholders who believe they have not received fair value for their stock as a result of a merger. However, P disavows any appraisal theory or remedy in this case.

---

7. LLC Mergers

a. Court Will Enforce Provisions of LLC Agreement Unless It Allows Breach of Fiduciary Duties

VGS, Inc. v. Castiel

2000 WL 1277372 (Del. Ch.) *aff'd mem.*, 781 A.2d 696 (Del. 2001).

Facts. Castiel (P) formed Virtual Geosatellite LLC ("the LLC"). The LLC's members consisted of Virtual Geosatellite Holdings, Inc. ("Holdings"), and Ellipso, Inc. ("Ellipso"), both controlled by P, and Sahagen Satellite LLC, which was controlled by Sahagen. Under the LLC agreement, Holdings held 63.5% of the equity of the LLC, Sahagen Satellite 25%, and Ellipso 11.5%. P had power to appoint, remove, and replace two of the three members of the board of managers, and therefore, the power to prevent any board decision that he opposed. The board of managers consisted of P, Quinn, and Sahagen. Sahagen and P had very different views on how the company should be run and disagreed constantly. Eventually, Quinn began to agree with Sahagen that P was a poor manager and should be ousted. Without notice to P, Quinn and Sahagen acted by written consent to merge the LLC into VGS, Inc. After the merger, Holdings and Ellipso had only a 37.5% interest in the corporation, and Sahagen Satellite had a 62.5% interest. P filed suit, arguing that the managers could only act by unanimous vote to approve a merger, and that he was entitled to notice of the vote.

Issues.

(i) Could board members approve the merger by a majority vote?

(ii) Was P entitled to notice?

Held. (i) Yes. (ii) Yes. Merger rescinded.

- The LLC agreement here is unique in that it allows action to be taken by a vote of the board of three managers rather than a vote of the equity interest. The agreement does not state whether the board must act unanimously or by majority vote. However, if a unanimous vote were required, many of the provisions of the LLC agreement would be rendered meaningless. For example, one section of the agreement states that Sahagen's approval is needed for a merger, consolidation, or reorganization of the LLC. This obviously implies that the other two board members were free to act on other matters upon only a majority vote. I find that the board of managers did have authority to act on the merger by majority vote.
- Neither the LLC Act nor the LLC agreement in this case requires notice to P before Sahagen and Quinn could act by written consent. Clearly, the members did not inform P because they knew he would veto the plan by removing Quinn from the board and appointing a friendly member in his place. Their success depended upon P not knowing of the vote.
- However, Sahagen and Quinn owed P a duty of loyalty and good faith. Under the circumstances of this case and the structure of this LLC, I find that Sahagen and Quinn's failure to give P advance notice of their merger plans breached their fiduciary duty of loyalty. Accordingly, I order the merger to be rescinded.

B. TAKEOVERS

1. Introduction

Control transactions serve as a mechanism for outsider monitoring of management. Necessarily, then, these transactions pose a conflict of interest for management. Consider these illustrations:

(i) An acquiring corporation's managers may favor a profit-reducing acquisition because expansion accompanied by a reduction in earnings volatility will reduce the risk that these managers will forfeit some of the value of their investment in their careers at the acquiring corporation and other "undiversified human capital" (which has no value to a public shareholder who can hold a diversified portfolio of investments);

(ii) A target corporation's managers may favor a profit-reducing transaction because of a promise of continued employment; or they may oppose it because they fear firing.

An individual, group, or corporation can obtain control of the productive assets of a "target corporation" by: (i) purchasing the target's assets, (ii) merging with it, or (iii) purchasing a controlling block of its voting shares. The first two transactions, however, require approval not only by the target's shareholders but by its board of directors as well. This explains why control block purchases serve as a vital mechanism for monitoring management. A potential control block purchaser will ordinarily prefer this transaction to a proxy fight in part because if a proxy fight results in an increase in share price, he would necessarily share this gain pro rata with other shareholders.

a. Tender Offers and Their Regulation

A tender offerer makes a conditional public offer, open for a limited period, to buy the target's shares, usually at a price well above market. The conditions, which will include at least (i) a minimum tender and (ii) no material change for the worse in the business or financial structure of the target, appear in the offering documents. The bidder may offer to pay cash or to exchange a package of its securities for all or some of the shares of the class sought. (In the case of a "partial bid," the bidder ordinarily reserves the right to accept more than the number of shares specified.) Acceptance requires depositing shares with a depository bank serving as the bidder's agent. If none of the contingencies entitling the bidder to cancel or reduce its offer occur or if the bidder waives its right to do so, this bank uses previously deposited funds to buy the tendered shares on behalf of the bidder.

Federal law, principally the 1968 Williams Act, which added sections 13 and 14 of the Securities Exchange Act of 1934, limits tender offers primarily by prescribing (i) the minimum period during which shareholders may tender, (ii) the disclosures that must be made in connection with a tender offer, and (iii) the withdrawal and "equal treatment" rights of tendering shareholders to their shares. State corporation law, particularly the law of fiduciary duties, serves as the principal limit on the conduct of target managements. Most states have enacted anti-takeover statutes, some of which, such as Pennsylvania's, virtually prohibit hostile offers.

b. Hostile Transactions

Because hostile transactions necessarily create a conflict of interest for the officers and directors of a target corporation, these transactions raise some difficult issues: Once a rejected suitor makes a hostile tender offer, what role, if any, should the target's officers and directors play? May they take actions to discourage the suitor from pursuing the tender offer? May they do so in order to induce the suitor to bargain with them rather than with dispersed, and thus perhaps less effective, shareholders? If the target's officers and directors may take such actions, under what standards should courts review them?

1) Early Doctrine

Cheff v. Mathes

199 A.2d 548 (Del. Ct. 1964).

Facts. Minority shareholder Mathes (P) filed a derivative action seeking to set aside the purchase by the company ("Holland") of its own securities from another corporation, Motor Products Corp. ("MP"). The company's sales and earnings had been declining; management had completed a reorganization, which it assumed would halt the decline. MP, owned by a man with a reputation for "raiding" other corporations, had purchased an interest in the company, then had inquired about a merger and sought representation on Holland's board. Holland's board consisted of the president and the legal counsel and others (Ds), all of whom owned stock in Holland. Ds voted to purchase the shares of Holland owned by MP at a price above the market price, based on the facts that: (i) if MP took over, it threatened to reorganize Holland's sales distribution system; and (ii) the threat of the takeover was causing poor employee morale and in some cases employees were quitting. P argued that the purchase was designed simply to perpetuate Ds in office, and the lower court agreed. Ds appeal.

Issue. Was the purchase of the corporation's shares undertaken for an improper purpose?

Held. No. Judgment reversed and case remanded to enter judgment for Ds.

- When directors face the threat of a corporation takeover and they purchase stock of the corporation, there is a conflict of interest (*i.e.*, the purchase may be to prevent a takeover and thus to perpetuate the directors or officers in office). When this occurs the burden of proof is on the fiduciaries to show that they have acted in good faith in the interest of the corporation and its shareholders.
- Directors who have a pecuniary interest in the corporation (such as the president and the legal counsel, since they received salaries) are held to a higher standard of proof than other directors.
- In this case, the facts support a showing that Ds had a proper business motive for the stock purchases; thus, their actions were in good faith. They had reasonable grounds to believe that a threat existed to corporate policy that they believed was in the best interests of the corporation (maintenance of the sales system).

Comment. Because corporate tacticians could easily manufacture policy conflicts, *Cheff* practically immunized almost all defensive tactics.

---

c. Defensive Tactics

1) Supermajority Provisions

A successful tender offeror typically eliminates a target's remaining shareholders through a "second-step" merger requiring shareholder approval (unless the bidder has acquired nearly all of the stock and can utilize a "short form" merger). A majority or a two-thirds vote ordinarily constitutes approval, but the articles may require more votes and perhaps an unusually large quorum, too. (The articles will also require this supermajority to amend this provision.) Such a provision discourages partial bids. Most corporation statutes permit a simple majority vote to adopt a supermajority provision, but the Revised Model Business Corporation Act ("RMBCA") and the American Law Institute's Corporate Governance Project would require the specified supermajority to adopt it.

2) "Fair Price" Provisions

These provisions provide for the waiver of one or more takeover obstacles if the bidder pays a "fair price" in the second-step transaction. They usually define "fair price" as at least equal to the highest of: (i) the highest price paid by the bidder for any shares acquired during or immediately before the tender offer; (ii) the highest price at which the stock has traded during some period; (iii) a price that is in the same proportion of the share price at the time that the second-step transaction was announced as the tender offer price was to the share price at the time that the tender offer was announced; and (iv) the product of multiplying the target's average earnings per share by the bidder's average price-earnings ratio. The definition may yield a second-step price significantly higher than the tender offer price, which deters shareholders from tendering.

Some fair price provisions provide that if the bidder fails to propose a second-step merger at a "fair price," target shareholders may insist that the target purchase their stock at that price.

3) Staggered Board Provisions

A provision in the articles dividing the board into classes, each elected in different years, may delay a bidder's acquisition of control—but only if the target's directors choose to remain on the board after a hostile bidder has acquired a majority of the stock.

4) "Shark Repellant" Bylaws

"Shark repellant" provisions typically: (i) require that any person wishing to bring any matter before the shareholders' meeting or to nominate directors must give the board advance notice; (ii) grant the board, but not the shareholders, the power to fill newly created board positions; and (iii) constrain shareholder action through written consent.

5) Poison Pills

a) A Good Illustration: The Original Pill

The target board used the power bestowed on it by a "blank check" provision in the articles to create a new class of preferred stock possessing a critical conversion feature (the "poison in the pill") and distributed this stock as a dividend to its common stockholders. The critical conversion feature enabled a holder of the preferred stock to convert it into an acquirer's common stock in a ratio that effectively permitted the holder to purchase the common stock at a steep discount. This "flip-over" feature would become operative, however, only if an acquirer were to purchase more than a specified percentage of the target's stock and subsequently acquire the target in a business combination, such as a merger or an asset sale. A bidder trying to minimize the threat of dilution might offer to buy all or nearly all of the target's shares. A bidder might also negotiate with the board because the "flip-over" provision typically empowered the board to "call" or "redeem" the preferred stock at a low price for a short period after a triggering event occurred.

When poison pills are challenged in a lawsuit, courts often focus more on the board's failure to redeem (or its selective redemption) than on the board's decision to adopt the pill.

b) Adaptations

(1) "Fair Price" Provision

The pill was made effective against bidders who declined to engage in a second-step transaction by adding a "fair price" provision to the redemption formula of the convertible preferred stock that entitled the holder to compel a buy-back from the target at a price equal to the highest paid by the bidder in acquiring target shares (the "flip in"). Triggering events were expanded to include a bidder's substantial open-market purchases, intercorporate transactions between the two firms once the bidder acquired control, or the bidder's failure to propose a second-step merger within a specific period.

(2) "Share Purchase Rights Plan"

The target distributes a dividend of warrants or "rights" to its shareholders that conditionally entitles all but the bidder and its affiliates to purchase the target's stock for a specified period. The condition is typically the announcement of a tender offer or a major stock acquisition. If the target is taken over, the "rights" become exercisable against the acquiror ("flip over").

(3) "Note Purchase Rights Plan"

Designed for use after a takeover campaign begins, this plan implements a "flipin" pill. The rights holder may compel the target to exchange the holder's stock for a valuable package of securities if a triggering event occurs, and passing a specified level of share ownership is usually one of the events. The package of securities exchanged will customarily consist of senior debt securities subject to financial covenants designed to interfere with the bidder's financing.

6) "Greenmail"

When a target's board purchases a potential bidder's stock for an above-market price, critics call the premium "greenmail." Claims that paying "greenmail" constitutes a breach of fiduciary duty, however, have met with little success. A well-counseled board usually creates a paper trail designed to show that continued shareholding by the bidder will likely disrupt operations, thereby endangering the value of the corporation. Most courts have deferred to the board's judgment under the business judgment rule.

7) Restructuring Defenses

To compete with the bidder, target management may offer its shareholders a package of cash or securities whose value arguably exceeds that of the package offered by the bidder. It may finance this package by selling or spinning off assets just as the bidder had proposed to do. Restructuring often involves substantially increased use of debt borrowed by the target and paid out to shareholders in cash or debt securities. Leveraged buyouts ("LBOs") and recapitalizations are the most common forms.

2. Development

a. Proportionality Review

Unocal Corp. v. Mesa Petroleum Co.

493 A.2d 946 (Del. 1985).

Facts. Mesa (P) began a two-tier "front loaded" cash tender offer for 64 million shares of Unocal Corporation (D) at $54 per share. The "back end" of the offer involved eliminating the remaining publicly held shares by an exchange of highly subordinated securities or "junk bonds." The board of directors of D met with their financial advisors to discuss the tender offer. In the opinion of the advisors, the offer was wholly inadequate. As a defense strategy, the advisors suggested a self-tender by D for its own stock at $70 to $75 per share. While D would incur substantial debt, D would remain a viable entity. D's directors adopted a resolution rejecting P's offer as grossly inadequate.

After another meeting, and on the advice of the investment bankers, D's directors adopted an exchange offer at $72 per share. The resolution provided that if P succeeded in acquiring 51% of the outstanding shares, D would buy the remaining 49% for an exchange of debt securities having an aggregate par value of $72 per share. The resolution excluded P from participating in the offer.

P brought suit challenging its exclusion from D's exchange offer. The trial court temporarily restrained D from proceeding with the offer unless P was included. The trial court recognized that directors could oppose a hostile takeover but that the directors had the burden of showing a valid corporate purpose and that the transaction was fair to all stockholders, including those excluded. After a hearing, the trial court granted P a preliminary injunction, finding that, while the directors' decision to oppose P's takeover was made in good faith, the business judgment rule does not apply to a selective exchange offer. The trial court certified this interlocutory appeal as a question of first impression.

Issue. Under the business judgment rule, may a corporation defend itself against a hostile tender offer by means of a self-tender for its own shares which excludes from participation the stockholder making the hostile tender offer?

Held. Yes. Judgment reversed and preliminary injunction vacated.

- A board of directors has the power to oppose a tender offer. The power of the directors to act comes from its fundamental duty and obligation to protect the corporation, including the stockholders, from reasonably perceived harm irrespective of the source. In the acquisition of its own shares, a Delaware corporation may deal selectively with its stockholders, provided the directors have not acted solely to entrench themselves in office. If the directors are disinterested and have acted in good faith and with due care, their decision will be upheld as a proper exercise of business judgment.
- The business judgment rule, which presumes that directors making a business decision acted on an informed basis in good faith and in the honest belief that the action was in the best interests of the company, is applicable in the context of a takeover bid. However, because of the danger that the board may be acting in its own interests in such a situation, the directors must show that they had reasonable grounds for believing that a danger to corporate policy and effectiveness existed

because of another person's stock ownership. This burden was met by the showing that the directors acted in good faith and upon a reasonable investigation of the facts pursuant to a clear duty to protect the corporation.

- To come within the business judgment rule, a defensive measure must be reasonable in relation to the threat posed. Concerns may include the inadequacy of the price offered, the nature and timing of the offer, questions of illegality and the impact of the sale on stockholders and others, such as creditors, customers, employees, and the community.
- While the exchange offer is a form of selective treatment, it is lawful and is reasonably related to the threats posed. D's directors concluded that the value of D's shares was substantially above $54 per share. D also determined that the "junk bonds" were worth much less than $54. The directors' objective was either to defeat P's inadequate tender offer or, if P succeeded, to provide $72 worth of superior debt to the remaining stockholders, who would otherwise be forced to accept the "junk bonds."
- P's participation in D's offer would have thwarted the purpose of the offer, as D would be subsidizing P's effort to purchase stock at $54 per share. Also, P is not within the class of stockholders D is seeking to protect. That some of the directors are stockholders does not alone create a disqualifying "personal pecuniary interest" to defeat the operation of the business judgment rule. The directors are receiving a benefit shared generally by all stockholders except P. If P is dissatisfied, P may use its voting powers to vote the directors out.

Comment. S.E.C. rule 13e–4 now forbids reporting companies from employing a selective self-tender. But the decision may have significant implications for use of the "flipin" pill, which grants all shareholders except the bidder valuable rights to purchase the target's stock at a discount (or to redeem their shares at a premium). Apparently, the discrimination inherent in such a pill may pass judicial scrutiny if the pill is "reasonable in relation to the threat posed"—although just what would be considered reasonable is difficult to predict.

---

b. Defensive Measures Constituting Breach of Directors' Duty

Revlon, Inc. v. MacAndrews & Forbes Holdings, Inc.

506 A.2d 173 (Del. 1986).

Facts. Pantry Pride (P) expressed interest in acquiring Revlon (D). D rebuffed all of P's subsequent attempts to discuss a friendly takeover. D's board of directors met to discuss the threat of a hostile bid by P. D's investment banker advised the board that P's proposed hostile tender offer at $45 per share was grossly inadequate. As a defensive measure, D's board adopted a proposal to buy five million of its 30 million outstanding shares. It also adopted a Note Purchase Rights Plan under which each of D's shareholders would receive as a dividend one Note Purchase Right ("the Rights") for each share of common stock owned, with the Rights entitling the holder to exchange one common share for a $65 principal note at 12% interest with one year maturity. The Rights would become effective whenever anyone acquired ownership of 20% or more of D's stock for cash at $65 per share. The Rights would not be available to such acquiror and, prior to the 20% triggering event, D could redeem the rights for 10¢ each. P made its first hostile offer at $47.50 per common share, subject to P's obtaining financing and the Rights being redeemed, rescinded, or voided. D's board advised stockholders to reject P's offer. D began a new offer for up to 10 million of its own shares, exchanging each share of common stock tendered for one Senior Subordinated Note ("the Notes") of $47.50 principal at 11.75% interest and one-tenth of a share of $9 cumulative convertible exchangeable preferred stock valued at $100 per share.

In view of D's exchange offer, P made a new tender offer of $42 per share, then raised it to $50 and then $53 per share. D agreed to a leveraged buyout by Forstmann. Under the terms of the agreement, each of D's stockholders would get $56 per share, D's management would purchase stock in the new company by exercising "golden parachutes," Forstmann would assume D's debt resulting from the issuance of the Notes, and D would redeem the Rights and waive the Notes covenant for Forstmann. Because of this agreement and the waiver of the Notes covenant, the market value of the Notes began to fall. D's directors received many complaints from noteholders and there were threats of litigation.

P made a new offer of $56.25 per share subject to nullification of the Rights, a waiver of the Notes covenant, and the election of three of P's directors to D's board. P met with D and Forstmann and announced that it would top any bid made by Forstmann.

Forstmann proposed a new offer of $57.25 based on several conditions. Forstmann demanded a lock-up option to purchase two of D's divisions at a price below actual value if another acquiror got 40% of D's shares. D was also required to accept a "no-shop" provision requiring D to deal only with Forstmann. Forstmann demanded removal of the Rights and Notes covenants and a $25 million cancellation fee to be placed in escrow and released to Forstmann if the new agreement terminated or another party acquired more than 19.9% of D's stock. There was to be no participation by D's management in the merger. In exchange, Forstmann agreed to support the par value of the Notes. Forstmann required immediate approval of the proposal or it would be withdrawn. D's board unanimously approved the proposal because it was for a higher price than P's offer, it protected the noteholders, and Forstmann's financing was in place. The covenants were waived.

P, which had originally sought injunctive relief from the Rights plan, filed an amended complaint challenging the lock-up, the cancellation fee, and the exercise of the Rights and Notes covenants. P also sought a TRO to prevent D from placing assets in escrow or transferring them to Forstmann. The trial court prohibited the transfer of assets and enjoined the lock-up, no-shop, and cancellation fee provisions of the agreement. The trial court found that D's directors had breached their duty of loyalty by making concessions to Forstmann out of concern for their liability to the noteholders. D appeals.

Issue. Were the defensive measures taken to avoid a hostile takeover consistent with the directors' duties to the shareholders?

Held. No. Judgment affirmed.

- The directors of a corporation owe fiduciary duties of care and loyalty to the corporation and its shareholders. When a board implements anti-takeover measures, there is a possibility that the board is acting primarily in its own interests. The directors must prove that they had reasonable grounds for believing there was a danger to corporate policy and effectiveness by showing good faith and reasonable investigation.
- In adopting the Rights plan, which gave shareholders the right to be bought out by the corporation at a premium whenever anyone acquired beneficial ownership of 20% or more of D's shares, D was protecting the shareholders from a hostile takeover at a price below the corporation's intrinsic value. The Rights plan was not unreasonable considering the threat posed. Thus, D's directors acted in good faith upon reasonable investigation. However, the usefulness of the plan was rendered moot by D's actions in redeeming the Rights conditioned upon consummation of a merger with Forstmann or to facilitate any more favorable offer.
- D's exchange offer for 10 million of its own shares was proper. The directors concluded that P's offer of $47.50 per share was grossly inadequate. The board acted in good faith on an informed basis and with reasonable grounds to believe there existed a threat to the corporation. However, when P increased its offer to $50 and then to $53 per share, it became obvious that the break-up of the company was inevitable. The duty of the directors changed from preserving the corporate entity to maximizing the sale value for the shareholders' benefit.
- The lock-up agreement with its emphasis on shoring up the value of the Notes was inconsistent with the directors' responsibility. Obtaining the highest price for the benefit of the shareholders should have been the directors' goal. By preferring the noteholders, the directors breached their

primary duty of loyalty. Concern for nonshareholder interests is inappropriate when the object is no longer to protect the corporation but to sell it to the highest bidder.

- A lock-up provision is not per se illegal. Those lock-ups that draw bidders into the battle benefit shareholders, but similar measures that end an active auction and foreclose further bidding operate to the shareholders' detriment. D's lock-up agreement ended the auction in return for very little actual improvement in the final bid. The principal benefit went to D's directors, who avoided personal liability to a class of creditors to whom the board owed no further duty. When a board ends an intense bidding contest on an insubstantial basis and a significant result of the action is to protect the directors, the action cannot withstand the enhanced scrutiny that *Unocal* requires of director conduct.
- The no-shop agreement is also impermissible because the board's duty was to sell the corporation to the highest bidder. The agreement to negotiate with only one buyer ended rather than intensified the bidding contest.
- P showed irreparable harm by establishing that, unless the lock-up and other aspects of the agreement are enjoined, P's opportunity to bid for D will be lost.

---

1) Under What Circumstances Does *Revlon* Require the Board to Auction the Company?

Because *Unocal*'s proportionality test is far more permissive of defensive tactics than *Revlon*'s value-maximization test, target management will almost never admit that sale of the corporation has become inevitable. *Ivanhoe Partners v. Newmont Mining Corp.*, 535 A.2d 1344 (Del. 1987), arose out of a hostile bid by Ivanhoe partnership (led by Boone Pickens, who had been characterized in *Unocal* as a "greenmailer") for Newmont. Newmont responded by declaring an enormous dividend ($33 per share), which enabled its largest shareholder (Consolidated Gold Fields, PLC) to purchase sufficient shares from arbitrageurs to raise its share holding from 26% to 49.7%. In conjunction with this dividend declaration, Gold Fields and Newmont entered into a "standstill agreement" limiting Gold Fields's representation on the board to 40%. Upholding these defensive maneuvers, the Delaware Supreme Court rejected the claim that they had transferred control of Newmont to management, much like a recapitalization might. *Note*: Perhaps the court perceived Newmont's board as trying to help shareholders deal with two pressure-filled partial bids: one from Ivanhoe, which had not specified when it would merge out the remaining shares or what it would pay, and the other from Gold Fields in the form of a "street sweep."

2) *Revlon* vs. the Business Judgment Rule

The boundary between *Revlon* and the business judgment rule becomes critical when management attempts to protect a friendly transaction, say by agreeing to a "lock-up" that will deter potential competing bidders.

3) *Revlon*'s Substantive Obligations

To obtain the highest price, the target board must possess sufficient information to properly assess the company's value, and structure the sale process so that the price obtained approximates this value.

4) Information

To assess a company's value, its board might: (i) rely on the information that the directors possess by virtue of their service on the board as augmented in the negotiation process; (ii) seek an opinion from its investment banker; (iii) retain an investment banker to seek bids ("shop" the company); or (iv) conduct a formal auction. According to the Delaware Supreme Court in *Barkan* v. *Amsted Industries*, 567 A.2d 1279 (Del. 1989), *Revlon* does not necessarily require a formal auction. Indeed, its opinion seems to suggest that the court will customarily defer to the board's decision.

The court observed that "[w]hen the board is considering a single offer and has no reliable grounds upon which to judge its adequacy, [it must] . . . canvass . . . the market to determine if higher bids may be elicited. When, however, the directors possess a body of reliable evidence with which to evaluate the fairness of a transaction, they may approve that transaction without conducting an active survey of the market. . . . [T]he circumstances in which this passive approach is acceptable are limited. . . . Here the Chancellor found that the advice of the Special Committee's investment bankers, when coupled with the special circumstances surrounding the negotiation and consummation of the management-sponsored leveraged buyout ("MBO"), supported a finding that Amsted's directors had acted in good faith to arrange the best possible transaction for shareholders." The court revisited this matter in *Paramount Communications, Inc. v. QVC Network, Inc. (infra).*

c. No Change of Corporate Control

Paramount Communications, Inc. v. Time Inc.

571 A.2d 1140 (Del. 1989).

Facts. In the mid-1980s, Time Inc. (D) began to pursue options for expanding its operations into the entertainment industry. One of the most important aspects of any deal for D was that it be able to retain its perceived journalistic integrity. D and Warner Communications, Inc. began discussing the possibility of a merger. Negotiations reached an impasse when the parties could not come to terms over the structure of the new board, but soon afterward negotiations resumed and came to what seemed to be a done deal. Paramount Communications, Inc. then entered the picture and made an all-cash offer to purchase all of D's outstanding shares for $175 per share. The next day D's stock rose from a $126 to $170 market price per share. D did not accept Paramount's offer, reasoning that the long-term benefit of the Time-Warner deal outweighed any short-term gain to be had by the increased stock price. Paramount responded with an offer of $200 per share, which D again refused. D's shareholders and Paramount (Ps) initiated separate suits against D, seeking to enjoin the Time-Warner deal.

Issues.

(i) Did the Time-Warner agreement effectively put D up for sale, thus triggering duties set forth in *Revlon, Inc. v. MacAndrews & Forbes Holdings, Inc., supra?*

(ii) Was the Time-Warner agreement a proper exercise of business judgment?

Held. (i) No. (ii) Yes. Judgment affirmed.

- The shareholder Ps allege that D's actions effectively put the corporation up for sale, requiring D to maximize immediate share value and to consider all offers on an equal basis. However, the Time-Warner agreement did not purport to change control of D and thus did not trigger any duties under *Revlon.* The agreement merely served to increase the scope of D's position in the marketplace, not to dissolve or break up the corporate entity as was the case in *Revlon.*

- When a board exercises defensive measures as did D in response to Paramount's offer, it must prove two things before the business judgment rule is applied to its decision. First, the board must prove that there were reasonable grounds to believe there was a danger to corporate policy and effectiveness. The board must also prove that the defensive measures used were reasonably related to the threat imposed. These are the duties imposed under *Unocal (supra).* D's board took an exhaustive and careful approach in deciding whether to enter into the Time-Warner agreement, keeping in mind the long-term interests of the corporation as it did so. As for P's offer, not only did the board find it to be of inadequate value, but great uncertainty existed as to whether D would be able to retain enough control of its business so as to keep its journalistic integrity.

---

d. Acquisition by a Controlling Shareholder/Defensive Measures Deterring a Competing Offer

Paramount Communications, Inc. v. QVC Network, Inc.

637 A.2d 34 (Del. 1994).

Facts. On September 12, 1993, Paramount's (D's) board approved a merger with Viacom. Viacom's chairman and CEO, Sumner Redstone, owned more than 91% of National Amusements, Inc., which owned more than 85% of Viacom's Class A voting stock and almost 70% of its nonvoting Class B stock. As part of this "Original Merger Agreement," D promised to amend its poison pill to exempt the proposed merger. The agreement provided that for each share of D, a holder would receive .1 shares of Viacom Class A voting stock, .9 shares of Viacom Class B nonvoting stock, and $9.10. This consideration would have provided a "modest change of control premium."

In the "No-Shop Provision" of the Original Merger Agreement, D promised to refrain from even discussing or encouraging any competing transactions unless it received "an unsolicited written, bona fide proposal . . . not subject to any material [financing] contingencies" and D's board determined that negotiations with the third party were necessary to comply with its fiduciary duties. D also promised that, if its board recommended a competing transaction or terminated the agreement because of one, or if its shareholders failed to approve the merger, D would pay Viacom $100 million ('Termination Fee") and either (i) sell to Viacom as much as 19.9% of D's outstanding stock for $69.14 per share—for which Viacom could pay with senior subordinated notes of "questionable marketability" (the "Note Feature")—or, if Viacom preferred, pay it, in cash, the difference between $69.14 and the market price of D's stock, no matter how high (the "Put Feature"). This "Stock Option Agreement" as well as the "No-Shop Provision," and 'Termination Fee," were designed to make it more difficult for a competing bid to succeed.

Viacom's Redstone attempted to discourage QVC from making a competing bid, but failed. On October 21, 1993, QVC announced an $80 cash tender offer for 51% of D's outstanding shares, upon the successful completion of which, remaining D holders would receive 1.4+ shares of QVC common stock for each share of D in a second-step merger. QVC made its offer conditional on, among other things, invalidation of the Stock Option Agreement. On the same day, QVC filed suit and requested a preliminary injunction against enforcement of the "No-Shop Provision," "Termination Fee," "Stock Option Agreement," and other defensive measures.

Because QVC's offer had a face value that was $10 per share greater than Viacom's, Viacom recognized that it would have to renegotiate the terms of its proposed merger in favor of D's holders. The "Amended Merger Agreement" called for Viacom to make an $80 cash tender offer for 51% of D's outstanding shares, upon the successful completion of which, remaining D shareholders would receive a package of Viacom securities for each share of D: .2+ shares of Class A voting stock, almost one share of Class B nonvoting stock, and .2+ shares of convertible preferred stock. This agreement gave D (i) the right to refuse to exempt Viacom's offer from D's poison pill if, because of a better offer, D's board concluded that its fiduciary duties required a refusal and (ii) the power to terminate the agreement if D's board withdrew its recommendation of the Viacom transaction or recommended a competing transaction. Except for these provisions, the Amended Merger Agreement was "essentially the same" as the Original Merger Agreement. Although QVC's bid gave Paramount "considerable leverage with Viacom," Paramount did not attempt to eliminate or modify the "No-Shop Provision," "Termination Fee," or "Stock Option Agreement."

On November 6, Viacom raised its cash tender offer to $85 and made a comparable increase in the amount of Viacom securities that holders of D shares would receive in a subsequent second-step merger. Later that day, D's board agreed to recommend this bid to its holders. On November 12, QVC raised its cash tender offer to $90 per share and made a comparable increase in the amount of QVC securities that holders of D shares would receive in a subsequent second-step merger. The face value of this bid exceeded that of Viacom's by more than $1 billion.

D's board met three days later to consider QVC's bid. D's executive vice president, a board member, had distributed to his colleagues a summary of "conditions and uncertainties" attendant to the offer, a summary that, according to one director's testimony, gave a "very negative impression of the QVC bid." Management also distributed an analysis of the dollar value of the securities that shareholders would receive pursuant to each bid, but the analysis did not reflect an estimate of the price that the securities would have when the shareholders received them. Instead, it reflected then-current prices, "which fluctuated depending upon which company was perceived to be the more likely to acquire Paramount." At the meeting, D's board concluded that QVC's November 12 bid would not serve the best interests of the stockholders, purportedly because the bid was "excessively conditional." (Several directors testified that they believed that a merger with Viacom would prove more advantageous to D's future business prospects.) D's board did not communicate with QVC about the conditions attached to the offer because the directors believed that the No-Shop Provision barred such communication until QVC obtained firm financing.

On November 16, the chancery court held a hearing in connection with QVC's request for a preliminary injunction. Three days later, QVC's CEO advised D's board in writing that QVC had obtained financing commitments and that antitrust law posed no obstacle to its tender offer. The chancellor granted the preliminary injunction, and D appeals.

Issues.

(i) Did the Original Merger Agreement obligate D's board to "seek the transaction offering the best value reasonably available to the stockholders" and subject the board's related conduct to "enhanced judicial scrutiny"?

(ii) Did the No-Shop Provision, Termination Fee, and Stock Option Agreement help realize the "best value reasonably available to [D's] stockholders" or did D's board have reason to believe that these defensive measures would do so?

(iii) If D's board cannot abide by the Amended Merger Agreement because of the directors' fiduciary duties, may Viacom obtain compensation from D as provided in the No-Shop Provision and the Stock Option Agreement?

Held. (i) Yes. (ii) No. (iii) No. Judgment affirmed.

- The Original Merger Agreement, if consummated, would have shifted control of D from a "fluid aggregation of unaffiliated stockholders" to a majority holder, one who could unilaterally change D's board's vision of a strategic alliance with Viacom.
- A shift in control would have deprived D's shareholders of the leverage to obtain another control premium. Therefore, since D's board initiated this potential shift, albeit unintentionally, D's shareholders became "entitled to . . . a control premium and/or protective devices of significant value"—even though D's board did not envision a breakup of D. Neither the Original Merger Agreement nor the Amended Merger Agreement included any "protective devices," so D's board became obligated to seek the transaction offering the best value reasonably available to stockholders.
- D's board also became obligated to discharge its fiduciary duties to this end regardless of the provisions in the merger agreements, including the No-Shop Provision. Because D's board agreed to a potential control shift for a modest premium, and to the No-Shop Provision, Termination Fee, and Stock Option Agreement, and because the board treated competing bidders QVC and Viacom

unequally, *Macmillan* requires enhanced judicial scrutiny. The board bears the burden of showing that it discharged its fiduciary duties.

- The board did not meet its burden with respect to process or result. The board clearly gave insufficient attention to the potential consequences of the defensive measures demanded by Viacom, particularly the unusual and potentially "draconian" provisions of the Stock Option Agreement such as the Note Feature and the Put Feature. By the time QVC made its tender offer, the board should have realized that this agreement, coupled with the Termination Fee and the No-Shop Provision, were impeding the realization of the best value reasonably available to D's stockholders. Yet the board made no effort to modify the improper defensive measures despite Viacom's willingness to renegotiate in light of the QVC bid. Nor did the board seek more information from QVC or negotiate with it, apparently believing, based on advice from D's management, that the No-Shop Provision barred such conduct and that the QVC offer was too conditional. Even when QVC revised its offer so that on its face it exceeded Viacom's by more than $1 billion, D's board declined to negotiate with QVC, paralyzed by this uninformed belief that the QVC offer was "illusory." In light of this difference between the two offers, D's board could not justify its conduct on the basis of its vision of a strategic alliance with Viacom because (i) the merger would have deprived the board of the power to implement its vision, and (ii) its uninformed process had deprived this vision of much of its credibility. (When assessing the value of noncash consideration, a board should focus on its value as of the date it will be received by the stockholders.)
- Because D's board breached its fiduciary duties when it agreed to the No-Shop Provision and the Stock Option Agreement containing "draconian" features, neither vested any rights in Viacom, a sophisticated party with experienced legal and financial advisors who knew of (and demanded) the unreasonable features.

---

e. Note on Subsequent Delaware Developments

Following the *Paramount* case, several other cases further defined the law in this area.

1) "Draconian" Measures Not Permissible

In *Unitrin v. American General Corporation*, 651 A.2d 1361 (Del. 1995), the Delaware Supreme Court held that a defensive measure approved by an independent board is permissible as long as it is not draconian (*i.e.*, coercive or preclusive). The court explained that a board is free to choose a defensive measure from alternatives that are within the range of reasonableness, and the court will not allow a plaintiff to argue that another measure would have been preferable.

2) "Dead Hand Poison Pills"

In *Carmody v. Toll Brothers*, 723 A.2d 1180 (Del. Ch. 1998), Toll Brothers employed a "dead hand poison pill," which provided that the pill could be redeemed only by those directors who had been in office when the shareholder rights constituting the pill had become exercisable. This was intended to foreclose a loophole available in standard poison pill arrangements in that it deprived any newly elected directors of the right to redeem the pill. A shareholder sued, challenging the validity of the pill, and the court held that the pill violated several provisions of Delaware law. First, it disenfranchised shareholders who wanted to elect a board committed to redeeming the pill. Secondly, there is nothing in Delaware law that would allow the creation of two classes of directors (one class having the power to redeem and the other not). The court held that the pill was preclusive in that the added deterrent effect of the dead hand provision made a takeover prohibitively expensive and effectively impossible.

3) "No Hand Poison Pills"

In *Mentor Graphics Corp. v. Quickturn Design Systems, Inc.*, 728 A.2d 25 (Del. Ch. 1998), Quickturn employed a deferred redemption provision under which no newly elected board could redeem the rights plan for six months after taking office if the purpose of the redemption was to facilitate a transaction with any person who proposed, nominated, or supported the election of the new directors to the board. Quickturn argued that the justification for this provision was to force any newly elected board to take sufficient time to become familiar with the company and its value before prematurely selling the company. The court found that Quickturn's board reasonably and in good faith attempted to protect the company from Mentor Graphics's offer, which it believed was inadequate. However, the court found that the pill was disproportionate to the substantive threat. The pill only foreclosed sale of the company to the initial bidder. Other potential buyers were not foreclosed. The Delaware Supreme Court affirmed on the grounds that the provision conflicted with section 141(a) of the Delaware corporations law, which confers upon any newly elected board full power to manage and direct the business affairs of the company. [Quickturn Design Systems v. Mentor Graphics Corp., 721 A.2d 1281 (Del. 1998)] Any limitation on the board's authority must be set out in the certificate of incorporation.

f. Clarification of *Revlon's* Categories of Bad Faith

Lyondell Chemical Company v. Ryan

970 A.2d 235 (Del. 2009).

Facts. Prior to the instant merger, Lyondell (D) was North America's third largest publically traded independent chemical company. Smith was CEO and many of the ten independent company directors were or had been CEOs of other similar companies. Blavatnik owns Basell, a privately held Luxembourg company, through his ownership of Access Industries. In April 2006, Blavatnik told Smith and later notified Lyondell's board that Basell wanted to acquire Lyondell for $26.50–$28.50 a share. D found the price too low; no other potential buyers approached the company during the next year. D prospered. In May 2007, an Access affiliate filed a Schedule 13D with the SEC, setting forth its right to acquire an 8.3% block of D's stock owned by Occidental Petroleum Corp. The Schedule also indicated Blavatnik's interest in possible transactions with D. D's board met immediately, recognizing that the 13D signaled to the market that D was "in play." The directors decided to "wait and see." In June, Basell announced its merger agreement with Huntsman Corp., a specialty chemical company. However, another offer was made to Huntsman, with which Basell decided not to compete. Blavatnik turned again to D and in July 2007 and after Smith refused his all-cash offer for $40 a share, Blavatnik moved to $44–$45 per share. Smith said he would present the offer, but he thought the board would reject it as D was not on the market. Smith said Blavatnik should give him his best offer, and later that day, Blavatnik offered $48 per share. Under the offer, Basell did not require a financing contingency, but D would have to agree to a $400 million break-up fee and sign an agreement by July 16, 2007. At a special meeting of the board on July 10, the board reviewed valuation material that had been prepared for the regular board meeting, discussed the offer, and the general situation, and asked Smith to get a written offer from Basell and more information about Basell's financing.

Blavatnik agreed to the board's request, but, because he only had until July 11 to make another bid for Huntsman, he asked Smith if the board would give a firm indication of interest by the end of that day. The board met on the 11th for one hour and decided it was interested in the offer and retained Deutsche Bank to negotiate with Blavatnik. Blavatnik announced Basell would not increase its offer for Huntsman; Huntsman terminated the merger agreement. During the next few days, negotiations ensued and D's board met again. It asked Smith to try to get better terms, *i.e.,* a higher price, a "go-shop" provision, and a reduced break-up fee. Blavatnik was shocked, but as a sign of good faith, he agreed to lower the break-up fee to $385 million. On July 16, the board met again. The bank, based on its review of valuation models with a range that did not even approach $48 a share, gave its opinion that the offer was "an absolute home run." Other advisors explained that notwithstanding the "go-shop" provision in the merger agreement, D could consider superior proposals under the "fiduciary out" provision. The bank said it believed there would be no better offer. D's board agreed to approve the merger and recommend it to the shareholders. Ninety-nine per cent of the shareholders approved the merger at a special meeting in November. A class action suit was filed by Ryan (P) and others alleging that D's directors breached their fiduciary duties of care and put their personal interests before those of D's shareholders. At trial, all claims were rejected except those focused on the process by which D was sold and the protection provisions in the merger provisions. The court found the directors were not motivated by self-interest or ill will. The trial court also found P might win at a trial on a breach of duty of care claim, but D's charter protects directors from personal liability for such a claim. Their breach of loyalty, however, is not exculpated. D appeals.

Issue. Are the directors entitled to summary judgment on the claim that they breached their duty of loyalty by failing to act in good faith?

Held. Yes. Judgment reversed.

- We must decide whether any arguable shortcomings on the part of the directors might implicate their duty of loyalty; their claims are one under *Revlon v. MacAndrews & Forbes Holdings, Inc., supra, i.e.,* the directors failed to obtain the best available price in selling the company.
- The trial court erred in its interpretation of *In re Walt Disney Co. Deriv. Litig.,* 906 A.2d 27 (Del. 2006), *supra,* where we examined "good faith" and held three different categories of fiduciary behavior are candidates for the "bad faith" label. The first is "subjective bad faith," where the conduct is motivated by an actual intent to do harm. The second is the opposite end of the spectrum and involves action taken solely through gross negligence, without malevolent intent. Gross negligence, without more, does not constitute bad faith. The third category falls between the first two; it is the intentional dereliction of duty, a conscious disregard for one's responsibilities.
- Trial court denied summary judgment so that it could obtain a more complete record before making its determination, but it reviewed the record under a mistaken view of the law. It imposed duties *on* the directors before they decided to sell or before a sale had become inevitable. It read *Revlon* as requiring a set of requirements that must be satisfied during the sale process, and it equated an arguably imperfect attempt to carry out *Revlon* duties with a knowing disregard of one's duties that constituted bad faith.
- All of Smith's negotiations, the board's reviews of valuation, seeking advice from third party experts and their awareness of market conditions fell short when the trial court deemed the board's efforts inadequate after the 13D was filed. The trial court called the board's failure to act "two months of slothful indifference." Because the board took no action to prepare for a possible acquisition, the merger was finalized in less than a week and the board met for only seven hours during that time.
- *Revlon* duties do not arise just because a company is "in play." They arise only when the company begins a transaction that will end in a change of control. The 13D did not put D on notice that Basell was interested in acquiring it. The directors met to decide whether they should take action and decided to just "wait and see" what ensued. That was appropriate under *Revlon*; *Revlon* came into play on July 10, 2007, when the directors began negotiating the sale.
- The trial court's focus should have been on the week during which the board considered Basell's offer. Then, they met several times, requested the CEO to negotiate better terms, reviewed D's value, the price offered and the possibility of obtaining a better offer. The sole *Revlon* duty is to

get the best price for the stockholders at a sale of a company. The trial court erred in its efforts to tell the directors how they must accomplish that and in questioning whether the disinterested, independent directors did everything they could have to get the best price. As a result of its erroneous interpretation of *Revlon*, the court was not able to conclude the directors had met their burden under that case.

- What the trial court should have asked is if the directors utterly failed to attempt to obtain the best sale price.

---

3. Extension of the *Unocal/Revlon* Framework to Negotiated Transactions

a. Shareholder "Lock-Up" Provision Not Enforceable

Omnicare, Inc. v. NCS Healthcare, Inc.

818 A.2d 914 (Del. 2003).

Facts. NCS Healthcare, Inc. (D) is a leading provider of pharmacy services to long-term care institutions. D experienced financial difficulties and was the object of competing acquisition bids by bitter rivals Genesis Health Ventures ("Genesis") and Omnicare, Inc. (P). D formed an independent committee of board members to negotiate any possible acquisition. The committee began negotiations with Genesis, which wanted an exclusivity agreement. P sent a proposal to D, but the board members felt the risk of losing the Genesis proposal was too substantial to begin discussions with P. Genesis improved its offer as a result of P's proposal. The committee voted to accept Genesis's proposal and recommended it to the board. The board resolved to recommend the transaction to the stockholders. Certain majority stockholders entered into a separate voting agreement with Genesis to approve the merger. P responded with a superior proposal and a lawsuit attempting to enjoin the D/Genesis merger. D's board withdrew its recommendation for the D/Genesis merger. However, the agreement provided that even if the board withdrew its recommendation, it must still submit the merger to a stockholder vote. Thus, success of the Genesis merger was predetermined by the voting agreements. This litigation was commenced to prevent the consummation of the inferior Genesis transaction.

Issue. Are the merger agreement and voting agreements valid and enforceable?

Held. No.

- We have assumed arguendo that the business judgment rule applies to the decision by D's board to merge with Genesis and that D's board exercised due care.
- The issues in this appeal involve the defensive devices that protected the Genesis merger agreement. The *Unocal* standard of review applies to defensive devices adopted by a board to protect a merger transaction even if that merger transaction does not result in a change of control. The deal protection devices need not all be in the merger agreement itself. Here, the agreement, combined with the separate voting agreements, provided a defense for the Genesis merger against any subsequent superior offers. Genesis made the voting agreements a non-negotiable condition precedent to its execution of the merger agreement.
- Under *Unocal*, D's directors must demonstrate that they had a reasonable ground for believing that a danger to corporate policy and effectiveness existed. Second, they must demonstrate that their defensive response was reasonable in relation to the threat posed. Here the minority stockholders, although not forced to vote for the Genesis merger, were forced to accept it because it was a fait accompli. The defense devises were preclusive and coercive. Thus we hold that the deal protection devices are unenforceable.

- Alternatively, the board did not have authority to accede to the Genesis demand for an absolute lock-up. The omission of a fiduciary out clause in the merger agreement completely prevented the board from discharging its fiduciary responsibilities to the minority stockholders when P presented its superior transaction. Defensive measures cannot limit or circumscribe a director's fiduciary duties.

Dissent. The court must respect the reasonable judgment of the board of directors and give effect to the wishes of the controlling stockholders.

---

4. Extension of the *Unocal/Revlon* Framework to Shareholder Disenfranchisement

a. Restructuring

Hilton Hotels Corp. v. ITT Corporation (Hilton H)

978 F. Supp. 1342 (D. Nev. 1997).

Facts. In late January 1997, Hilton Hotels Corporation (P) announced both a $55 per share tender offer for the stock of ITT Corporation (D) and plans for a proxy contest at D's next annual meeting. In mid-February, D's board, consisting of nine outside directors and two inside directors, formally rejected the tender offer. The board then proceeded to sell several non-core assets and to oppose the takeover before Nevada, New Jersey, and Mississippi gaming regulators. In mid-July, the board announced its "Comprehensive Plan" to split D into three, assigning D's hotel and gaming business—about 93% of its then current assets—to "ITT Destinations." Under the plan: (i) D's board would become the board of ITT Destinations; (ii) the directors would serve three-year terms with one-third of the board standing for election each year; and (iii) repeal of this "staggered" or "classified" board scheme or removal of a director without cause would require a shareholder vote of 80%. The board announced that it would implement this plan without obtaining shareholder approval, which neither the Nevada statute nor D's governing documents expressly required (although in 1995, D's board submitted a planned division of the company to the shareholders for approval). Subsequently, the board adopted in large measure the business strategy advocated by P. Shortly after the board announced its Comprehensive Plan, P announced an amended tender offer of $70 per share, which the board rejected. At the meeting, the Goldman Sachs advisors hired by the board opined that the market valued D's shares under the Comprehensive Plan at $62 to $64. Subsequently, the board offered $70 per share for 26% of D's shares, using borrowed funds. In late August, P requested a preliminary and permanent injunction enjoining the Comprehensive Plan.

Issue. In the face of P's tender offer and proxy contest, could D's board implement its comprehensive plan without obtaining shareholder approval?

Held. No. Injunctive relief granted.

- Because this case involved both a tender offer and a proxy contest, the proper legal standard, in the absence of Nevada statute or case on point, is a *Unocal/Blasius* analysis as articulated in *Stroud v. Grace*, 606 A.2d 75 (Del. 1992) and *Unitrin, Inc. v. American General Corp.* In assessing a challenge to defensive actions by a target corporation's board of directors in a takeover context, a court should evaluate the board's overall response, including the justification for each contested defensive measure, and the results achieved thereby, and when the defensive actions are inextricably related, a court must evaluate them collectively as a unitary response to the perceived threat.
- The board made no showing that P would pursue a corporate policy different than the board sought to implement through its Comprehensive Plan. During the months preceding the hearing,

the board largely adopted P's proposed strategy. D did not show that P would be unable to run D or be ineffective in doing so. That some Sheraton franchise owners would be unhappy if P were to enter into certain management contracts was neither fundamental nor pervasive enough to constitute a "threat" to D's corporate policy or effectiveness.

- P's offer of $70 a share did not qualify as a "threat" because: (i) contrary to D's claim, this price did reflect a control premium as evidenced by the Goldman Sachs opinion solicited by D's board that the market valued D's shares under the Comprehensive Plan at $62 to $64, and (ii) D itself was offering to buy back about 26% of its stock at $70 a share while planning to burden its remaining shares with much more debt.
- D's board failed to meet its burden under the first prong of the *Unocal* test of showing "good faith and reasonable investigation" of a threat to corporate policy or effectiveness. After P announced its tender offer, the board did not meet with P's representatives.
- Even in good faith, a board may not take ordinarily permissible actions if its primary purpose is to disenfranchise the shareholders in light of a proxy contest. The following circumstantial evidence, considered together, demonstrates that the primary purpose of D's Comprehensive Plan was to disenfranchise its shareholders.

  The first bit of evidence is the ***timing*** of the plan. The board announced its Comprehensive Plan well after P's initial tender offer. The board did claim that it had contemplated a spin-off or asset sale earlier, but it made no such claim about the adoption of a classified board. The plan would have dramatically restructured D in little more than two months, two months before a scheduled annual meeting at which shareholders would have voted on an annually elected board.

  The second piece of evidence is the ***entrenchment*** of the board the plan would offer. D's directors who approved the Comprehensive Plan in time to avoid the shareholder vote that otherwise would have occurred at D's 1997 annual meeting would take much more protected positions as directors of ITT Destinations.

  The third piece of evidence is the board's ***inconsistency***. The planned rapid implementation of the board's plan coupled with the board's opposition to P's tender offer is inconsistent with the board's argument defending its postponement of the 1997 annual meeting from May to November, which was that the delay would give shareholders more time to inform themselves and to consider the implications of their vote.

  Finally, the last important piece of circumstantial evidence is the board's ***past behavior***. The board did put its 1995 division of the company to a shareholder vote.
- Installing a classified board for ITT Destinations, a company that would encompass 93% of D's current assets and 87% of its revenues, would at least cause D's current shareholders to lose their existing right to replace a majority of D's incumbent board members for one year. Because of the inherent conflicts of interest that arise when shareholders are not permitted free exercise of their franchise, a board's unilateral decision to engage in defensive measures that purposefully deprive shareholders of their vote cannot pass muster under *Unocal* and *Stroud* without a "compelling justification." The board offered no such justification, stating only that it declined to seek shareholder approval of its plan to avoid market risks and other business problems as its advisors suggested. That the plan might generate additional benefits for shareholders did not remedy the fundamental flaw of board entrenchment. Thus, this defensive measure was preclusive and coercive under *Unitrin*.
- The right of shareholders to vote on directors at an annual meeting is a fundamental principle of corporate law, and it is not outweighed by the interests listed in Nevada Revised Statutes section 78.138—interest related to non-shareholder constituencies.

---

b. "Blank Check" Preferred Stock

In *Unilever Acquisition Corp.* v. *Richardson-Vicks, Inc.*, 618 F. Supp. 407 (S.D.N.Y. 1985), the board of a target corporation (Richardson-Vicks) responded to a hostile tender offer by creating a new class of preferred stock, each share of which would carry 25 votes per share unless transferred to a new holder, in which case it would carry only five votes per share. This practically precluded the hostile bidder from buying control so long as a significant minority fraction of the shareholders did not tender their shares. The district court ruled that such a fundamental change in voting rights required a shareholder vote, in part because it discriminated against incoming shareholders.

c. The "De Facto Merger" Doctrine

An issue analogous to the one raised by *Unilever Acquisition Corp. v. Richardson-Vicks, Inc., supra*, may arise when a transaction would function in a particular setting much like a merger, but is not listed as a "fundamental change" in the relevant statute. Some courts insist that shareholders be accorded the same voting and appraisal rights that they would have had had the transaction been structured as a merger; hence, the name of the doctrine. The California General Corporation Law codifies this result by conferring the same basic voting and appraisal rights on shareholders in all "reorganizations."

5. What Voting Power Should a Share Carry? Rule 19C–4 and the One Shareholder/One Vote Controversy

a. Exchange Rules and Issuing Stock

As a condition of listing, the New York Stock Exchange ("NYSE") requires companies to seek shareholder approval for issuing stock if issuing it could either work a change in control or increase outstanding common stock by 18.5%. From the 1920s to the mid-1980s, the NYSE refused to list a company's common stock unless each share of any class of such stock had exactly one vote. The American Stock Exchange and NASDAQ (the National Association of Securities Dealers' automated quotation service) competed by accepting common stock listings from companies with shares having disparate voting rights (within limits). This competition seriously threatened NYSE revenues, however, only when the top management of many publicly held companies developed techniques for defeating or deterring takeovers which employed stock with limited voting rights or multiple votes. Against this background, General Motors's 1984 decision to finance its acquisition of Electronic Data Systems Corp. by issuing common stock with one-half vote per share prompted the NYSE to declare a moratorium on enforcement of its rule and appoint a committee to review "qualitative listing standards." Many companies then followed GM's example.

6. State and Federal Legislation

a. State Regulation

CTS Corp. v. Dynamics Corp. of America

481 U.S. 69 (1987).

Facts. Indiana passed the Control Shares Acquisitions Act, which applied to businesses incorporated in Indiana that have: (i) 100 or more shareholders; (ii) their principal place of business, their principal office, or substantial assets within Indiana; and (iii) either: (a) more than 10% of their shareholders resident in Indiana; (b) more than 10% of their shares owned by Indiana residents; or (c) 10,000 shareholders resident in Indiana. An entity acquires "control shares" in such a corporation whenever it acquires voting power to or above 20%, 33.3%, or 50%. Voting power of these acquired shares is only granted on petition and approval of a majority vote of all disinterested shareholders of each class of stock. The acquirer can request a meeting for such a vote within 50 days; if voting power is not granted, the corporation ***may*** buy back the stock, or if no petition calling for a vote is asked for, the corporation can buy back the stock.

Dynamics owned 9.6% of CTS Corporation, an Indiana corporation. CTS elected to be governed by the new Act. Dynamics tendered one million shares of CTS, which would bring its interest to 27.5%. Dynamics sued, alleging that the Act violated the Commerce Clause and was preempted by the Williams Act. The district court agreed with Dynamics; the circuit court affirmed. Dynamics appeals.

Issues.

(i) Does the federal Williams Act preempt Indiana's state law?

(ii) Does the state law violate the Commerce Clause?

Held. (i) No. (ii) No. Judgment reversed.

(i) The state law is not preempted by the Williams Act.

- The state law is consistent with the intent of the Williams Act—it protects the shareholders against both management and the tender offeror. Neither contending party gets an advantage; it does not impose an indefinite delay on tender offers; it does not impose a government official's view of fairness on the buyer and selling shareholders. The shareholders can evaluate the fairness of the proposed terms.
- If the tender offeror fears an adverse shareholder vote, it can make a conditional offer, accepting shares on condition that the shares receive the voting rights within a certain time period.
- The Williams Act does not preempt all state regulation of tender offers, or state laws that limit or delay the free exercise of power after a tender offer (example: staggering the terms of the members of the board of directors).

(ii) The state law does not violate the Commerce Clause.

- The state law does not discriminate against interstate commerce by imposing a greater burden on out-of-state offerors than Indiana offerors.
- The law does not adversely affect interstate commerce by subjecting activities to inconsistent regulations of more than one state. It applies only to corporations incorporated in Indiana.
- It is an accepted practice for states to regulate the corporations it creates. Thus, it is appropriate for the state to regulate the rights that are acquired by purchasing the shares of the corporation in order to promote stable relationships among the parties involved in the state's corporations.
- It is not for this Court to decide, or the intent of the Commerce Clause to promote, any specific economic theory—*i.e.*, whether tender offers are good or bad.
- There is no conflict with the provisions or purposes of the Williams Act.

Concurrence (Scalia, J.). If the law does not discriminate against interstate commerce or risk inconsistent regulation, then it does not offend the Commerce Clause. It is irrelevant whether it protects the shareholders of an Indiana corporation.

Dissent (White, Blackmun, Stevens, JJ.). The law undermines the policy of the Williams Act by preventing minority shareholders in some cases from acting in their best interests by selling their stock. Thus, the law directly inhibits interstate commerce (*i.e.*, the interstate market in securities).

Chapter VIII Corporate Debt

A. Debt Instruments

Debt is a promise to pay back an investment with interest as provided in a contract. The claims of debtholders are almost always superior to the claims of holders of common stock, preferred stock, and other equity interests. A short-term debt instrument is called a ***note***. A long-term debt is called a ***bond*** if it is secured by a mortgage on corporate property or a ***debenture bond*** if it is unsecured. In the context of a publicly held corporation, the contract governing a debt instrument is called an ***indenture***. The indenture limits the corporation's right to take specified actions that might put the debtholders at more risk. (It may also give the corporation the right to ***call*** a debt instrument, *i.e.*, repay the holders early.) In a sense, these provisions—and the common shareholders' incentive to maximize the value of the corporation—serve as a substitute for a vote, which debtholders almost always lack. A corporate trustee is usually appointed to enforce the indenture's terms.

B. Arising Issues

1. Debtor Sells Substantially All Assets

Sharon Steel Corporation v. Chase Manhattan Bank, N.A.

691 F.2d 1039 (2d Cir. 1982), *cert. denied*, 460 U.S. 1012 (1983).

Facts. UV Industries ("UV") issued debentures with interest rates low enough that their market value totaled less than their face value. Several years later, in March 1979, UV fashioned a plan to liquidate that, under the tax laws in effect at the time, had to be accomplished in 12 months to avoid a tax on the sale of its assets. One of UV's three lines of business, carried on by subsidiary Federal Pacific Electric Company and comprising 60% of UV's operating revenue and 81% of UV's operating profits, was sold in March 1979 to Reliance Electric Company for $345 million. UV's second line of business, made up of oil and gas properties and generating 2% of UV's operating revenues and 6% of UV's operating profits, was sold in October 1979 to Tenneco Oil Company for $135 million. UV's third line of business, composed of metal mining and manufacturing, run largely by subsidiary Mueller Brass Company, and comprising 38% of UV's operating revenues and 13% of operating profits, was sold in November 1979 along with UV's liquid assets to Sharon Steel Corporation ("Sharon") for $107 million plus subordinated debentures with a market value of $353 million. The issue arose whether the liquidation of UV rendered the debentures due and payable, an effect that could benefit the shareholders, but hurt Sharon. Sharon asserted that a boilerplate successor obligor clause included in the indenture, permitting Sharon's assumption of UV's public debt from one of the indentures upon the sale by UV of "all or substantially all of its assets, applied to Sharon's benefit. The trial judge disagreed and held that the debentures were due and payable, and Sharon appeals.

Issue. Does a boilerplate successor obligor clause protect lenders as well as borrowers?

Held. Yes. Judgment affirmed.

- Boilerplate provisions such as the one used here are not peculiar to the parties or the particular indenture at issue and, therefore, are a matter of law and not of fact to be decided by a jury. Uniformity of interpretation of such provisions aids in the efficient working of capital markets.
- Contract language is the starting point in interpreting successor obligor clauses. Sharon argues that, in November 26, 1979, it purchased all of what UV owned by that point, and that, thus, it purchased "all or substantially all of UV's assets for purposes of the clause. Such a literal interpretation of the phrase, however, is unhelpful apart from a reference to the underlying purpose to be served. Successor obligor clauses protect not only the borrower's ability to merge, liquidate, or sell its assets but also protect lenders by assuring a degree of continuity of assets. A borrower which sells its assets cannot continue to hold the debt; it must assign the debt or pay it off. Allowing Sharon's interpretation would severely impair the interests of lenders, enabling a borrower to engage in a piecemeal sale of assets, with concurrent liquidating dividends to that point at which the asset restrictions of an indenture prohibited further distribution. We hold that, to protect the lender, boilerplate successor obligor clauses do not permit assignment of the public debt unless "all or substantially all of the assets of the company ***at the time the plan of liquidation is approved*** are transferred to a single purchaser.
- Here, UV's shareholders approved the plan of liquidation on March 26, 1978. Using that date as a reference, it is clear that the assets owned by UV on March 26, 1978, and later transferred to Sharon, constituted only 51% of the book value of UV's total assets. Thus, for purposes of the successor obligor clause, "all or substantially all of UV's assets were not transferred to Sharon. Therefore, the clause is not applicable in the present case, and the debentures are due and payable.

---

2. Incurrence of Additional Debt

Metropolitan Life Insurance Company v. RJR Nabisco, Inc.

716 F. Supp. 1504 (S.D.N.Y. 1989).

Facts. In late 1988, Johnson, then CEO of RJR Nabisco ("RJR Nabisco"), proposed a $17 billion leveraged buy-out ("LBO") of shareholders at $75 per share. After a bidding war developed among Johnson's investment group, the investment firm of Kohlberg Kravis Roberts & Co. ("KKR"), and others, a special committee of RJR Nabisco's directors, which was established to consider the bids, recommended that D accept the KKR proposal—a $24 LBO under which RJR Nabisco's outstanding stock would be purchased at $109 per share. Metropolitan Life Insurance Company ("MetLife") and Jefferson-Pilot Life Insurance Company ("Jefferson") (Ps) owned RJR Nabisco bonds of substantial value. MetLife also owned 186,000 shares of RJR Nabisco common stock. Ps filed suit, asserting that RJR Nabisco misappropriated the value of their bonds to finance the LBO and to distribute a windfall to its own shareholders, in effect drastically impairing the value of Ps' bonds. Ps moved for summary judgment on their count against RJR Nabisco of breach of implied covenant of good faith and fair dealing and against both RJR Nabisco and Johnson on their count entitled "In Equity." At the heart of these issues lies Ps' assertion that RJR Nabisco violated an ***implied*** restrictive covenant of good faith and fair dealing—not to incur the debt necessary to facilitate the LBO and thereby betray its alleged reassurance at the time it bargained with Ps that it had a "mandate" from its board of directors to maintain its preferred credit rating. RJR Nabisco defended the LBO by pointing to express provisions in the bond indentures permitting mergers and the assumption of additional debt, provisions known to the market and to Ps, who are sophisticated investors.

Issue. In the absence of an express covenant restricting the incurrence of new debt and there being no perceived direction to that end from the express covenants, will the court imply a covenant that prevents the LBO?

Held. No.

- The indentures at issue address the eventuality of a merger, but while they impose related restrictions not at issue in this case, they contain no restriction that would prevent the LBO. Under certain circumstances, courts will consider extrinsic evidence to evaluate the scope of an implied covenant of good faith. The provisions at issue here, however, are admittedly boilerplate provisions that are interpreted uniformly in this circuit under *Sharon Steel Corporation v. Chase Manhattan Bank, N.A. (supra)*.
- In contracts, including bond indentures, covenants are implied directly from the provisions of the indenture, and cannot grant holders rights that are inconsistent with the rights expressly set forth in the indenture. Here, the indentures guarantee the periodic and regular payment of interest and the repayment of principal; there is no language supporting a finding of the promise of the additional benefits Ps would have the court imply.
- Because Ps' equity claims are premised on their unsuccessful contract claims, they cannot survive.

Comments.

- Another issue that arose in this case involved "negative pledge covenants," covenants prohibiting debtors from mortgaging certain of their assets to another lender without providing " 'equal and ratable' mortgage protection to the obligations covered by the covenant." A debtor who violates such a covenant is in default, resulting in the acceleration of its repayment obligation. Some of RJR Nabisco's obligations contained negative pledge covenants but also included a "cure period" of 90 days during which RJR Nabisco could attempt to cure the default. Ps asserted that some of RJR Nabisco's actions violated the negative pledge covenant. RJR Nabisco sought a declaratory judgment that it had not violated the covenant, as well as an order tolling the cure period while awaiting the court's decision. On appeal, the Second Circuit noted that the provisions of the covenant were unambiguous and included no mention of tolling during litigation, but allowed for a stay of the running of the cure period to allow for necessary discovery.
- While the court also dismissed some of Ps' claims under securities law, its decision left various claims pending, including claims of fraud and fraudulent conveyance. Eventually, the case was settled, restoring a significant amount of the value the bonds lost as a result of the LBO. Under the terms of the settlement, RJR Nabisco offered Ps cash, common stock, new debt securities, and a shortened duration for a portion of the debt already held. Additionally, RJR Nabisco paid Ps' legal fees and expenses.

---

3. Debt Exchange Offer Not Permissible Under the Terms of the Documents Governing Debt

Bank of New York Mellon v. Realogy Corporation

2008 WL 5259732 (Del.Ch. Unpublished Memorandum Opinion).

Facts. Realogy (D) was publically traded until it was taken private by an affiliate of Apollo Management (Apollo). D includes Century 21, Coldwell Banker, and Sotheby's. D issued several debt instruments in order to provide the large amount of debt financing necessary to complete Apollo's acquisition. Under the Credit Facility (in simple terms, the Credit Agreement), Level I, with a total principal amount of $3.92 billion, is the most senior debt, secured by a first lien on all of D's assets. The terms of this debt ("accordion feature") permit D to issue additional debt obligations up to $650 million to new lenders on the same terms as the other Level I debt. Level II is unsecured debt whose obligations differ only in terms for payment of interest. The "Cash Notes" ($1.7 billion) with interest at 10.50 percent require semi-annual interest payments. The "Toggle Notes" ($582 million) with interest at 11.375 percent, allow D to pay in cash or pay in kind (PIK). Payment in kind is accomplished by issuing new notes for the interest due on the old notes on the same terms as the original notes. Level II and Level I notes are "pari passu." In liquidation, the two share pro rata in the available proceeds, by the face value of their claims. Because the Level II debt is unsecured, there might not be anything left to share after Level I notes have exercised their lien. Level III debt is $875 million with 12.375 percent interest, unsecured and subordinated to Level I and Level II debt. Since its debt-financed purchase by Apollo, D has had financial difficulties. Level II Cash Notes now trade at just under 18 cents on the dollar; the Toggle Notes at about 13 cents on the dollar, and the Level III notes just below 12 cents on the dollar.

D proposed debt refinancing on November 13, 2008. Eligible noteholders are invited to participate as lenders under a new $500 million term lending facility, consisting of Term C and Term D loans under the accordion feature of the Credit Facility. These loans would be secured by a second lien on all of D's assets. Rather than cash, these loans would be funded with delivery of existing notes. For each $100,000 in term loan commitment, Level III debt holders would be required to deliver $277,477.48 in principal value; Level II Cash Notes $198,709.68; and Toggle Notes $212,030.08. A priority provision put Level III holders first with an entitlement to take up to $125 million of the new notes, Level II Cash Notes holders for the difference between $500 million and the amount taken by the Level III holders, and Toggle holders for the remaining amount. The new notes would be pari passu to the existing indebtedness under the Level I Credit Facility and the Level II notes. They would also be secured, giving the new holders a higher priority in any bankruptcy proceeding than any of the Level II or Level III notes.

On November 24, 2008, the attorney for a majority of the Level II Toggle Noteholders asked that D confirm in writing that it would terminate the proposed exchange transaction, alleging breaches of the indenture governing the Toggle Notes ("Indenture"). D replied it would go forward.

On November 26, 2008, Bank of New York Mellon (P), the Trustee, for the Level II Toggle Notes made a similar demand of D, alleging a breach of Section 4.12 of the Indenture. The parties filed cross motions for summary judgment.

Issue. Does the proposed transaction violate the Level II Indenture?

Held. Yes. Judgment for the Plaintiff.

- Section 4.12 provides that D may not grant any liens to secure new loans other than those allowed under the Level I Credit Facility's accordion provision.
- Because they are not funded in cash, P argues that the new loans D proposes cannot be loans under the Credit Facility.
- P claims the meaning of the word "loans" permits only cash borrowing. A loan is "an advancement of some valuable property in exchange for a promise to repay. . . ." There are many examples of commercial loans not funded with cash; further, such "hyper-technical arguments seem out of place." In another attempt to advance his argument, P either relies on the references in the Facility to loan denominations in terms of amounts of currency, or other procedural and ministerial provisions. The references to currency are not convincing. The references to administrative provisions are equally unconvincing. P says the language in the Facility that provides that as part of the required notice of a borrowing request, D must specify the place and number of the borrower's account to which monies are to be disbursed. Because there must be a bank account, P argues, there must be a cash requirement. The purpose of the requirement is simply to provide the process for initiating a loan. If we interpreted the language differently, we would prohibit other transactions clearly anticipated and authorized by the same Facility. Other

of P's circuitous reasoning and interpretation further fuels our doubt in P, a non-party urging an absurd result, solely for its own benefit.

- P's second argument is that the proposed transaction is prohibited because the Credit Facility provides D cannot engage in the proposed transaction unless the new term loans fit the definition of "Permitted Refinancing Indebtedness." Specifically, "no Permitted Refinancing Indebtedness shall have different obligors, or greater guarantees or security, than the Indebtedness being Refinanced." The proposed exchange offer—replacing unsecured notes with second lien term loans—would give the new debt greater security than the refinanced debt. D relies on a carveout to the above provision that allows new security to be added to the refinancing indebtedness to the extent allowed under the Facility's negative covenants. Generally, these covenants forbid liens on D's property, but they permit liens created under the Credit Facility itself. Since the new loans would be issued under the "accordion" feature of the Credit Facility, D argues the liens are created under the Credit Facility and thus come within the carveout for permitted additional security. P counters that such an interpretation is so broad that the exclusion it modifies would be rendered meaningless.
- An interpretation of the exclusion to the "Permitted Refinancing Indebtedness" that requires no more than compliance with the covenants adds no substance to the definition. The exclusion would be "mere surplusage." We prefer P's interpretation which permits refinancing indebtedness to be secured only if the debt being financed could itself have been secured under the terms of the Credit Facility.

4. Exchange Offers

a. Introduction

Indentures typically provide that amendments may be made by a vote of a specified percentage of the bondholders. Generally, however, the indenture will proscribe the voting of debentures that are "owned" by the debtor itself. If the debt is publicly issued, the Trust Indenture Act of 1939 prohibits amendments altering the "core terms" of the agreement, *e.g.*, interest payments, the amount of principal, or the duration of the indenture, absent the unanimous consent of the bondholders.

b. Exchange Offer and Consent Solicitation

Katz v. Oak Industries, Inc.

508 A.2d 873 (Del. Ch. 1986).

Facts. Katz (P) owned long-term debt securities issued by Oak Industries, Inc. (D), a manufacturer and marketer of components; a producer of certain communications equipment; and a manufacturer and marketer of laminates and other materials. Faced with serious financial trouble, D's board of directors authorized steps to buy the company time to become more profitable. To reduce an annual cash interest obligation on its $230 million of outstanding debentures, D offered to exchange the debentures for a combination of notes, common stock, and warrants, resulting in the exchange of approximately $180 million principal amount of the debentures. D also entered into two agreements with Allied-Signal, Inc. ("Allied"): (i) for the sale of the materials segment of D's business for $ 160 million in cash ("acquisition agreement"); and (ii) for the sale of 10 million shares of D's common stock and warrants to purchase additional common stock for $15 million cash ("stock purchase agreement"). Under the stock purchase agreement, as a condition to Allied's obligation, at least 85% of the aggregate principal amount of all of D's debt securities must have tendered and accepted the exchange offers that are the subject of this lawsuit. D had six classes of such long-term debt, and if the condition was not met, Allied had just an option but no obligation to make the purchases provided in the stock purchase agreement.

The exchange offers in question were made as part of the restructuring and recapitalization contemplated by the agreements with Allied. D extended an exchange offer to each of the holders of its long-term debt securities, including a common stock exchange offer available only to some holders and a payment certificate exchange offer available to all holders. Under the latter, securities would be exchanged for a payment certificate in an amount less than the face value of the securities. The payment certificate exchange offer was also subject to conditions, including that the holder tendering securities to take advantage of the offer also consent to proposed amendments to the relevant indentures. If implemented, the amendments would have the effect of removing significant protections to all holders of D's debt securities. The amendments, however, were necessary for D to have the power to close the stock purchase agreement. P filed a class action to enjoin the consummation of the payment certificate exchange offer, asserting that the offer was a coercive device and constituted a breach of contract.

Issue. Was it unlawful for D to condition an exchange offer on the holders' consent to amendments to the terms of the indentures?

Held. No.

- The mere fact that a corporation makes an offer that will benefit its own stockholders "at the expense of the holders of its debt does not suggest a cognizable legal wrong. Similarly, the existence of "coercion" itself is not unlawful. P must show that a legal wrong has been committed. P contends that the obligation of each party to a contract to act with good faith towards the other with respect to the subject matter of the contract has been breached by the structure of D's exchange offer. Here, P must show that, had the parties at the time of contract negotiated with the exchange offer in mind, they would have expressly agreed to prohibit contractually the linking of the giving of consent with the purchase and sale of the security.
- Nothing in the indenture provisions that grant bondholders the power to veto proposed modifications to the indenture implies that D may not offer an inducement to bondholders to consent to such amendments. Significantly, such an implication where, as here, the inducement is offered on the same terms to all holders of the affected securities, would be wholly inconsistent with the strictly commercial nature of the contractual relationship.
- Nor does the provision that D may not vote debt securities held in its treasury supply a ground to find D's conduct wrongful. P asserts that the structure of the offer permits D to dictate the vote on securities which it could not itself vote. The purpose of the provision is to protect against the issuer voting in favor of modifications that would benefit the issuer but be detrimental to bondholders. Here, the linking of the offer and the consent solicitation does not involve a risk that bondholder interests will be affected by a vote involving anyone with a financial interest other than a bondholder's interest. The consents will be granted or withheld only by those with a financial interest shared by all bondholders, and the incentive to consent is available to all bondholders.
- Finally, the contractual provisions granting D the power to redeem the securities at a price set by the relevant indentures is irrelevant here. The present offer is not the functional equivalent of a redemption. A redemption is an act that the issuer may take unilaterally. Here, rather than acting unilaterally, D is extending an offer that it hopes will be a financially attractive alternative to holders. This process cannot be said to constitute a subversion by D of its negotiated provisions regarding redemption of its debt.

Comment. An alternative approach would be to have the debtor make a tender offer of a percentage of the obligations after successfully voting to eliminate the restrictive covenants.

---

5. Redemption

Morgan Stanley & Company v. Archer Daniels Midland Company

570 F. Supp. 1529 (S.D.N.Y. 1983).

Facts. Archer Daniels Midland Company (D) redeemed $125 million of debentures, which carried a 16% interest rate and were due on May 15, 2011. Morgan Stanley & Company (P) had purchased some of the debentures within the month immediately prior to D's announcement that it would redeem the debentures in two months. The boilerplate language in the debenture and trust indenture provided that D could not redeem the debentures "from the proceeds, or in anticipation, of the issuance of any indebtedness . . . if . . . the interest cost or interest factor [is] less than 16.08% per annum." More than one year prior to D's redemption announcement, D borrowed $50,555,500 at a less than 16.08% interest rate, and more than two months prior to the announcement, D borrowed $86,400,000 at a less than 16.08% interest rate. P asserted that these facts constituted proof that, in violation of the agreement, the redemption was being funded at least indirectly from the proceeds of borrowing at less than a 16.08% interest rate. In the period prior to the redemption, D raised money through the issuance of common stock that it used to fund the entire redemption. P maintained, however, that this fact was an irrelevant "juggling of funds" used to circumvent the protections afforded investors under the agreement. The parties filed cross-motions for summary judgment.

Issue. Under this typical indenture agreement, is the early redemption of preferred stock lawful when it is funded directly from the proceeds of a common stock offering?

Held. Yes. D's motion for summary judgment granted.

- Under *Sharon Steel Corporation v. Chase Manhattan Bank, N.A. (supra)*, the interpretation of boilerplate language should be left to the court as a matter of law. The existing authority on the issue presented by the case at bar provides that the early redemption of preferred stock is lawful under typical indenture agreement language when it is funded directly from the proceeds of a common stock offering. Significantly, this authority existed and was therefore available to the parties at the time the indenture agreement was drafted.
- It is undisputed that D directly funded the redemption through the issuance of common stock. Thus, as a matter of law, the redemption was lawful under the terms of the indenture agreement.

Comment. In a footnote, the court recognized that such a redemption could arguably violate the boilerplate language at issue if, contemporaneously with the redemption, a defendant issued new, lower-cost debt and then used the proceeds to repurchase the common stock issued ostensibly to fund the redemption.

Table of Cases